# Dallas Cowboys
## *The First Twenty-Five Years*

### Carlton Stowers

Taylor Publishing Company

DALLAS, TEXAS

**Library of Congress Cataloging in Publication Data**

Stowers, Carlton.
  Dallas Cowboys: the first twenty-five years.

  1. Dallas Cowboys (Football team) I. Title.
GV956.D3S753 1984 796.332′64′097642812 84-16152
ISBN 0-87833-448-3
ISBN 0-87833-449-1 (deluxe)

Printed in the United States of America.

# Table of Contents

# Acknowledgements

Assembling a book of this nature is much like putting together a jig-saw puzzle whose pieces are scattered hither and yon. Were it not for the help of a number of people who had necessary and important pieces it might never have come together. Thanks are in order to E. L. McGee, who designed the book, giving it a texture and flow; Dave Pelletier, whose enthusiastic research was invaluable, artists and cartoonists Merv Corning, Greg Battes and Bob Taylor, whose illustrations say a great deal about the Cowboys as well as their own remarkable gifts; and, of course the numerous members of the Dallas Cowboys organization who were never too busy to lend help to the project along the way.

Among the many gifted photographers whose works are collected here are Ron Scribner, Russ Russell, Bukki Erwin, David Woo, John Rhodes, Skeeter Hagler, Jay Dickman, John Mazziotta, Jim Laughhead and Bob Friedman. And for additional photography help a bow is necessary to Dave Boss and the staff at NFL Properties. The Dallas Public Library was also there when needed.

Bill Sansing made his contribution. And book-wise folks like Jim Black, Wayne Stokes, Kevin Howe and Pierce Watters helped the project get off the ground and finally made it fly.

Jimmy Parker's reflections were as fun as they were helpful; same with the stories told by Clint Murchison, Jr. And the many former Cowboys players who added an anecdote here and there.

In fact, as you read the book and come across a name, you can rest assured that person made a contribution of some sort. And, as is always the unfortunate case, there are those who have not been formally recognized. Hopefully they know how much their help has meant.

Without each and every one of them, the puzzle would never have come together.

# Foreword

*by James Michener*

For any professional sports team to weave an unbroken skein of winning seasons is unusual. And for that team to stand at the very top in the competition, year after year with its share of league and world championships, is a remarkable accomplishment. The New York Yankees did it in baseball. The Boston Celtics are doing it in basketball. And for many years the Montreal Canadiens dominated ice hockey. Unquestioned champions, these teams won a harvest of accolades which come to few.

In football the great success story has been the Dallas Cowboys who have stood either at the top or close to it for eighteen successive seasons. Pittsburgh and Miami have had visits to the top but neither team has equaled the Cowboys' record for consistent performance.

The Cowboys' record is impressive because it has been achieved by a *team*, not an individual, and it is much more difficult to inspire a collection of forty-nine professional athletes to maintain a consistent standard than it is for an individual to achieve supremacy in the first place and then to sustain it. Bill Tilden in tennis, Joe Louis in boxing, Jack Nicklaus, Arnie Palmer and Gary Player in golf were able to extend their tremendous individual careers, but it took the Dallas Cowboys to do the same as a collective team. Their feat is doubly difficult when one considers the relatively brief career of the individual football player and his susceptibility to injury. The football team has to renew itself every five or six years.

The Dallas record is awesome and the despair of the competition. 'How do they do it?' sportswriters in other cities ask and the answer seems to be four-fold: 'Find an owner like Clint Murchison, Jr. who will put up the cash without trying to run the team. Get yourself the best general manager in the business, say Texas E. Schramm, and let him run things. Hire one master coach like Tom Landry and stay with him through bad years and good for a quarter of a century. And because the rules will prevent championship teams from drafting high, search for a talent scout like Gil Brandt who can find football talent in the free-agent badlands. Most

important, keep that team-of-four together for 25 years.' The speaker left out one vitally important component: 'Find a great quarterback, like a Roger Staubach, who is not injury prone.'

The Cowboys have had only one head coach. Their continued success is a reflection of his football genius and his ability to hold a group of wildly individualistic superstars together. Tom Landry was hired in 1960, and the fact that the Cowboys stayed with him through the disastrous first five years is a tribute to the management, because in those seasons Landry went 18-46-4. In his first year the team lost ten straight before managing a 31-all tie with New York. And it was not until the sixth season that the team broke even, seven wins against seven losses.

A Cowboys fan had to have faith in 1965 if he believed that his team was about to launch an unmatched record for excellence. But there were intimations of greatness if one looked at the able manner in which the management was using its first and second draft picks: Bob Lilly, Lee Roy Jordan, Mel Renfro, Craig Morton.

Equally important was the cleverness of the coaches in spotting hidden talent far down the list: Roger Staubach a tenth-round pick, Jethro Pugh an eleventh, Walt Garrison a fifth. These were brilliant choices, as was the acquisition of Dandy Don Meredith.

Nothing better exemplifies the long-range approach of the Cowboys than their willingness to gamble on the United States Naval Academy graduate, Roger Staubach in the 1964 draft. An excellent quarterback in college, Staubach had obligated himself to serve four years on active duty with the Navy before he would be available to play football. In those four years anything might happen, including Staubach's possible decision not to return to football when his military hitch was over. But the Cowboys took the big gamble and got themselves one of the premier players of all time.

In the meantime, they found themselves with one of the most genial professional athletes, Dandy Don Meredith, and my association with the team begins with him. Don and I are partners in an interesting business venture — trying to revive a dead radio station — and I can testify to his craziness, his warmth and his make believe poor-boy cleverness. I cannot imagine a more unlikely combination than austere Tom Landry the disciplinarian and dipsy-doodle Don Meredith the consummate playboy, but for nine frenzied seasons they made it work, and the dynasty was on its way, launched by the stern coach and the amiable clown prince.

Watching the Cowboys from afar in the years when I was working on my book on sports in America, I discussed with many experts the mystique of the Dallas team and these generalizations surfaced repeatedly: 'The Cowboys are able to convince their players that when they put on a Dallas uniform they become part of a class outfit. Their scouts have an uncanny skill in identifying talent that will fit the Dallas mold. This team has a more solid community support than others. And through the years this has created a belief that the Cowboys can go into the closing minutes of any close game and win it with some miracle play.'

Among these classic finales were the unbelievable 'Hail Mary' pass in the 1975 playoff against Minnesota, a 50-yard desperation toss from Staubach to Drew Pearson; the Thanksgiving Day thriller against Washington in 1974; and the big finishes against San Francisco in 1974, Washington in 1979, and Atlanta in 1980. Each now a classic of football lore.

Meanwhile, the superlative drafting continued, with the Cowboys picking up such first-round dazzlers as Calvin Hill, Billy Joe DuPree, Randy White and Ed Jones, and late-round sleepers like Dennis Thurman and Herb Scott. And in the fine tradition of the management, skilled free agents like Michael Downs, Dextor Clinkscale, Anthony Dickerson and Everson Walls were rescued from oblivion. The more I study the Cowboys, the more credit I give their scouting team and their management.

Terry Donahue, the college coach at UCLA said: 'I think if you had to sum up the Dallas Cowboys organization in one word it would be *class*. If you had to sum it up in two words it would be *first class*.'

The Cowboys mystique is no accidental thing. It has been carefully crafted for twenty-five years by Tex Schramm, one of the best administrators in all of professional sports. He knew exactly how he wanted to build an image of a team that drew its support from the entire Southwest, even nationally to some degree. He did it with creative ideas, a commitment to long-term success, and a shrewd understanding of public relations and promotions. And it worked.

Like all organizations that hit it big, the Cowboys also had their share of unplanned good luck. In 1978, NFL Films editor Bob Ryan, searching for a tag for that year's highlight film, christened Dallas 'America's Team,' and the name stuck. It was justified, because like the old New York Yankees in baseball, the Cowboys represented to many fans across the country the apex in skill, popularity and winning tradition. When the NFL peddles football souvenirs, Dallas items lead the sales by a huge margin. In television and radio coverage of their games, the Cowboys win immense audiences, and their popular newspaper, *The Dallas Cowboys Weekly*, prints an English edition of 100,000 each issue, plus another 300,000 in Spanish translation for sale in Mexico, where Dallas has become the adopted home team.

Of course, when the Cowboys acquired the title 'America's Team,' the twenty-seven other teams were bound to get angry and some harsh words have been thrown around. This year a publication has appeared trying to cast ridicule on the claim: *The Semi-Official Dallas Cowboys Haters' Handbook*. Every aspect of the Dallas operation is lambasted and some great punchlines are tossed about, but as with all lampoons, nobody takes the trouble to write one unless the subject is famous and very much in the public eye.

But the Cowboys do pay a price for their notoriety, because every opponent has an extra incentive to blast 'America's Team,' which makes the Dallas schedule one of the toughest in the NFL.

Another of Schramm's ideas took shape in 1976 when the Dallas Cowboys Cheerleaders became 'America's Darlings.' Other NFL teams had groups of beautiful young women leading cheers and decorating the playing fields, but somehow the

Dallas lovelies caught the national imagination. I always thought it was because the world-famous Apache Belles from Tyler and the Kilgore Rangerettes had alerted America to the fun and beauty of the Texas marchers, but at any rate, the Dallas cheerleaders quickly became a sensation, with appearances on national television, roles in two movies and their colorful performances on the popular television show 'Love Boat.' Last year more than two thousand beautiful girls tried out for 36 positions.

Outside Texas, people rarely understand the emotional value of the Cowboys to the state and especially to Dallas. In 1963 the city suffered a body blow when President John F. Kennedy was assassinated here by a drifter from out of state, and many accused Dallas of the crime. It was at this point that the Cowboys began to capture the imagination of first the city, then the state and finally the nation. Football helped erase the stigma of the tragedy, so that in 1983 when the Gallup Poll conducted a nationwide sampling to find an answer to the question 'What is the first thing that comes to mind when you think of Dallas, Texas?' twenty-eight per cent of those polled replied 'The Cowboys.' They outdistanced even the lurid television show.

John Steadman, sportswriter for a Baltimore newspaper, offered an explanation: 'The Cowboys are one of the most remarkable organizations in sport. They don't always win the championship but, most emphatically, they carry themselves with a dignity and a professionalism that sets them apart from the rest. It's not even a contest. Everything about the team is pointed toward perfection.'

My official affliation with the Cowboys started when I moved to Texas to do some writing and friends warned me: 'If you want to be happy in this state you must support God, the Republican Party and the Dallas Cowboys, not necessarily in that order.' Even though I knew this was prudent advice, I had to explain: 'As a longtime football fan and a sometime resident in other cities, I will cheer lustily for the Cowboys except when they play Boston, New York, Pittsburgh, Philadelphia, Baltimore, Washington, Miami or Denver.' I had known coaches, owners and players in all those cities and could not easily switch my allegiance!

My friends were satisfied with my answer: 'You'll grow to forget the others. The Cowboys have no equals.' And they were right. During my first year I noticed the mixture of joy and sincerity with which a true-born Texan fan loves his Cowboys, and I have respect for that kind of partisanship. But it was not until the early stages of the 1983 season that I became a convert, for in a chain of unbelievable games the Cowboys surged back from inescapable defeat to win nail-biting victories. I can support a team like that.

One of the unforgettable football games I've attended was that Wild Card game against the L.A. Rams on the bone-chilling day after Christmas, 1983. I was permitted to sit in the box of Clint Murchison, Jr. who was watching the last game the team would play under his ownership. Having bought the franchise in 1960 for $600,000 he would soon be selling it for $60,000,000 plus another $20,000,000 for the stadium lease. If anything testified to the popularity of the Cowboys, those figures did, a growth of 33-to-1 over a quarter of a century.

The final day was marred by two misfortunes: the Cowboys were knocked out of the play-offs, 24-17, and the weather was so incredibly cold that all the toilets in the stadium froze except one. With 43,521 in attendance the lines became very long.

As a new season starts under new management the Cowboys face the task of extending a notable tradition. Roger Staubach is gone, my good friend Dandy Don is long gone, Bob Lilly and Mel Renfro are merely names enshrined on the Ring of Honor, Clint Murchison, Jr. is no longer the respected owner, and Tom Landry can't go on forever. But the lure of a splendid tradition can.

It will be exciting to see what the new ownership will come up with, what surprises to equal the Cheerleaders, what great draft picks to keep the winning tradition alive. I will expect the final moments of any game to be as thrilling as the last-minute miracles of the past.

*James A. Michener*
*Austin, Texas, August, 1984*

# Years of Struggle: 1960-1965

Originally they were to be called the Dallas Rangers, and their first steps were tentative, often comical, and rarely successful. The Dallas Cowboys, the only National Football League expansion franchise ever launched without benefit of a player draft, looked every bit the newborn team they were. They lost like clockwork and hardly looked worth the $600,000 purchase price anted up by owner Clint Murchison, Jr., his brother, John, and business partners Bedford Wynne, T. L. Wynne and Fritz Hahn.

The first team was, with precious few exceptions, a band of castoffs, has-beens and never-wases; a roguish collection of characters even Damon Runyon would have had difficulty creating with his fictional genius. The team offices were shared with an auto club, and sounds of contract negotiations mixed with the enthusiastic voices of customers mapping vacation plans. Practices were held in a tired, rundown baseball stadium, Burnet Field, except when flooding made it impossible. On such occasions, various city parks were used.

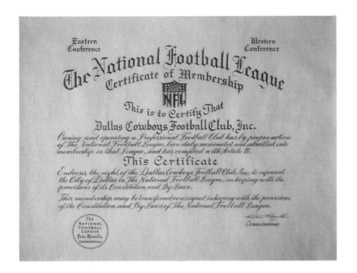

Yet despite the tribulations they faced at virtually every turn, the Cowboys were endowed with youthful optimism. Eager to lure the city into a love affair with pro football, they mailed out 200,000 letters to potential season ticket holders, hoping to fill the Cotton Bowl on Sunday afternoons. There were, in that initial season, 2,165 takers.

And for every eager young player like Don Meredith and Eddie LeBaron who reported to that 1960 pre-season training camp in Forest Grove, Oregon, there were dozens of old-timers like Bobby Luna and John Gonzaga and Woodley Lewis. The younger players, making their first attempt at pro ball, were baffled by the complex system head coach Tom Landry was bound and determined to install. Veterans who had seen their better days in other NFL camps, rebelled against it, collectively pleading they were too old to learn new tricks.

The first season, marked by frustration, poor attendance, and an on-going territorial war with another new team in town — the American Football League Dallas Texans — was into its eleventh week before defeat was avoided. And even then it did not come in the form of victory.

"I'll never forget the date," says Murchison. "It was December fourth and we went to New York and tied the Giants, 31-31. Since it was the first time we'd managed to do anything but lose, I badly wanted to celebrate and do some bragging. So I went to El Morocco that night, looking for someone to talk football with. But hard as I looked, I couldn't find anyone interested in hearing about the day the Cowboys finally failed to lose a game. And, believe me, it was a story I really wanted to tell."

Back home, the team received its first heroes' welcome. At the airport two fans waited to greet them. One carried a hand-painted sign, which read, "Well Done Cowboys."

During the ensuing years of growth — the pioneer years — the Cowboys battled a variety of adversaries. The AFL Texans drained off badly needed revenue and fan interest. Landry continued a frantic search for the caliber talent he needed to field a competitive

BOB LILLY
DALLAS COWBOYS

DEFENSIVE TACKLE

*Though the won-lost records would not show it in those early days, the Cowboys did have their moments — and their heroes. Defenders like Warren Livingston (41), Jerry Tubbs (50) and Dickie Moegle (47) did their best to keep the score down (above) while running back Don Perkins (below) fueled the Cowboys' running game.*

*By 1963 the Cowboys quarterbacking corps was a mixture of experience and promise. Front to back are Eddie LeBaron, Don Meredith and Guy (Sonny) Gibbs.*

13

team, trying out virtually anyone who remotely resembled a football player — and some who didn't. Quarterback Eddie LeBaron, who stood only 5-7, was delighted when a wide receiver named Cleveland (Pussyfoot) Jones reported to the new training camp facilities at St. Olaf's College in Northfield, Minnesota. Jones, on tiptoes, stood 5-4.

The media had a field day with the backgrounds of those wearing Cowboys uniforms. Ollie McClay, a fullback, was more talented at the piano than picking up tough yardage, defensive back Kyle McFarlane was making the transition from rodeo cowboy to football, and linebacker Gene Babb had been an art teacher and Golden Gloves boxer.

Landry, trying everything, including a shuttle of quarterback LeBaron, who had been lured out of retirement following an impressive career with the Washington Redskins, and Meredith, the Texas good ol' boy who had made headlines at Southern Methodist, managed to break into the win column in 1961. The team ended the season with a 4-9-1 record and impressed no one.

For every positive step they took, there were two negative ones. And while the quality of players was gradually improving, the mad search for more continued. "In those early training camps," LeBaron remembers, "I would be throwing passes to guys I'd never seen before. And after that practice I never saw them again. It seemed there was a Greyhound bus-load of new players coming and going every day."

It was in the 1962 season that the frustrated little LeBaron endured an afternoon that would become part of NFL lore, playing a part in an infamous play that will forever stand in the record book. In a game against the Pittsburgh Steelers, he sailed a 99-yard touchdown pass to Frank Clarke, but an official threw a flag on guard Andy Cvercko who had been caught holding in the endzone. Thus instead of a touchdown Dallas was penalized and the Steelers were awarded a 2-point safety.

There were a lot of those kinds of days. When only 12,642 bothered to come out to the Cotton Bowl to watch Dallas play the Chicago Bears, there was legitimate reason to wonder if the early-day clouds did, in fact, have a silver lining.

While the Cowboys improved to a 5-8-1 record that year, they gained little ground on Lamar Hunt's Texans who had brought the AFL championship to Dallas that same year.

Still, those closest to the organization had reason for optimism. Landry's multiple set offense was beginning to take form and the draft was providing talent like Bob Lilly, George Andrie, and Lee Roy Jordan. A radio contract was signed and in '63 the Cowboys games would be heard throughout a four-state (Texas, Louisiana, Arkansas, and Oklahoma) area. And, there were rumors following the '62 campaign that the Texans were moving out of Dallas, headed for Kansas City.

As the Cowboys entered their fourth year of existence, *Sports Illustrated's* Tex Maule stepped out on a limb and, while praising the offensive fire-power Dallas owned, picked them to win the conference championship. Dallas traveled off to its new training camp site, in Thousand Oaks, California, entertaining visions of grandeur for the first time. What resulted was a 4-10 season, which set fans to howling.

*Even on the sidelines little Eddie LeBaron looked the part of a lawyer. Wide receiver Bill Howton was Dallas' leading receiver in 1961 and 1962.*

15

"People were getting tired of waiting till next year," president and general manager Tex Schramm remembers. "They were ready for us to start winning and there was a growing list of people around town who had decided we weren't going to be able to do so with the coach we had. I finally went to Clint and talked with him about it and he made it very clear right away how we felt about the job Landry was doing."

Rather than launch a search for a new coach, Murchison chose to quiet the disgruntled by making it clear Landry was, and was going to be, the coach of the Dallas Cowboys. To emphasize his point, he signed Landry to a new 10-year contract which was unprecedented in professional sports. "That," Murchison said, "should quiet people down."

While the Cowboys would still not threaten the .500 win-loss level in '64, the caliber of performance improved noticeably. Trades and productive drafts improved the manpower situation dramatically. "In the first few years," says Dick Nolan, a player-coach in the early days of the franchise, "we simply didn't have the people you had to have to win. We had some very good players, but not enough of them. Even in the first couple of seasons I think Tom was looking several years down the road. He had a plan he was certain would work. But to accomplish it, he had to get the right people in the right spots."

*By 1963 some were saying that the Cowboys' defense was strong enough to merit championship consideration. And the offense, directed by a high-stepping Don Meredith was getting better.*

*Linebacker Dave Edwards (52) brought cheers from the sparse Cotton Bowl crowd with this interception return against the New York Giants. Fellow linebacker Jerry Tubbs (50) prepares to help clear the way. When Dallas fans began to grumble about the record of the Cowboys' young coach, Tom Landry, owner Clint Murchison (right) quieted things by extending him an unprecedented 10-year contract.*

By 1965 there was evidence that he was making progress toward that goal.

The scouting department, directed by Gil Brandt and aided by the help of computers, had already earned a reputation for seeking out players from small colleges who had backgrounds in sports other than football. In '64, for instance, they had picked Olympic sprint champion Bob Hayes in the seventh round, then spent their tenth round pick on a Naval Academy quarterback named Roger Staubach. Though it would be five years before he would complete his military obligations and be free to try to earn a place with the Cowboys, the Dallas organization felt the long-shot was a wise investment for the future.

"One of the most drastic changes we've gone through since those days," says Landry, "is the fact we're no longer able to spend draft selections on what I call development players. Back in the early days, when we weren't winning and knew we probably weren't going to for a while, we could afford to sign a basketball player or a track man and let him develop. Or we could use a pick on someone like a Staubach who might or might not want to play five years down the road. That was a fun part of the game then. But, once you get to a position where you're contending for a championship, you can't afford to do some of the things we did in the draft then."

It would be 1965 when the Cowboys closed out with three straight wins to end the season at 7-7. The .500 mark had been reached and there was a bonus attached to the accomplishment. After five years the Dallas Cowboys' season extended beyond the regulation 14 games.

The three-game sweep of Philadelphia, St. Louis, and New York in the final weeks of the season earned Dallas the runner-up spot in the NFL Eastern Conference and a berth in the Miami-based Playoff Bowl against the Baltimore Colts. In time, the Playoff Bowl would fail to survive the criticism it received from the press and fans. It was dubbed the Runner-up Bowl, the Losers' Bowl and pointed to little more than a meaningless stage show which pumped additional dollars into the NFL coffers.

"Most of the criticism of the game was probably justified," Tex Schramm would later admit, "but for us, at the time, it was almost as exciting as going to a Super Bowl. After five years of getting nowhere, it was a sign that we were getting somewhere. We were thrilled — and proud — to be playing in the game."

That the Colts thoroughly dominated Dallas, winning 35-3, took little edge from the fact the year had been a success. They had won as many as they lost and attendance at the Cotton Bowl had averaged 55,559 per game.

The Cowboys, it seemed, had finally arrived.

*Seven times he ended the season as Dallas' leading rusher, but the closest running back Don Perkins ever came to the magic 1,000-yard season was in 1962 when he gained 945.*

*From 1963 to 1968 Don Meredith was the man atop the Cowboys passing statistics. In '68, a year when he threw for a club record 2,500 yards, he ranked second in the NFL.*

*Chuck Howley would become one of the NFL's premier linebackers during his 12-year career with the Cowboys.*

21

# Signs of Success: 1966-1970

*For the first time, the Cowboys were ready to challenge the league's best.*

For those with a penchant for history, it is duly recorded that the year 1966 marked the beginning of one of the longest-running success stories in professional sports history. It was then that the Dallas Cowboys shed their adolescent shortcomings and matured into a team capable of challenging anyone in the league. Even Vince Lombardi's remarkable Green Bay Packers.

The break-even season of '65 had been a step in the right direction; still, it had not marked Dallas as a winner. It had, on the other hand, sparked new interest in the future. Ticket manager Kay Lang delighted in the knowledge that season ticket sales doubled, climbing over 15,000 before the first home game.

What head coach Tom Landry would put on display was the first ever Cowboys team with all the ingredients he'd been hoping to collect since that first training camp in 1960. Offensively he had incredible firepower with Don Meredith and Olympic sprint champion Bob Hayes teaming to wreck NFL passing records. On the ground there were fullbacks Don Perkins and Walt Garrison and a promising newcomer named Dan Reeves. Defensively, the likes of Bob Lilly, Chuck Howley, Lee Roy Jordan, Mel Renfro, and Cornell Green formed the backbone of a unit that was finally judged solid.

What would result was a 10-3-1 season that would lure sellout crowds to the Cotton Bowl and earn the Cowboys the level of prestige that they had long sought.

It would also earn them the right to host the famed Packers for the NFL Championship. First, however, there would be a long list of awards for the Cowboys to collect. Landry was recognized by *The Sporting News* as the Coach of the Year, then received the same citation from the Associated Press and UPI. Meredith was honored with the Bert Bell Award and four players — Lilly, Howley, Green, and Hayes — were selected to various All-Pro teams.

Kicker Danny Villanueva put things into proper perspective when he said, "For all these years we've been labeled losers. But, hey, look where we are now."

In the two weeks leading up to the championship game there was, throughout the nation, much speculation on the pressure the still relatively inexperienced Cowboys would be dealing with. Green Bay, seasoned and methodical, had a dozen players on its roster who had been in four championship games since 1960. The Cowboys had little idea what to expect from a game where so much individual playoff money was on the line.

As things got underway on that New Year's Day, it appeared the forecasters knew what they were talking about. Green Bay jumped into a 14-0 lead before Dallas' offense even touched the ball. But, to the surprise of many, there was little sign of panic from the Cowboys. With just over five minutes remaining, Green Bay owned a 34-20 advantage but in just over a minute Meredith whittled the gap to just seven points on a 68-yard bomb to Frank Clarke.

On the sidelines, Landry was convinced his team could win it all if only they could force the obviously tiring Packers into overtime. It almost came to pass.

After the Cowboys' defense held, Clarke got wide open again and Meredith threw what appeared to be a tying touchdown pass. Safety Tom Brown, however, deliberately fouled Clarke at the two-yard line. So it was first-and-goal with 52 seconds remaining. Perkins narrowed the distance to one yard on first down. Then tackle Jim Boeke moved before the ball was snapped, a five-yard penalty that moved the Cowboys back to the six. In the mixup of the false start by Boeke, a Packer had somehow stuck a finger in Reeves' eye. On second down, when Meredith lofted him a short swing pass, Reeves saw two footballs — and didn't catch either.

Meredith connected with Norman at the two on third down, leaving one final chance to draw even with the suddenly vulnerable Packers. But a rollout pass never got a chance. Green Bay linebacker Dave Robinson got to Meredith before he even had a chance to locate a receiver. Don threw wildly to a point in the end zone where he hoped someone might be — and Tom Brown intercepted.

After all the tension and suspense, the Cowboys had fallen short in their first chance to claim a championship. The Green Bay dynasty continued.

It was fitting, then, that the same two teams should meet a year later to renew the championship war. This time, many were suggesting, Dallas should be free of the concerns that generally precede such an encounter. Having completed the regular season with a 9-5 record, the Cowboys had, in fact, warmed up for the title game with a stunning 52-14 victory over Cleveland in the Eastern Championship game.

What was to transpire on December 31, 1967, was one of the most remarkable games in NFL history, one which would earn legendary status and be given a name. Even today fans know of what you speak when you mention "The Ice Bowl."

It would be the coldest day ever recorded by the Green Bay, Wisconsin, weather bureau. At 8 a.m. on game day the temperature was minus 16 degrees. And before game's end it would have fallen to minus 20 with a chill factor of minus 41.

And, while the ice rink surface of Lambeau Field and the frostbite weather would considerably hamper the wide-open Dallas offense, the Cowboys battled the Packers on even terms. Eight seconds deep into the final period, in fact, Dan Reeves threw a 50-yard option pass to wide receiver Lance Rentzel for a touchdown that would lift Dallas into a 17-14 lead.

The Pack, seeking its third straight championship, was far from ready to give up, however. And, with just under five minutes remaining quarterback Bart Starr launched a drive that carried his team to the Dallas one. On third down he called for his team's final time out and trotted to the sidelines to confer with Lombardi. A field goal, which would surely tie the game and force an overtime, was quickly ruled out in favor of a play called 31 Wedge, a rarely used quarterback sneak. The Packers would go for broke.

With just 16 seconds remaining, Starr followed the block of guard Jerry Kramer into the endzone. Once

*With a last minute field goal, Danny Villanueva provided Dallas with a 31-30 victory over the Washington Redskins in 1966 and helped them gain a playoff berth for the first time in the franchise's history.*

*Finding running room against arch-rival Cleveland was a particularly demanding chore for the Cowboys in the mid-sixties. The first of the Dallas quarterback controversies came when a gifted passer from the University of California named Craig Morton arrived in 1965.*

again the Packers had survived. Dallas had again come up short at the goal line in the fading seconds.

The Ice Bowl results brought about a new attitude toward the Cowboys. It was agreed they were talented and exciting, that they were a team on the verge of greatness. But, many wondered, were they capable of winning the Big One?

The question would, in days to come, haunt the entire organization.

It grew louder as the Cowboys flexed their muscles with 12-2 and 11-2-1 season records in 1968 and '69, but fell to the Cleveland Browns in the Eastern Conference Championship games. First it had been Green Bay, now the Browns. It began to appear Dallas was destined to be the most talent-blessed bridesmaid in NFL history. So frustrating did the situation become that Meredith, in the prime of his career, announced his retirement the summer after the '68 loss to Cleveland.

The quarterbacking was turned over to strong-armed Craig Morton, while a gifted young Naval Academy graduate named Roger Staubach would serve as his apprentice.

For the Cowboys, the sixties ended much as they had begun. In the 1969 Playoff Bowl in Miami they would only go through the motions, losing to the Los Angeles Rams, 13-0.

It was in the seventies that professional football grew to full maturity, bursting on the national consciousness like no other sport before it had ever done. Over one hundred million people would gather in NFL stadiums during the course of the decade to pay homage to a game which had captured the fancy of media from coast to coast.

With the battle against the upstart American

Football League over, resolved by a merger which found the NFL realigned into a National and an American Conference, the television cameras could again focus squarely on one league. And, realizing that more and more advertising dollars were waiting out there to be spent, ABC-TV adopted an NFL idea which would serve as the touchstone of the game's emergence as the national pastime.

They called it "Monday Night Football."

It was in November of 1970, before a sellout crowd in the Cotton Bowl, that the Dallas Cowboys made their debut with Cosell & Co.

Unanimously picked to win their division and, perhaps, make it all the way to the Super Bowl, the Cowboys were anxious to earn their spot in the just-beginning decade with a performance that would demonstrate to millions of viewers how far they had come in just ten years of existence.

What occurred, however, was one of the most dismal performances in the organization's history. People sat dumbfounded as Dallas could do nothing right against the St. Louis Cardinals. What was going on down on the unusually warm floor of the Cotton Bowl gave every appearance of being something less than a fair fight. And as the travesty continued, much of the blame was directed at quarterback Craig Morton, heir to the quarterbacking duties following Don Meredith's surprising retirement.

By the fourth quarter the boos had turned to a chant and eyes moved from the playing field to the announcers' booth where Meredith was working as a color analyst for the Monday Night team. "We want Meredith," the chant went. Don leaned out the open window, smiled, and said, "No way!"

By game's end Dandy Don, whose announcing

Pete Gent (top right) was a standout Michigan State basketball player who developed into a dependable receiver. Running back Walt Garrison (bottom right) was a rodeo standout at Oklahoma State before gaining football stardom with the Cowboys. With the arrival of Craig Morton (14), Tom Landry suddenly had the luxury — and headache — of two outstanding quarterbacks (above). And for all of them, the early day Dallas Cowboys cheerleaders, made up of boys and girls from Dallas high schools, lent support.

*The Cowboys' defense was making strides with the likes of Cornell Green (34), Bob Lilly (74), Larry Stephens (77), Chuck Howley (54), Maury Youmans (78) and George Andrie (66). The flex defense was gaining in stature and causing problems for offenses throughout the NFL.*

polish would eventually earn him an Emmy, admitted genuine concern for his former teammates. The Cardinals would win, 38-0, and those who had seen it wondered what all the furor over the growing powerhouse in Dallas was all about.

From that night of horror, however, would come one of the most critical turnarounds in Cowboys history. Owners of a 5-4 record after nine games, Dallas was pronounced dead in the following morning's editions. Certainly no team could play as poorly as it had and return to make any manner of a run for the money.

"Landry realized that everyone was pushing too hard," recalls All-Pro defensive lineman Bob Lilly, "so he relaxed everything. For the only time in my career with the Cowboys, I heard him tell everyone to just have fun. Shoot, we even started playing volleyball and touch football once a week instead of running windsprints and sitting in meeting rooms."

In what must remain one of the greatest coaching moves of his career, Landry pulled his talented team back together, and five weeks and as many wins later they had ended the regular season with a 10-4 record and were back in the playoffs.

For good measure, they defeated Houston, 52-10, in the regular season finale.

Then, in round one of the playoffs, the Dallas team showed its defensive muscle by defeating Detroit for the Divisional Playoff title, 5-0, as Mike Clark booted a 26-yard field goal and George Andrie and Jethro Pugh dumped Lions quarterback Greg Landry in the endzone for a two-point safety.

A week later the ten-year dream of the franchise would become reality as the Cowboys, defeated San Francisco for the NFC Championship and the right to participate in Super Bowl V.

In Miami, however, misfortune would again descend. To this day historians refer to the Cowboys-Baltimore Colts match as the Blooper Bowl, pointing to a record 11 turnovers during the game

*As per the Landry philosophy, the championship Cowboys teams were built on defense. All-Pro safety Cliff Harris (below), it seemed, managed to get his hands on the ball as much as some members of the Dallas offense.*

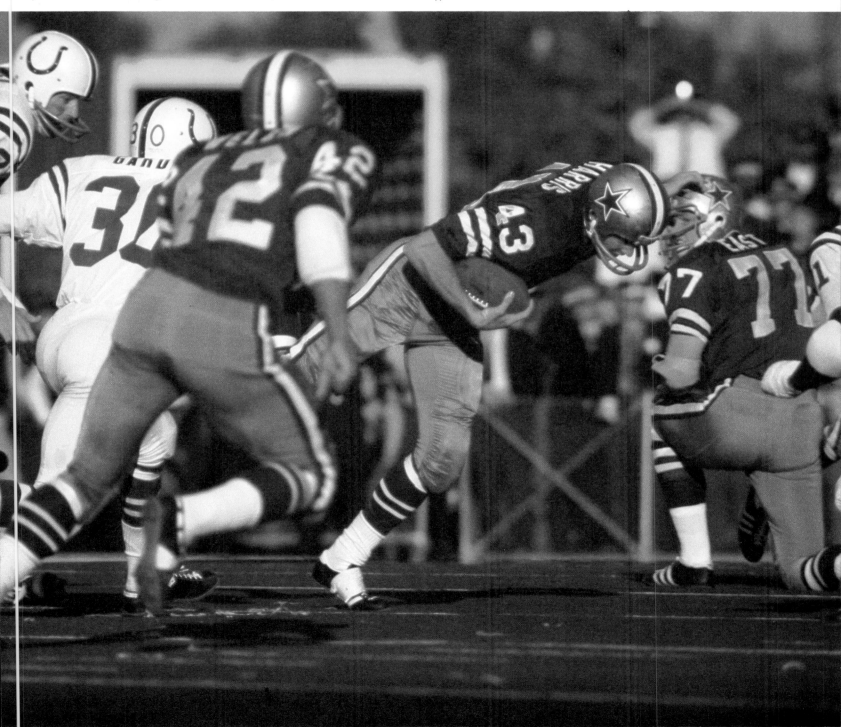

*Even Baltimore's legendary Johnny Unitas found the swarming Doomsday Defense, sparked by Jethro Pugh (75), Bob Lilly (74) and George Andrie (66), a difficult thing to handle.*

32

(Colts 7, Dallas 4). It was the Dallas mistakes that proved most costly, however. A Craig Morton interception set up one Baltimore touchdown and a controversial fumble by Duane Thomas at the Colts' two-yard line early in the second half had denied the Cowboys the opportunity to take control of the game at a point when they were already leading 13-7.

In truth, Dallas center Dave Manders had recovered Thomas' fumble. But, when Baltimore defensive lineman Billy Ray Smith began yelling "Baltimore's Ball!", official Jack Fette signaled a Colts recovery.

It wasn't the only zany happening of the day, however.

After the Cowboys had moved to a 6-0 lead, Baltimore quarterback Johnny Unitas threw over the middle to Eddie Hinton who leaped high, just getting a hand on the ball. Deeper in the secondary, Dallas' Mel Renfro also jumped to try for the interception. However, the ball sailed on downfield, into the hands of John Mackey. Officials ruled the ball had been touched by Renfro, thus making Mackey eligible to make the reception and earn credit for a 75-yard touchdown.

Finally, with just five seconds remaining on the scoreboard clock, Baltimore rookie Jim O'Brien came

on to kick a 32-yard field goal that gave the Colts a 16-13 victory.

No sooner had the ball cleared the uprights than Lilly took off his helmet and threw it half the length of the Orange Bowl field. Clearly, getting to the Super Bowl had not been enough for the Cowboys.

*Calvin Hill, the first 1,000-yard runner in Dallas history, strikes a sideline pose with player personnel director Gil Brandt, who was more than eager to take a chance on drafting someone from Yale in the first round. Even with a little interference from an official Don Perkins picks up good yardage.*

The "new-look" Cowboys Cheerleaders were on hand in Miami when Dallas made its Super Bowl debut against the Baltimore Colts.

As time went by the protection quarterback Don Meredith received steadily improved to championship caliber.

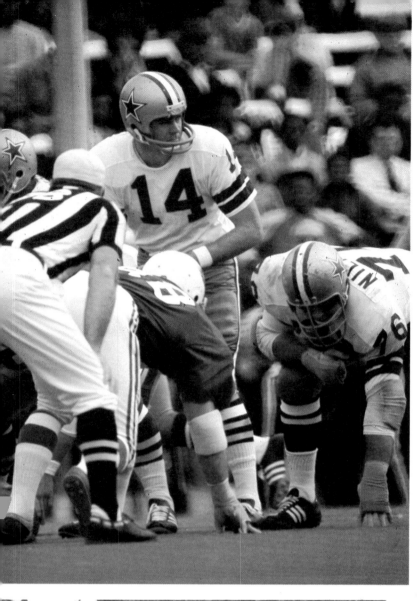

Craig Morton (left) became a commanding figure at the line of scrimmage and the team of Don Meredith and Olympian wide receiver Bob Hayes (below) was the most lethal passing combination in the league. Then, there was the running contribution of a durable halfback named Dan Reeves (30).

# The Championship Years: 1971-1979

*In the decade of the 70s, the Cowboys proved themselves to be champions of the league.*

With the Packers Dynasty having faded, relegated to the bygone sixties, the NFL awaited a new champion to emerge and rule the coming decade. More than one expert felt that new ruler would be the Dallas Cowboys. Having climbed to the top in the National Football Conference, they had but one final step to make before assuming the rank that owner Clint Murchison, Jr., had hoped for a decade.

To further polish the image of his team, Murchison moved it into new quarters during the 1971 season. On the outskirts of Dallas, the state-of-the-art Texas Stadium beckoned to fans. And the promise of a special season drew them like a magnet. Even Tom Landry had difficulty hiding his enthusiasm. "I felt we had an excellent season in 1970. But just as soon as it was over I couldn't help but think ahead to '71. I felt strongly that it was going to be a great year for us."

And, despite controversies and disruptions, the Cowboys blossomed much as Landry had expected. After winning all six of their pre-season games, their only concern seemed to be the brewing quarterback controversy which would provide fuel for hometown argument. Morton was being seriously challenged by Staubach, and Landry had sidestepped a final decision by insisting that he actually had "two starting quarterbacks."

Then there was another difficulty to attend. Young Duane Thomas, brilliant in his rookie season, had returned as a rebellious, angry young man. He called Landry a "plastic man, no man at all," said Gil Brandt was a "liar," and made note of the fact Schramm was "sick, demented and completely dishonest."

Schramm laughed off his slur, "Well, two out of three ain't bad."

Throughout the season Thomas would march to a different drummer, abiding by a different set of rules. He spoke only on rare occasions. But on Sundays he played up to the same championship level as his teammates. "Looking back," says Landry, "I think one of the most satisfying things I've experienced as a coach was the manner in which the rest of the team accepted the way I tried to deal with Duane. Everyone seemed to realize that he had some special problems and went along with the manner in which I handled them."

By the time the Cowboys raced through a seven-game winning streak in the last half of the regular season, Thomas was more novelty than distraction. And Staubach, a gambling, scrambling quarterback, had established himself as Dallas' quarterback of the future.

The Cowboys took an 11-3 record into the playoffs, then scored impressive wins over Minnesota (in the Division Playoff) and San Francisco (for the NFC title) to earn a return trip to the Super Bowl. This time their opponent would be the upstart Miami Dolphins.

"Never, in my career," reflects Hall-of-Famer Bob Lilly, "have I ever been a part of a team so prepared to play a game as I was that Super Bowl in New Orleans. I don't think there was a man on the roster who even considered the possibility of losing that

game. We had paid our dues and felt our time had come."

On a day when the Cowboys played as near-perfect a game as they ever had, they crushed the Dolphins, 24-3, rewriting numerous Super Bowl records along the way. They rushed for over 250 yards while the Doomsday Defense allowed the frustrated Dolphins just 185 total yards for the day. And Staubach, earning his fourteenth straight victory as a Cowboys starter, was cited as the game's Most Valuable Player.

"There are few feelings in the world like winning the Super Bowl," Staubach says. "There were guys on that first championship team who had been around for some time, who had been through a lot of the hard times necessary to build a team to where we were in '71. I was pleased for them more than anything else — them and Coach Landry."

Back-to-back Super Bowl appearances, then, clearly made the Cowboys the odds-on favorite to reign as the team to beat for years to come. Careful drafting had enabled them to prepare new talent to fill holes that would soon be left by retirements. On paper, at least, they were head and shoulders above those standing ready to challenge their status as World Champions.

Thus it was that they entered the '72 campaign as the NFL's premier team. But things did not get off to a smooth start. During the pre-season Staubach suffered a shoulder injury which sent him to the sidelines and Morton back into the No. 1 spot. And the backfield lost some of its punch when Thomas was traded away to the San Diego Chargers. His absence would, however, hardly be noticed as a brilliant halfback from Yale, Calvin Hill, took up the torch in his fourth year and became the first Dallas player ever to rush for 1,000 yards in a season.

And there was the manner of heroics which would, in time, become a Cowboys trademark. In the

*All-Pro cornerback Cornell Green insists he was never beaten by an opposing receiver. Sometimes they just got lucky. Ignoring the efforts of Pittsburgh defender Donnie Shell, wide receiver Drew Pearson goes up for yet another of his circus-like catches. It was a last minute victory over the Washington Redskins that produced this rare show of emotion from quarterback Roger Staubach.*

Divisional Playoff with the San Francisco 49ers, a team which had pounded them 31-10 in the regular season, they seemed on the brink of elimination, trailing by 15 points late in the third period.

Concerned that his offense was getting nowhere, Landry summoned Morton to the bench and inserted Staubach. And, with just a minute and a half to play he had pulled them to within five points of a 49ers team which had begun a premature celebration. Almost magically, the Cowboys gained possession of an on-side kick and Staubach began to display the last-minute mastery which would become his trademark. In the final minute he drove Dallas downfield, capping the drive with a touchdown pass to Ron Sellers. With two touchdowns in a span of only 38 seconds, he had engineered a 30-28 victory that vaulted Dallas into the NFC title game for the third straight year.

This time, however, there would be no Super Bowl. Flat after the miracle finish in Candlestick Park, the Cowboys traveled to Washington where they would lose, 26-3. It would be George Allen's Redskins who would carry the NFC banner into Super Bowl VII.

In 1973 the Cowboys, favored to regain the spot taken from them by the Redskins, experienced much the same fate. Despite an impressive 10-4 season in which Landry would achieve his 100th victory as the Cowboys coach, Dallas would again be stopped one game shy of a third Super Bowl trip. This time it would be the Minnesota Vikings who would defeat them in the conference championship game, 27-10.

A year later the disappointment would turn to turmoil. The hoped-for dynasty appeared to have feet of clay. Veteran defensive star Chuck Howley retired, Craig Morton was traded to the New York Giants, and Calvin Hill signed a contract with the

newborn World Football League, saying he would play out the remaining year on his contract, then leave for Hawaii.

The Cowboys would, in effect, never get started, losing four of their first five. By season's end they had barely managed to remain in the win column, going 8-6 and failing even to make the playoffs. Throughout the league there were whispers that the Cowboys had peaked and were now headed in the direction of the Packers. Too many key players were gone. It was time for the rebuilding process to get underway.

Dallas accomplished that with one brilliant draft, one in which a dozen talented rookies — among them the likes of Randy White, Bob Breunig, Herb Scott, Thomas Henderson, Pat Donovan, Randy Hughes, and Scott Laidlaw — made the team. They were called the Dirty Dozen.

And their task would be monumental. Before the new season began Dallas could count what amounted to an all-star team's worth of departures. Bob Lilly, Walt Garrison, and Cornell Green had retired, Bob Hayes had been traded, and Hill left for the WFL.

Concerned that his running game would be sub-par, Landry went to the drawing board and dusted off an old formation he had unsuccessfully tried to

*A member of the famed Dirty Dozen, defensive tackle Randy White (54) became the finest defensive player in the NFL.*

sell to Meredith in the early sixties. It was called the Shotgun, and Staubach welcomed it enthusiastically.

It was, then, the presence of the most outstanding crop of rookies in the team's history, a new formation, and the fact they were able to pull off yet another last-minute miracle, which turned a rebuilding year into yet another Super Bowl season.

In Minnesota for the Divisional Playoff, Dallas found itself an eight-point underdog to the Vikings and, in fact, trailed 14-10 late in the fourth period. With just 44 seconds remaining in the game, Dallas faced a fourth-and-16 situation in its own end of the field.

From there, however, Staubach, working out of the Shotgun, connected on two straight bombs to wide receiver Drew Pearson. The last one, a lofty floater which the Tulsa free agent hauled in despite being closely guarded by Vikings defender Nate Wright, would cover the final 50 yards needed for the 17-14 victory. Staubach's name for his throw, ("That's my Hail Mary pass") became part of Cowboys lore. And it would pave the road for a 37-7 win over the Rams for the NFC title and a match against AFC champion Pittsburgh in Super Bowl X.

The match-up of the Cowboys and Steelers in Miami would serve as Round One of the most heated rivalry the decade would enjoy.

Dallas held to a slim lead through three quarters before Steelers quarterback Terry Bradshaw began to connect with a corps of gifted receivers, moving his team out to a 21-10 lead. And, while Staubach put on some last-minute heroics, drawing the Cowboys to within four points with just over a minute remaining, the day belonged to the Steelers.

Before, during and after the game there would be angry exchanges. Dallas players publicly suggested the Steelers played the game on the razor's edge of the rules. Pittsburgh players spoke, in turn, of aggressive play and intimidation. That the aggressive Steelers could have played the entire Super Bowl game without drawing a single penalty drew particular anger from Cowboys players and officials. Pittsburgh had led the league in penalties during the regular season. There was little doubt that no love would be lost between the two teams in days to come.

A year later the Steelers were back in the Super Bowl but the Cowboys, following an impressive 11-3 season, stumbled in the opening round of the playoffs, losing to the Los Angeles Rams, 14-12, in Texas Stadium.

The Dallas-Pittsburgh rivalry would continue to be battled from afar in '77 as the Steelers, plagued by injuries, were eliminated from the picture long before enthusiasm for Super Bowl XII began to build. The Cowboys, on the other hand, enjoyed one of their finest seasons in history.

Except for a mid-season slump, which saw them lose back-to-back games to St. Louis and, somewhat ironically, the Steelers, Dallas showed all the characteristics of a team capable of going through an entire season undefeated. With a new weapon added to the running game — rookie Tony Dorsett — Dallas posted a 12-2 season record, winning eight in a row, losing two, then closing with four straight victories. In the playoffs, they dominated, easily brushing aside Chicago, then Minnesota to earn a

*Calvin Hill came running out of Yale, earning himself a starting job in his first pro season, and was cited as the league's Rookie of the Year.*

ticket to New Orleans where they would meet an old friend. The opponent would be the upstart Denver Broncos, quarterbacked by former Cowboy Craig Morton.

It would be one of the championship game's most decisive triumphs as the Dallas defense immobilized Denver with sacks and interceptions. Staubach, meanwhile, was brilliant. So, too, was the Cowboys defense. Before the 27-10 victory was claimed, Dallas defensive linemen Harvey Martin and Randy White had already been judged the co-MVPs from a rather lengthy list of Cowboys candidates, including defensive back Randy Hughes and Staubach.

The Cowboys had gained ground in their on-going battle with the idle Steelers. A year later, they would match talent again, battling for yet another Super Bowl trophy.

Once again the verbal pre-game jousting took on the tone of a heavyweight title bout. Super Bowl XIII was to serve as the comparison of what writers were labeling Cowboys Cool and Steeler bullyism. Cowboys linebacker Thomas (Hollywood) Henderson got the ball rolling by suggesting that the Steelers' Bradshaw was several I.Q. points shy of genius level. "The guy," Henderson said, "couldn't spell cat if you spotted him the 'c' and the 'a.'." You get the idea.

By halftime the Steelers led 21-14 and there was every indication that the game would develop into one of the best of all championship match-ups. Then, however, Dallas suffered two unfortunate mishaps, which allowed Pittsburgh to take command.

In the third period, when momentum was badly needed, the Cowboys methodically drove to the

*A hometown hero, defensive end Harvey Martin annually led the Dallas defense in quarterback traps.*

Steelers' 10-yard line before Staubach threw to
reserve tight end Jackie Smith for what appeared to
be a sure six-pointer. Smith, who had come to Dallas
after a storied career with St. Louis, was wide open
but the ball slipped from his grasp, incomplete. Thus
the Cowboys had to settle for a Rafael Septien field
goal instead of the 21-all tie that had seemed a
certainty just seconds earlier.

Then, in the final period, Bradshaw sent wide
receiver Lynn Swann deep from his own 44-yard
line and lofted a high, floating pass down the right
sidelines. Dallas defender Benny Barnes was with
Swann, stride-for-stride, and the two collided. An
official signaled interference on Barnes, giving the
Steelers the ball at the Cowboys' 22. Seconds later
Franco Harris ran in for a touchdown. It would be
that touchdown, set up by a questionable call, which
provided Pittsburgh with a lead the Cowboys could
not surmount. Despite a two touchdown comeback
engineered by Staubach, the Cowboys would come
up shy, losing 35-31.

The Steelers, three-for-three in Super Bowls,
would add a fourth championship the following year
as Dallas closed out the decade on a down note,
falling to Los Angeles in the last two minutes of a
Divisional Playoff.

Still, no team, not even the Steelers, could claim
the winning percentage Dallas had accumulated in
the 10-year period. And there was no other team in
the game who could point to five Super Bowl
appearances in the same time span.

"I would be lying if I said I wasn't disappointed
that we didn't beat the Steelers," said Schramm, "and
I was disappointed when we didn't make it to Super
Bowl XIV because that would have given us a chance
to be looked back on as the team of the seventies. The
Rams almost upset the Steelers, and the Rams were
only a 9-7 team. If we could have won that Super
Bowl, a sixth apperance and third championship, it
would have surpassed the Pittsburgh achievements."

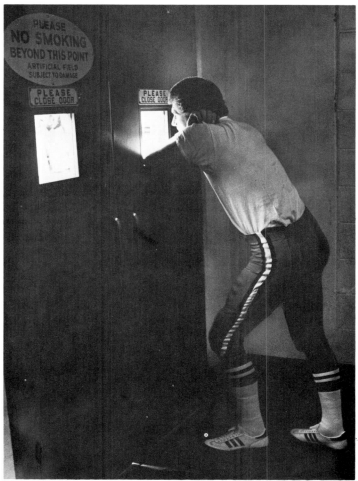

*After celebrated years with the St. Louis Cardinals, tight
end Jackie Smith closed out his career with the Dallas
Cowboys in 1978, dreaming of a trip to the Super Bowl.
Unfortunately, many remember him only as the man who
dropped a Roger Staubach pass in the end zone against the
Pittsburgh Steelers in the championship game.*

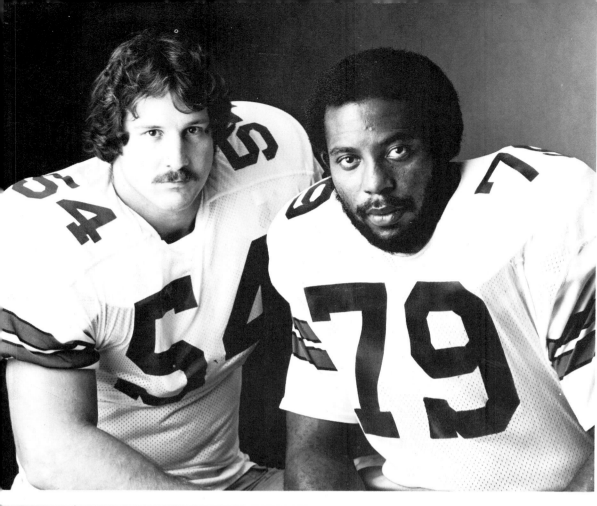

The stars and big plays in Cowboys history have been many. Who can forget quarterback Roger Staubach (top left) launching a bomb in Super Bowl XII, then marveling as wide receiver Butch Johnson (bottom left) made a diving catch? Defender Randy White was all over Denver quarterback Craig Morton that day (below). Randy White and Harvey Martin (left) were named MVPs of the game for their incredible defensive effort.

49

# The Tradition Continues: 1980-1985

As the Dallas Cowboys celebrated their twentieth birthday there were those ready to signal the end of an era. It had, as the 1980 season began, been a gradual but steady downward path taken by the team since that Super Bowl triumph over Denver following the '77 season.

The next year, it was pointed out, they did make it back to the Super Bowl but lost. Then, the following season ended at the divisional level. And all the while new threats were being issued in their own NFC Eastern Division by the likes of Philadelphia and Washington.

Such, it is worth noting, is the manner in which the Dallas Cowboys had come to be measured. Records of 11-5 and 12-4 were not judged successful unless they led to the addition of another Super Bowl trophy. "We had reached a point," says president and general manager Tex Schramm, "where people expected us to go to the Super Bowl every year. Which is fine. That's what we expected of ourselves. The goals of the Dallas Cowboys are different from those of a lot of teams in the league. To us, there is no success unless we win it all. Maybe that's not the way to approach it — perhaps that creates too much pressure on everyone — but it has long been a part of our philosophy. And it will continue to be."

As the eighties got underway there was another element which caused Dallas loyalists genuine cause for concern. Gone was Roger Staubach, the magnificent architect of so many thrilling come-from-behind victories, the man who had directed the offense each time Dallas had brought home a Super Bowl trophy. Retiring after the conclusion of the 1979 season, his formal announcement drew over 200 members of the media, was the subject of a special supplement of one of the Dallas newspapers, and was the lead item on the evening network news.

Staubach, the man who had, throughout the seventies, epitomized the personality of the Cowboys, was leaving sizable shoes to be filled. The man who would have to try to rise to the occasion was Danny White.

And even as heralders of doom insisted the Cowboys could not continue along their winning ways without him at the controls, Staubach heaped praise on the man who would inherit his job. "One of the things that made it easier to come to the decision on my retirement," he says, "was the fact I knew full well that Danny was ready to take over and do an excellent job."

It is doubtful, however, that any player has been more watched than Dallas' new quarterback in his initial season as the starter. Regardless of the Sunday results, he could count on having his performance compared to those of Staubach. Members of the media even compiled charts to show comparisons of everything from yardage to touchdown passes to the number of interceptions each had thrown at particular stages of their career. White laughed it off, resigned to life in Staubach's shadow. He would accept it for a while.

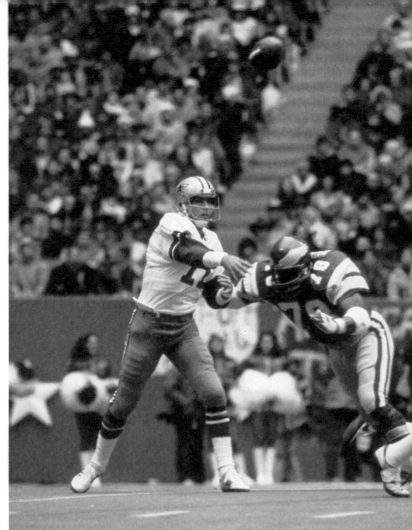

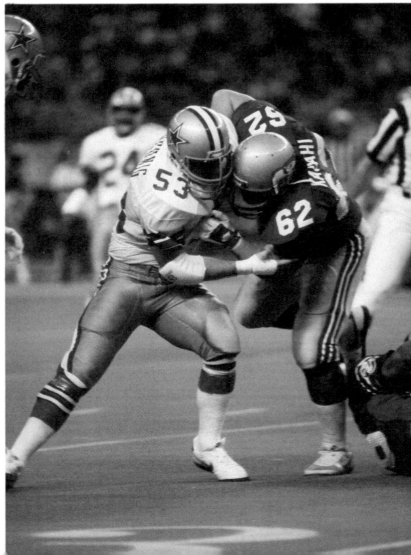

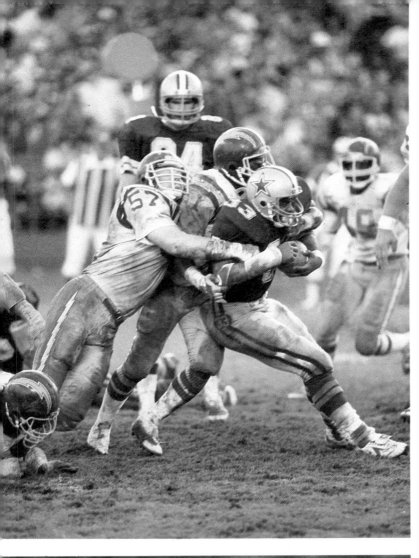

There would come a time, however, when he would demand to be judged on his own merits. And with that in mind he set about to erase every passing mark in the Dallas Cowboys record book. And during his four-year tenure as the starting quarterback, White would direct the team to 37 victories and suffer only 19 defeats.

The defeats, however, were of such a nature as to cause history to beg to repeat itself. Remember how fans wearied of Don Meredith and cried out for Craig Morton? And how when Morton ran into difficulties the call went out for Staubach?

Now, as the decade rushes toward the midway point with no addition to the Cowboys' trophy case, there are those looking beyond White to the next heir apparent. Such is the nature of the job, of the game, and those who follow it.

Still, it is worth noting that White and the Cowboys made three straight trips to the conference championship game, in 1980, '81 and '82, before the season's end, one win shy of a sixth Super Bowl appearance.

In his inaugural year, in fact, White had given every indication that the Cowboys would not miss a beat in Staubach's absence. Not only did he lead the team through a 12-4 regular season record but would also demonstrate the manner of clutch play Dallas followers had come to expect of their quarterbacks.

It was in the 1980 Divisional Playoff in Atlanta that White managed a miracle of his own.

Having lost the Eastern Division title to Philadelphia, Dallas was forced to take the wild card route through the playoffs. After brushing aside Los Angeles, it traveled to Atlanta to face the NFC West champions.

On a bitterly cold afternoon the hosts showed precious little mercy in the early going, building a 24-10 lead, which they would carry into the final 15 minutes of play.

Just over four minutes remained when White jolted the Fulton County Stadium audience to attention. The score had stood at 27-17 when the Cowboys seemed to click into the "two-minute drill" that Staubach had made legendary. White was

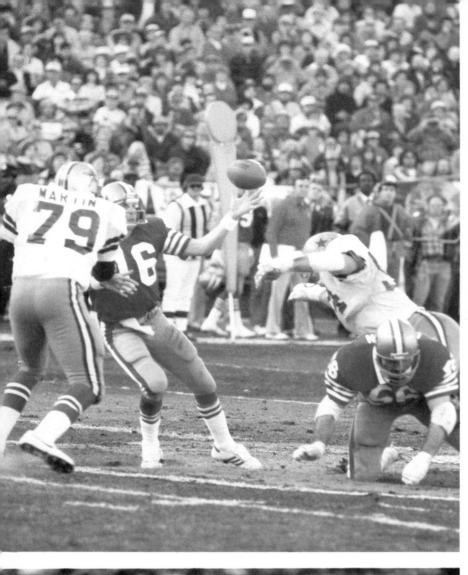

suddenly carving at the Falcons' defense, capping a drive with a 14-yard touchdown pass to Drew Pearson, the same man who had been on the receiving end of so many of White's predecessor's desperation passes. Only 1:48 remained when the Dallas offense gained possession for one last attempt at salvaging the day. White needed only a minute of it before he again connected with Pearson for a score that lifted Dallas to a 30-27 victory.

It was, beamed Landry, the Cowboys' third miracle. The others, of course, had taken place in San Francisco, then in Minnesota, orchestrated by Staubach. This one, however, belonged to White.

The following week, however, the Cinderella story would end as the Eagles, a team the Cowboys had soundly defeated in the regular season finale, won the NFC title game and advanced to the Super Bowl.

White was quick to point out that none of what he had accomplished in his first season at the helm was significant inasmuch as he failed to attain the goal he and his teammates had set. "Until I'm able to put a Super Bowl ring on everyone's finger," Danny said, "there's no way I can be satisfied."

The statement, in retrospect, is the birthplace of much of the Cowboys' frustration in recent years. A year later they were back in the NFC Championship game, this time facing a new opponent, Bill Walsh's San Francisco 49ers.

And again disappointment would slap "America's Team" across the face. With Dallas leading and the clock ticking away the final minutes, quarterback Joe Montana launched a miracle drive of his own, finally connecting with receiver Dwight Clark in the endzone to give the 49ers a 28-27 victory.

In Dallas the grumbling began. Once more there was public concern over the team's ability to win the big one. Danny White was aware that the question was, by and large, being directed to him.

And so, in his third year, he again went in search of the Holy Grail in a season that perhaps should not even have been. After but two games of the 1982 campaign the NFL Players' Association went on strike, stunning a nation which had come to hold its sports heroes above auto workers and teamsters. For eight agonizing weeks there was no NFL football and disenchantment visited fans, front offices, and the players.

And, just as serious discussion of cancellation of the remainder of the season got underway, the strike issues were resolved and play resumed. Since there would be only nine regular season games, league commissioner Pete Rozelle announced a first-time-ever Super Bowl tournament format to replace the traditional playoffs. Dallas, 6-3 for the year, again was a wild card sort of entry into a post-season crap-shoot that would require them to win four games if they hoped to regain the world championship.

By the time they reached the NFC Championship game their believers had regrouped. Surely there was no way the Cowboys could arrive at the same well three straight times and go away thirsty. Perhaps the shortened season would taint the Super Bowl championship, but the Cowboys were eager to have it any way they could get it.

But this time, in Washington's RFK Stadium, there was never any doubt. No fluke calls, no harrowing last-minute finishes. The Redskins triumphed, 31-17,

Dallas' fastest wide receiver since Bob Hayes is Ohio State-ex Doug Donley (above left), a teammate who quarterback Danny White (above) will be looking for more regularly now that Drew Pearson has retired. The newest stars on the defensive front are All-Pro cornerback Everson Walls (upper right) and Bill Bates (lower right) who was voted the Specialty Teams Player of the Year in his rookie season.

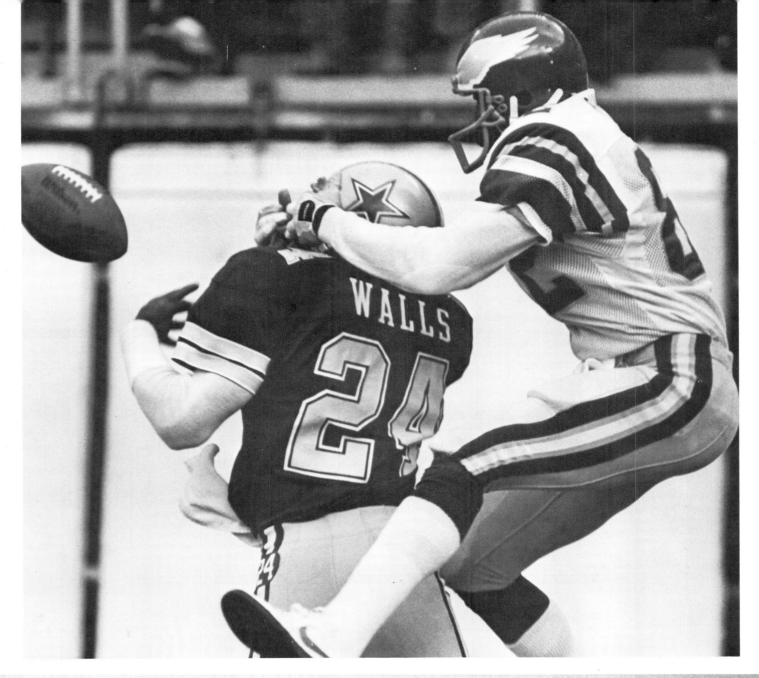

and would go on to become the new world champions. Dallas' problems were compounded by the fact starting quarterback Danny White was kayoed in the waning stages of the first half. While backup Gary Hogeboom would come on to spark something of a rally, directing Dallas to a pair of touchdowns, interceptions would eventually be his — and the team's — downfall.

It would, in fact, be the Redskins who would emerge as the roadblock to the Cowboys' success in '83 as well. Despite a 12-4 regular season, Dallas was forced into the wild card bracket as the Redskins captured the NFC East with a 14-2 mark. And in one quick playoff week the Cowboys were out, losers to the Los Angeles Rams.

There is, now, talk of changes, of a new assertiveness and a renewed attitude toward the goals the team still hopes to achieve in the eighties. Tom Landry has made it clear that training camp would again become a demanding, unyielding grind. "Fort Landry," they called it in 1983. And there are echoes from the mid-sixties in the demands he is now making of his team, his assistants, and of himself.

There is, then, more than a hint that things will be different in the days to come. Of course, there is the new ownership, headed by Dallas businessman H.R. (Bum) Bright; there are plans for a new workout site and corporate headquarters at the Valley Ranch. And, no doubt, there will be new faces wearing the Cowboys uniform. Prior to the '84 season, for instance, Harvey Martin called it a career; so did Pro Bowl offensive lineman Pat Donovan.

On the other hand, there are the still-fresh faces of such promising performers as Everson Walls, Howard Richards, and others. In time they will become a part of the Cowboys' legacy, the folklore of one of the winningest teams in the history of professional sports.

"Our goal has not changed," says Schramm. "The Super Bowl is always what we strive for."

*Fullback Ron Springs finds running room against the Washington Redskins.*

*Seeing running back Tony Dorsett in the open spaces has become a familiar sight to Dallas Cowboys followers.*

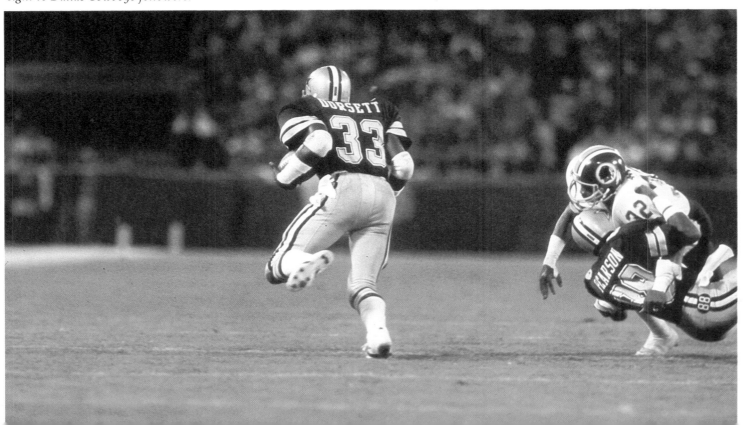

# The Organization

While there is little argument that winning is the primary ingredient for success in the world of professional sports, the Dallas Cowboys' climb can be charted in areas well removed from win-loss percentages and titles earned. Once the struggling days of the early sixties were behind them, they assumed the role of pacesetter — daring to be different as the corporate truism goes. And in their daring, adventurous approach to the molding not only of a championship team but a championship-caliber organization, they've gained status as one of the nation's best-known enterprises.

"It all starts with winning," declares Cowboys president and general manager Tex Schramm. "Without that, nothing else of a successful nature would be possible." Thus the reading of each Sunday's scoreboard is the foundation upon which the Cowboys organization is built. Eighteen consecutive winning seasons, then, is what sets them apart. But, it is a record which begets other records. The Cowboys regularly play to sellout crowds, at home and on the road; they own virtually every television rating high-water mark that's kept; products bearing their insignia account for 28 percent of all sales of NFL Properties, the league clearinghouse for everything from T-shirts to tumblers; The Dallas Cowboys Weekly, a publication begun nine years ago to better spread the word about the team, enjoys a paid circulation nearing 100,000; the Cowboys Cheerleaders have, with overseas armed forces tours, made-for-TV movies, books and posters, become almost as recognizable as the team they cheer for; and players, both past and present, seem in constant demand as broadcasters, speakers, or to endorse products ranging from iced tea to grocery store chains.

All of which is to say the Cowboys have a salable product and they market it better than any professional sports franchise in business today. And Schramm, for one, is working on that. A man with a keen sense of history, he admits concern about how the Dallas Cowboys will be viewed by historians.

"I'd like for people to remember us like they do the great Yankees teams of the Twenties, Thirties and Forties," he says. "Now there was an organization, one you could use as a blueprint, an example to follow. The great players would come and go and so would the managers and coaches. But they kept their status because the organization maintained its excellence.

"You know, we were the first team ever to win Super Bowls with almost completely different teams," he adds. "We've been able to maintain a high level of performance while going through rebuilding years. Teams like the New York Giants, Baltimore, and Green Bay had their moments at the top but when their players got old, they crumbled."

The fact the Cowboys have advanced to the playoffs for the last nine straight years underscores Schramm's observation.

The achievement of such long-range success did not occur by accident. It was, in fact, carefully planned 25 years ago. Clint Murchison, Jr., an astute businessman who was quick to admit his knowledge of the technical aspect of football was no better than

*What others say about the success of the Dallas Cowboys organization:*

*EDDIE LeBARON, general manager, Atlanta Falcons: "To me the big secret to the Cowboys' success is their continuity. Sure, there were lots of setbacks in those early days but Tom Landry was always there to coach, Tex Schramm was always there to run the team, and Gil Brandt was always there to handle the personnel. They were — and still are — the right people in the right jobs. Winning can be simple if you have those ingredients. That and always being able to think ahead."*

*CURT MOSHER, public relations director, St. Louis Cardinals: "It's a well-known fact that Dallas has always made a concerted effort to be a pacesetter in professional football. Tex Schramm is the man who always wanted to find new ways to do things better and with a little more flair. And that rubs off. It is evident in Gil Brandt's scouting program and in Tom Landry's coaching. They're all pacesetters in their particular areas. In an atmosphere of success like Dallas has developed, you can do a lot of things with a little more confidence."*

*AL WARD, NFL executive: "In Dallas they already knew how they were going to handle success even before they became successful. Everyone was aware that once you start winning, that's the time to get on your high horse and get to work. It was all a part of their plan. And it has worked beautifully. The thing that has always impressed me most about the Cowboys organization is the way they utilize their time. It has always been important to get as much out of every day as possible. I think that was one of the things that got them to the top so quickly."*

*It all begins in the drafting room where president and general manager Tex Schramm, player personnel director Gil Brandt, and head coach Tom Landry select players to man future championship teams. And the man who put it all in motion a quarter century ago is Clint Murchison, Jr., shown (at left) pulling the ball away from kicker Rafael Septien.*

that of the average fan, felt the shortest route to success was to follow the simple business rules which had worked for him in other areas. "What you do," he says, "is hire the best possible people you can find to run your business, then step back and let them run it. And unless you have evidence they aren't getting the job done, you leave them alone."

The result has been a remarkable stability within the executive ranks of the Cowboys. Of the four individuals who formed the foundation of the franchise back there in 1960, three remain, doing the same jobs they were originally assigned to do. And, in a sense, the success of those three is a legacy of the one man now absent from the picture, Murchison.

Following the 1983 season, he sold the team to a group of businessmen headed by H.R. (Bum) Bright. And Bright, quick to recognize the old axiom which insists that if something ain't broke, don't fix it, has repeatedly stated that he will, as did Murchison, remain in the background. "I see no reason for me to get more involved in the day-to-day operation of the team than is necessary," he says. "The people who are running the Dallas Cowboys have been doing an exceptional job for a long time. Why would anyone want to change that?"

69

At the time the Cowboys were beginning to gain the attention and admiration of a football-crazed nation, they were, as Schramm puts it, the perfect heroes for the time. "Once our popularity got going," he says, "we wanted to be sure that it continued. I feel we're more image-conscious than any other team in the league. We try to do everything first-class from top to bottom. We don't cut corners, and we've attempted to be as innovative in the front office as the team has been on the field."

Schramm smiles as he reflects on the impact that his own business philosophy and guidance have had on the Cowboys. "As far back as I can remember," he admits, "I dreamed of the opportunity to take a team from scratch and build it. So I guess you could call my job a dream come true."

It's a far cry from his original aspiration to become a sportswriter. A journalism major at the University of Texas, he worked as a $35-a-week member of the *Austin American-Statesman* sports staff during his undergraduate days before moving west to become the public relations man for the Los Angeles Rams in 1947. There he worked his way up to general manager and assistant to the president, hiring a young man named Pete Rozelle (now NFL commissioner), to fill his old job in the PR department.

But, disenchanted with the power struggle that had developed among Ram owners, he left the club in 1957 to play a part in the big sports boom then occurring in the television industry. Joining CBS, he got the job of assistant director of sports and was put in charge of handling the first telecast ever of the Winter Olympic Games. It was Schramm, for example, who originated the idea of using an anchor reporter for covering major events; CBS's anchorman for the Winter Games telecast would be Walter Cronkite. Schramm's reputation in the sports world grew. While at CBS, he turned down jobs with the NFL Detroit Lions, the Detroit Pistons of the National Basketball Association, and the Montreal Alouettes of the Canadian Football League. He also made it known he was not interested when talk began of his becoming commissioner of the NBA.

Only when mutual friends brought him in touch with Clint Murchison was his enthusiasm for sports management rekindled. He had, he admits, always felt he would return, but only under the right circumstances. What the big money man from Dallas was offering was a big gamble — and Schramm jumped at it.

"When Clint hired me," Tex says, "we weren't even sure we'd have a team, so the people at CBS told me that if things didn't work out I could come back to my old job."

Schramm, however, pursued his new challenge without so much as a look back. With Murchison's blessings, he set about to hire those people he felt would best help a new team get from blueprint to the playing field. He hired a little-known, part-time scout named Gil Brandt to seek out players and sign them to contracts. One of his choices coach was Sid Gillman, an established NFL name, but he ultimately decided to seek out the services of a young former defensive coach of the New York Giants named Tom Landry.

Along the way, Murchison gave Schramm a free hand, voicing trust in his judgment.

Today, a quarter century later, the names are the same; only the titles have changed slightly. Schramm is president as well as managing general partner; Brandt is vice-president in charge of personnel; and Landry remains as head coach, enjoying the longest tenure of anyone now in the business.

It is that long-standing relationship, many say, which has provided the backbone of the Dallas success. Unlike the in-and-out shuffle so common to the other NFL front offices, there's a feeling of permanence with the Cowboys. And, asserts Schramm, that's the way it should be.

"We don't have anyone looking over the other fellow's shoulder here," he says. "We have qualified people hired to do a particular job. It's our philosophy that to be able to function at their best, people have to have a certain sense of stability. If someone doesn't really know how long he's going to be around he is more likely to make a decision to sacrifice the future for the present. We don't want that."

A man both outspoken and insightful, Schramm wields substantial power in the NFL. For instance, he was chairman of the owners' negotiation committee during the first of many disputes with the NFL Players' Association. He's chairman of the league rules committee and has been honored as the NFL Executive of the Year. It was Schramm who negotiated the NFL-AFL merger.

They are all, he says, parts of that dream he held to for so long.

Though he majored in business administration and had decided to seek some kind of management position before being summoned to Dallas, Tom Landry avoids the hard-core business side of the team operations. He and his assistant coaches are a building's length removed from the offices of the administration staff. It is a plan not without design.

"I'm aware of the business phase of the organization," says Landry, "but my job is to coach. There is nothing that Tex, Gil, or any of those people do that I could do half as well. They have their jobs to perform and we coaches have ours. Running a professional football team properly is hard work for everyone, and it's all related. When you break it down, the ticket manager and the equipment manager both have to do their jobs well or things begin falling apart. And, frankly, I don't know anything about selling tickets or making sure we have the proper equipment."

By the same token, there are no suggestions of plays coming to Landry from the owners or the general manager. They own and they general manage; Landry's the coach.

Thus if, as Schramm says, none of the Cowboys' success was possible if the team didn't win, one would have to lend a large measure of praise to the contribution Landry has made.

"Without a doubt," Schramm says, "Tom Landry is the best. He and I work well together on those things we have to deal with jointly, but I made it a point not to jump into his area of responsibility for the simple reason I don't know that much about it."

Landry, on the other hand, is quick to hand off praise to Schramm: "When you think about the success of the Cowboys," he says, "you have to remember it was Tex who built the organization."

Late in 1959 when he saw the need to sign free

agents for the hoped-for upcoming season, Schramm thought of Gil Brandt, a baby photographer who had done some part-time scouting for the Los Angeles Rams. He called and asked if Brandt might help in signing some players and was astonished when he accomplished the assigned mission so quickly. Schramm gave him another assignment which was carried out just as swiftly, and Brandt's been a key member of the Cowboys organization ever since.

Today he is generally recognized as the top player personnel director in the NFL. "He is," says a fellow scout, "the man who revolutionized our business. He poked around at the little colleges no one had ever heard of and gathered information on players who weren't on anyone's list. He's a guy who was quick to spot the great athletes who hadn't played a down of college football but were prospects just the same. The list goes on and on."

Brandt pursues his job with a dedication that borders on fanaticism. His office and home number are the same. In a room next to his office is a virtual library of notes and statistics on college players, many of them who won't be seniors for several seasons yet. Not only does he want to know a player's height, weight, and number of yards gained, but also his background, interests, the names of his immediate family, his girlfriend — even the make and model of car he drives.

To accomplish such titanic fact-gathering, he keeps a staff of scouts on the road or on the phone year-round. He even hires knowledgeable Dallas-area high school coaches to spend their evenings in the Cowboys' offices, grading films obtained from colleges throughout the country.

In recent years Brandt's responsibilities have gone well beyond the selection of players. He has inherited player contract negotiation duties from Schramm and has gained a reputation as a fair but hard-bargain dealer.

*Doug Todd heads up the Cowboys' public relations staff.*

*Joe Bailey, vice-president in charge of administration, has been associated with the club since 1961.*

"There are a lot of things which come under consideration when we're talking contract," Brandt points out, "but there are a few basic yardsticks we adhere to. The Cowboys don't have a lot of players who have the kind of contracts which makes headlines, but I don't think we've ever been accused of being pinch-pennies either.

"What we try to do is look at the entire team, not just the individual. For instance, all the incentive clauses we build into a player's contract are team-oriented rather than based simply on individual merit and accomplishment. And, we always judge a player's contribution to the team when we determine his salary. I think it is safe to say our salary budget compares favorably with any other team in the NFL. But, unlike some others, what we strive for is overall fairness."

In the most recent NFL salary survey, the Cowboys ranked ahead of all other teams in the league.

It is but another sign of successful business management on the part of the Cowboys.

Had this text been written in masthead order, the name of Clint Murchison, Jr., would have appeared first on the list of key people who have made the Cowboys what they are today. But, offered a choice, this is where he would have preferred to be.

For twenty-four years the diminutive millionaire was the behind-the-scenes partner in the Cowboys' success story.

"To a certain extent," he says, "I always avoided publicity. Certainly I've never sought it out. I never felt my name being in the papers was going to sell tickets or win games. Besides, I'm basically a shy person. I'm little [5-7] and when a little guys pops off, he's liable to get his nose busted. Actually, though, I was pretty active in the operation of the team for the first eight or ten years.

"But as time went on and things began running smoothly, I stayed out. I quit going to the owners' meetings for the simple reason they got too big and weren't much fun anymore.

"Tex and I always had a good understanding, a good relationship, personally and in business. If something came up that he felt I needed to know about, he gave me a call. I always felt comfortable with that. I've always felt it best to let people who know what they're doing run things. In my estimation, it is the only way you can run a business. When you start second-guessing executives, they're going to rebel and eventually quit. The people who run the Cowboys know what they're doing. They're regarded as the best in their respective fields. And I always felt they should be allowed to do their jobs without interference from me."

"You know," says Schramm, "I don't ever recall his asking me what the amount of any player's contract was. He was never concerned with that. He was comfortable leaving that part of the operation to us. And his philosophy permeated the whole organization and was one of the major reasons for our success."

Clearly, the organization which Bum Bright and his group of investors purchased in the spring of 1984 is a solid one.

*Key figures in the creation of the Cowboys franchise were NFL Commissioner Pete Rozelle (above left), Tom Landry (center), and Tex Schramm. Former owner Clint Murchison, Jr. and partner Bedford Wynne (right) watch their team from a sideline vantage point.*

72

# An Interview With Tex Schramm

When Clint Murchison, Jr., began to put the organization together that would eventually be known as the Dallas Cowboys, he reached out to the New York offices of CBS-TV for a man to direct the day-to-day operation of the club he hoped to own.

Advised by Chicago Bears owner-coach George Halas that Texas E. Schramm, a Californian with strong ties in the Lone Star State, would be an ideal man to serve as general manager of his team, Murchison summoned him to Dallas.

And Tex was eager to make the trip. It was, in a sense, a homecoming for the enthusiastic young man whose career had already wound through the newspaper business, ten years with the Los Angeles Rams front office, and three as assistant director of sports for CBS. Even before Murchison's call, in fact, Schramm had been aware of the possibility there might be a new franchise in Dallas. And he wanted to be a part of it.

Which he has now for a quarter of a century, watching the Cowboys climb from losers to winners, from unknowns to one of pro sports' best-known organizations.

*When Clint Murchison first contacted you with the idea of moving to Dallas to become a part of a new team, did you have reservations about its chance for success?*

I was in New York, working for CBS in September of 1959, when I began hearing stories that there would be, in all probability, an expansion team in Dallas and that Clint Murchison and Bedford Wynne were the people interested in owning it. The idea interested me, so I called a friend in Dallas, Bill Sansing, and asked if he would see what he could find out. He, in turn, contacted Field Scovell and Field got in touch with Clint and Wynne. That's how my name got in the pot.

A few weeks later I was invited down to talk with Clint about his plans to get a team for Dallas. At the time it was rumored that the Chicago Cardinals were for sale and I told Clint that from a purely financial standpoint I thought an expansion team would lose as much, or more, money in the formulative years as it would cost to be an existing team. Deep down, however, I was excited about the opportunity to start a team from scratch. And, during the course of our conversation I gathered that was Clint's preference. A week or two later he called to say he was ready to proceed and offered me a job.

I was excited about the whole idea but since there was no promise Dallas was actually going to get a team, I had to consider the situation carefully. Finally, I went to the executives at CBS and told them of the possibility of Dallas coming into the NFL and Clint's offer. At the time I was in charge of production of the first Winter Olympics, to be held in Squaw Valley. They told me to continue with my work on the Olympics and also pursue the Dallas opportunity. See, it wasn't going to be determined until January whether Dallas would get a franchise or not. I wanted the job badly but was relieved that CBS told me that if things didn't work out I had a job there.

*In those early days, when the team was still in its formative stages, did you have a timetable for success in mind?*

I had no timetable, but I had total confidence that we would eventually be successful. The methods and philosophies I had learned during my ten years with the Los Angeles Rams had provided me with what I felt was a pretty good formula for success. And I had the opportunity to look at the operations of other NFL teams during the three years I spent at CBS. Probably those three years were very important because they enabled me to step back from being involved in just one pro football operation and judge the things others were doing.

One of the things I recognized while with the Rams was the need for a thorough scouting system. We had one, but we still didn't win as consistently as I thought we should. What it boiled down to was the fact we were bringing in so many good young players that we weren't giving the older players time to really mature and gain the experience necessary for a championship team. I also recognized that in scouting you can gather so much information that you can't utilize it properly. I also felt that people in football have their own inbred prejudices and opinions of what makes a good player. Such subconscious preconceptions affect objectivity in grading players for the draft.

While I was with CBS I was introduced to the computers which we used during the Winter Olympics. Our studios were in the IBM building and I began talking with some of their people about the possibility of using computers to evaluate players. I felt if it would work, it would answer two major concerns I had about evaluating talent — dealing with a large volume of information, then making proper use of it.

*Did the Cowboys become winners more quickly than you had anticipated?*

I never thought of our progress in those terms. Each year I felt we were making big strides. I was confident that we had the proper cast of people in Tom Landry and Gil Brandt, so we all felt it was just a matter of time. Sometimes, when you're young you tend to go on blind confidence, and I think that was pretty much our attitude in those early days.

Truthfully, the winning, the turnaround, happened rather unexpectedly. In 1965 we went 7-7 and to the Playoff Bowl in Miami. I doubt you'll ever see a happier group of people than we were when that happened. I think we all felt it was going to be better and better from that point on. And it was. The next year we made it to the NFL Championship game.

*Is there a moment in the club's history that you would pinpoint as the most important milestone to date?*

There have been two milestones, really. The most significant in our history were the two championship games against Green Bay. Here we were, an expansion franchise, playing a legendary team for the league championship. It was then that we formed a lot of the roots for the popularity we

were to later enjoy around the country. We started out as the underdog and people rallied to us. And, I think, they were attracted by the fact we weren't an ordinary kind of team. The Cowboys then were a collection of athletes from all walks of life. We had track men, basketball players, a finger-snapping quarterback. People seemed to really pick up on the personality of the team.

And, though we lost both the games to the Packers, they were exciting games. The Ice Bowl, in fact, was to become one of the most famous in NFL history. That we were a part of the league's history at such a young age was something we benefited from.

I think those two games sort of set a pattern for the Cowboys. Even in losing we gained confidence in ourselves. So did the general public. It was then, I think, that people began seeing us as the team of the future.

*But there would be several years of near-misses after that. Dallas was tagged the team that couldn't win the big one. What were your feelings when Dallas won its first Super Bowl?*

It was one of the greatest feelings of relief and satisfaction I've ever known. I think the same applied for everyone in the organization. That 1971 season was one of the most grim I've ever been involved in. I've never seen so many people so dedicated to accomplishing something. There was no joking, no horsing around. You could feel the intensity.

The game itself was almost anti-climactic. It was one of the greatest games Dallas has ever played. And afterwards, everyone knew that the monkey was finally off our backs. We had reached the point where winning wasn't enough. To be recognized in the manner we wanted, we had to win it all, to be the Super Bowl champions. Once that was accomplished everyone felt a great deal better. And it put us in a position of setting newer, higher goals.

*You've been regarded as an innovative president and general manager throughout your career with the Cowboys. Are there accomplishments which have given you more personal satisfaction than others?*

In my role with this club, the most satisfying thing is the consistency of our success over the years. That, to me, should be the number one objective of any sports organization. I'll always get the greatest pleasure from realizing we've had 18 winning seasons and been in the playoffs 17 times, things like that. In a sense, the five Super Bowls and two championships are just icing on the cake.

*Your contributions haven't been restricted to the building of the team, though. You've also been something of a pacesetter in what, for lack of a better phrase, would be called the entertainment side of pro football. Like the Cowboys Cheerleaders, for instance.*

You've always got to be concerned with the show-business side of things. What we've tried to do is give the fans more than their money's worth. You begin, obviously, with a quality team. But there is more. I think we've got the finest stadium in the country for people to come to. And the Cheerleaders have become something of an institution. I simply felt we needed something more colorful to attract people's attention during time-outs and lulls in the game. Quite honestly, I never dreamed the Cheerleaders would become the phenomenon they are. People all over the world know about them. After our girls were so successful every other team in the league — with a few exceptions — began cheerleader tryouts. One year, it was about the hottest topic in the league. And they were all imitating what we were doing. Which was fun since I hold to the philosophy that imitation is the highest form of flattery.

*If you would, generally outline the progress of the NFL in the last 25 years. What do you think has brought about the greatest advancement in the game?*

First and foremost is the explosion of television coverage. The popularity of pro football had been building since the end of World War II and continued through the fifties. Back then, though, we were getting only limited television coverage, generally in areas where the game wasn't being played. What that did was help it to become a national game.

Starting in the sixties the TV exposure increased and eventually the sport grew to the point where it eclipsed baseball. That's when things really got rolling.

Also, I think the interest generated by the war with the AFL and the eventual merger helped. Then the advent of the Super Bowl and our current system of playoffs solidified the game in the minds of the fans.

That got us into the seventies with a full head of steam and the quality and popularity of the game really took off. The next big step was Monday Night Football, taking the game into homes in prime time and adding greatly to its stature.

Also significant is the fact our rules and

competition committees have kept up with the changing times. As players got bigger and faster, the game became more sophisticated. The coaches, in turn, altered the game to maintain a high level of quality. And along the way we've changed rules which have enabled them to do so.

And, I think timing has had a great deal to do with the NFL's success. We were a game right for the times.

*You've had a front row seat from which to view the coaching career of Tom Landry. What changes have you seen in his approach to the game? And what do you feel will be the greatest legacy he will leave when he retires?*

Tom has always been a paradox. He's very innovative in his coaching yet has always had the ability to mix that with a great understanding of the value of experience and application of the fundamentals. On one hand you hear that we're the cold, computerized team; yet on the other, we've got an outstanding record and have been an exciting, ever-changing team. Tom has always been one of the most progressive when it comes to change when change is needed. In a sense he's like two men. When looking at the defense he is very demanding, very disciplined, wanting a regimented, solid style of play. Yet on offense he has been the leader in things like the multiple formation, motion, the Shotgun, the unexpected.

It is as if he enjoys building a defense which he feels is unbeatable, then sitting down and working and working to find the way to beat it. When all is said and done I think the thing people will have to remember about Landry is his ability to constantly change with the times.

*What has been your philosophy so far as dealing with players is concerned? Have you had favorites over the years? And what kinds of changes have you seen in the athletes who play for the Cowboys?*

Except when I've negotiated contracts I've rarely dealt with the players individually. That's never been part of my job. My responsibility is to provide the proper atmosphere and resources for those who do deal directly with the players. Mine is more of a supportive role. And I've attempted to create the type image for the organization that is conducive to winning.

*You would like to be more personally involved with the players but it is very difficult.*

Actually, in the earlier days there was a closer relationship among all members of the organization — front office, coaches, players. Everyone had a common goal. We were all fighting to gain recognition for the team and for the sport. Unfortunately, that kind of relationship changed with the advent of player agents. In came a third party who didn't have any involvement in the goals of the players or the organization.

Now there's too much emphasis on money. To the athlete, I'm afraid, money has become the accepted gauge of success more than accomplishments on the field.

*Has that developed as the most frustrating part of the game today?*

Not really. Your greatest frustration comes from the things you have no control over. For instance, you can work all year trying to get everything in order, to provide yourself every opportunity in the world to win. You put in the time, the effort, and the dedication, then the ball bounces the wrong way at the wrong time and determines the success or failure of your efforts.

For instance, I was greatly disappointed that we didn't get to the Super Bowl in 1979. One little tipped pass against Los Angeles determined our fate for the whole year. If we had made it to the Super Bowl and won, we would have been judged the Team of the Decade, something I felt we had a right to claim.

But in this line of work you have to forget the frustrations and disappointments of last year and get to work on next year. It's a never-ending cycle; and that's what makes it enjoyable.

*Most of this book deals with a celebration of the past 25 years. What thoughts do you have on the next 25?*

Well, in the first place, they'll have to get along without me at some point during the next quarter century, I'm afraid.

I'm not much at predicting, but I'd have to say there will be some problems the sport will have to deal with in the years to come, mainly because changes seem to come so fast now. But generally I see the success and popularity of pro football continuing to grow.

I suspect we'll see a lot of changes from the TV standpoint. The game will get even faster, even more sophisticated. For instance, I think you'll see even more specialization on the part of athletes playing the game. And I think you'll see electronics playing a

bigger role. Coaches may have direct radio communication with the quarterback on the field instead of using the messenger system or hand signals. And with the growth of crowd noises in the indoor stadiums, it may be necessary to equip the quarterback with some kind of amplification so he can call audibles at the line of scrimmage. And, yes, the officials might be wearing wrist televisions so they can watch replays before making penalty calls.

The uniforms and protective equipment will become lighter and more stylized — and safer. It won't be long before every player will be wearing some kind of knee protection; something that won't affect his mobility but will provide him protection against what is the most critical injury area we have in the game today.

And, at some point in the next 25 years, I think you'll see the game being played outside the United States on a regular basis.

*How would you like Tex Schramm to be remembered by the NFL historians?*

I'd like to be remembered as someone who played a role in creating something unique. I've never made any bones about my belief that history is important and that I'd like to be a part of it. I think everyone who has been a part of the Cowboys organization in the last 25 years will have something special to look back on. They — we — will be looked on and referred to as members of the Dallas Cowboys during a time period when a lot of great things happened. I'm delighted to have been a part of it.

# Fielding a Team

*It was in 1968 when the famed Dallas Cowboys scouting computer appeared to have blown a fuse, tempting them to draft a player who wasn't, well, exactly what they thought they were getting.*

*Dave McDaniels, a wide receiver from little Mississippi Valley State, had been overlooked by the swarm of scouts who had left no college campus unturned in their search for talent. He has size, intelligence and moved his 6-4, 200-pound frame through a 40-yard dash in 4.5 seconds according to a Cowboys scout who personally clocked him.*

*Brandt, then, was beside himself when he was told that McDaniels was still available when it came time for Dallas to make its second round draft selection.*

*The following summer, however, McDaniels arrived at the Thousand Oaks, Calif., training camp and ran the 40 as if his legs were tied together. The best clocking he could manage was five seconds flat. Brandt, outraged, stormed off in search of some explanation.*

*What he was to find out eventually was that the previously reported 40 time had been attained over a 35-yard course. "But," says Brandt in retrospect, "we learned something from it. A tape measure, 40 yards long, is now a standard tool of our trade."*

It is a team said by many to have been assembled by computer, instructed by computer and, some say, perhaps even motivated by computer; a talent-blessed roster whose heart and soul is a bank of supplied facts and figures, tapes, high voltage, and print-outs. Labeled the team of the Scientific Seventies, they served as a prime example of the direction professional football was headed. So much a business that it seemed hard to call it sport; so much of a sport it is hard to call it business.

Nowhere within the width and breadth of the National Football League — America's entire sports spectrum, for that matter — is there a more serious, set-jawed, grim pursuit of the degree of excellence that is to be found within the offices which house the Dallas Cowboys. There is a constant, non-stop search for the slightest edge, that fine line which elevates the Danny White-Tony Dorsett-Randy White Cowboys a notch above the rest of the pro football world.

In the early sixties, while still laying the foundation for a dreamed-of dynasty, Dallas officials found the fifth ace in the deck. In a move that was to revolutionize the game as we know it today, Dallas plugged electronics into the brain, brawn, blood, sweat, and tears of sport.

The computer came to the NFL. And the shockwaves are still being felt.

"We have," says president and general manager Tex Schramm, "developed a reputation that is not totally fair to our people. Sure, we use computers; everyone does. But they are only an aid. For instance, we don't actually draft off the computer as some people seem to think. The computer is just another tool our people use. There is no way you can ever replace the judgment and talent of people. It is people, not computers, who have made our approach successful."

"Football," admits a highly regarded NFL scout who opted not have his name associated with his statement, "is a copycat game. And the Cowboys are the most copied team in the league. Some years ago, they decided to clock prospective players at 40 yards rather than 100 and within six months everyone was following suit. They went out and drafted a great basketball player like Cornell Green, turned him into a defensive back, and suddenly everyone's taking a hard look at basketball players. Word got around they were using computers to evaluate college players and mapping game plans and everyone else in the league was suddenly busting his equipment getting down to wherever they sold computers."

The steady flow of talent which arrives in the Cowboys camp annually is a testimony to the quality of material the Dallas scouting department has been feeding into the computers. And rival defenses have had great difficulty finding fault with the Cowboys' game plans over the years.

Coaches watch film of an upcoming opponent, charting each play [offense and defense] of a game on specially designed pads. By the time they have finished, they've recorded formations, down and

**1960**

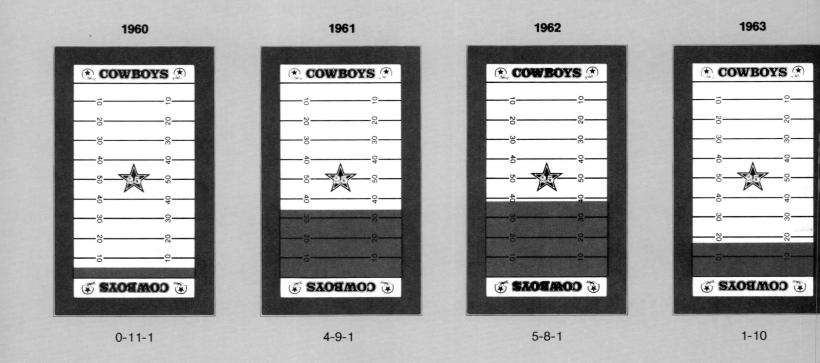

0-11-1

**1961**

4-9-1

**1962**

5-8-1

**1963**

1-10

COWBOYS

**1972**

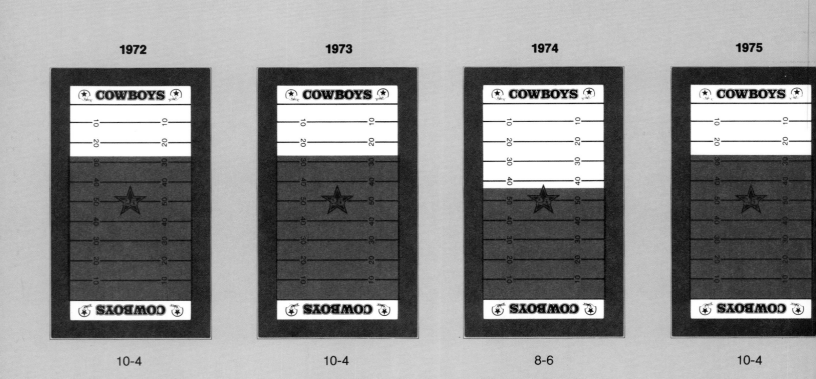

10-4

**1973**

10-4

**1974**

8-6

**1975**

10-4

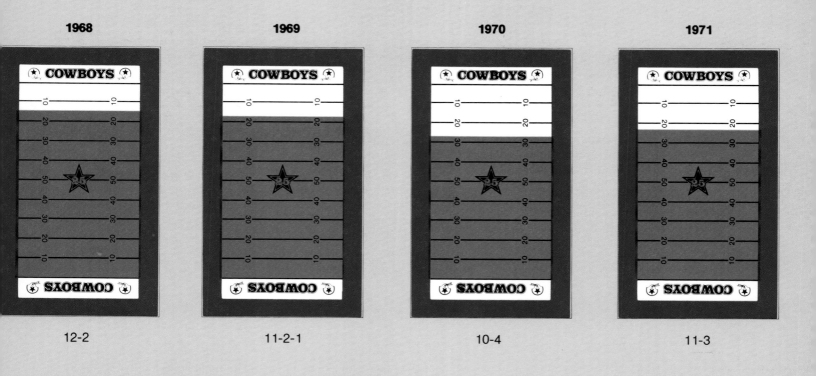

**1968**

COWBOYS

12-2

**1969**

COWBOYS

11-2-1

**1970**

COWBOYS

10-4

**1971**

COWBOYS

11-3

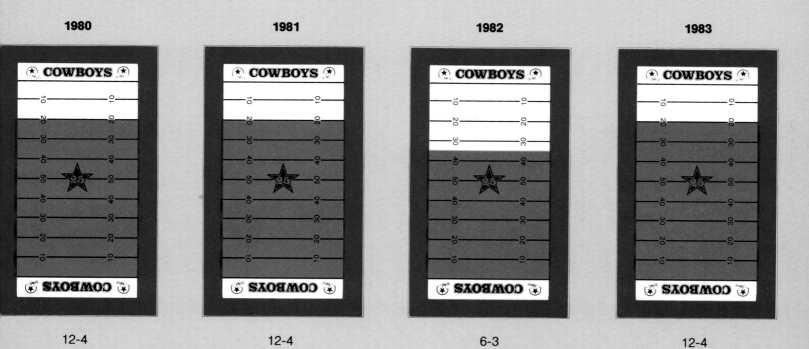

**1980**

COWBOYS

12-4

**1981**

COWBOYS

12-4

**1982**

COWBOYS

6-3

**1983**

COWBOYS

12-4

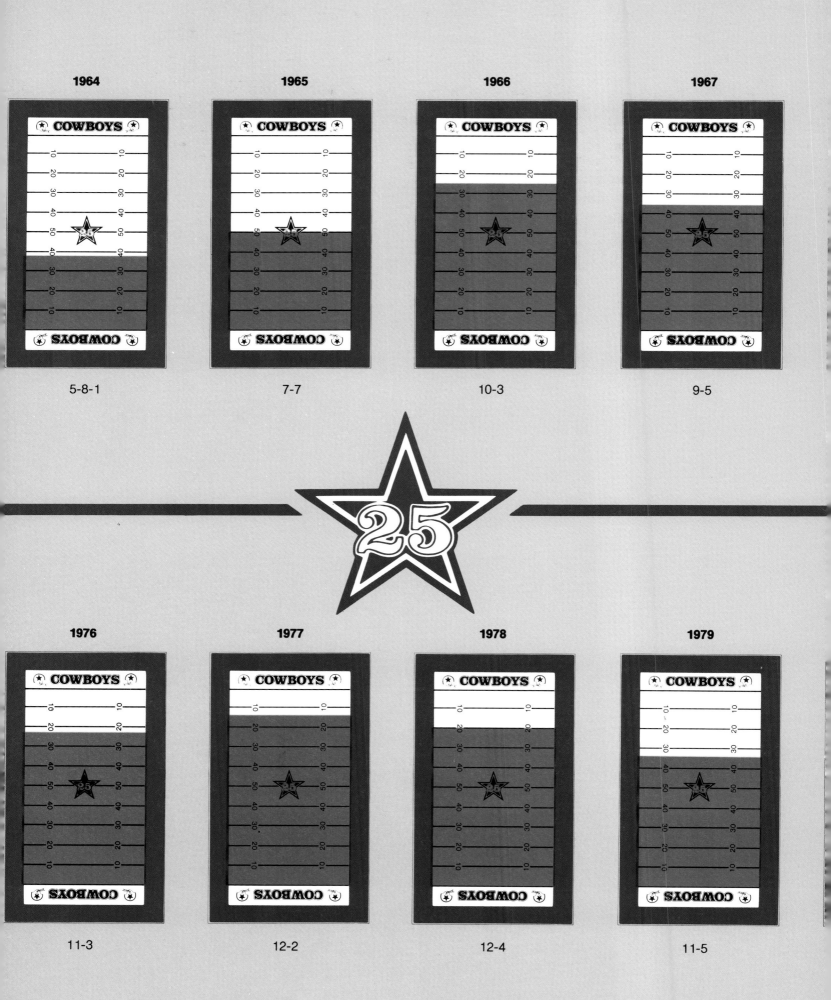

**1964**

COWBOYS

COWBOYS

5-8-1

**1965**

COWBOYS

COWBOYS

7-7

**1966**

COWBOYS

COWBOYS

10-3

**1967**

COWBOYS

COWBOYS

9-5

**25**

**1976**

COWBOYS

COWBOYS

11-3

**1977**

COWBOYS

COWBOYS

12-2

**1978**

COWBOYS

COWBOYS

12-4

**1979**

COWBOYS

COWBOYS

11-5

distance and time of the game in which each particular play was used. Also programmed are such things as whether certain plays were called when the team was ahead or behind, whether the first unit was in and which side of the field the play originated from. The total game — weather conditions, everything — is recorded.

If it all sounds terribly complicated, so be it. So advanced are the Cowboys, computerized methods that the old card-punch system was long ago scrapped in favor of one of the first scanner models. The forms filled out by the coaches are "scanned" by the electronic eye and all information then transferred to tapes.

On Monday mornings, after every possible scrap of information on an upcoming opponent has been gathered, charted, and categorized, the computer receives the information. Thirty-five minutes later a 200-page, book-style scouting report is ready, to be distributed to the players and coaches the following day.

"Of course, it is unreasonable to ask a player to wade through 200 pages of statistics, charts and diagrams," says special assistant Neill Armstrong, "so he's asked to study only that part of the report which applies to his particular area of responsibility.

"Our chief goal is to eliminate as much work as possible, yet still realize maximum results There is nothing in a computerized scouting report that our coaches couldn't do themselves with proper time to assemble it. This way, however, they're freed to deal

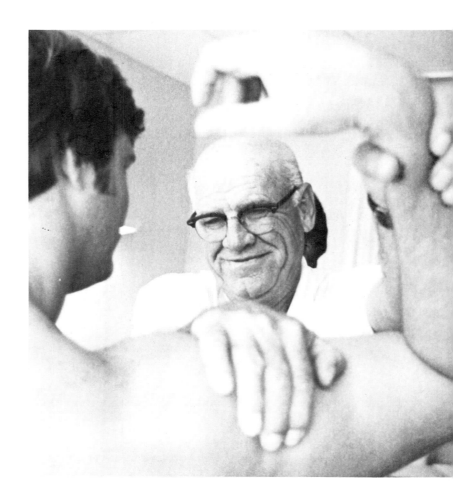

*From the hapless 0-11-1 record of the Cowboys' first year to their steady string of 12-4 seasons in recent years, the Cowboys won-lost record shows how things have changed over the years. Dr. Marvin Knight (right) is among those who attend the Cowboys' medical needs. Then there is the all-important decision-making that goes on annually during the college player draft.*

with other things necessary to get the team ready for a game."

It is difficult to gauge the advantage such high-speed electronic efficiency provides the Cowboys, particularly in view of the fact all others in the league now use much the same system. If, in fact, there is an edge it would lie in the fact Dallas has had longer to refine its program than have others.

"It's a little like the country club golf tournaments they have," player personnel director Gil Brandt says. "You have guys who they put in the third flight, some in the second, better ones in the first, and the best in the championship flight. We like to think we're the club champion in this particular phase of the game."

If rival teams will not concede that Dallas is the champion of game-plan blueprints, they are bound by the record to point to the Cowboys organization as one of the best at spotting college talent that is ofttimes overlooked until Dallas' turn to announce its selection.

The cases in point are numerous. In 1969 one of pro football's leading scouting combines, BLESTO, had Calvin Hill of Yale rated as the 12th best player in that year's collegiate crop. Eleven other running backs were rated above him. The Cowboys, however, entertained more positive feelings and selected him as their No. 1 draft pick. He would finish his first season in the NFL as Rookie of the Year. Lest you call it a fluke, recall that West Texas State running back Duane Thomas was tapped by the Cowboys after 22 other teams had called out their first round preferences. You get the idea.

Then there are the free-agents — young men who were ignored in the draft but signed on by Dallas and given a chance to make a place for themselves in pro ball. From those ranks have come the likes of Cliff Harris, Drew Pearson, Everson Walls, Michael Downs, Benny Barnes, *et al*. "People have questioned the fact we sign so many free agents each year," says Brandt, "but we feel it is a good investment. If you

*On the California Lutheran practice fields each summer, draft selections and free agent rookies make their bids to earn spots on the Cowboys roster.*

can sign 80 or 90 kids and find just one Everson Walls, it has been well worth it."

It was the high hopes of just such coups that sent Cowboys president and general manager Tex Schramm off to secure the services of Service Bureau Corporation, a subsidiary of IBM, in 1960. He suggested they develop a method of applying computers to the numerous problems of scouting. Primary among his reasons for wanting to venture into the electronic realm was to eliminate the emotion that sometimes hinders a scout's judgment. "For instance," he explains, "I would be prone to overlook some of a player's weaknesses if he had blazing speed. Landry gives high priority to character. Then, there are scouts throughout our system who might have prejudices against certain coaches or areas of the country. All of these things — and more — we felt were apt to result in poor judgment.

"And we were gathering too much information on players for our people to handle. By the time we had a draft list whittled down from, say, 2,000 to 300, it was still very difficult to rank that final group from one to 300. Since it took a man at least an hour to read and evaluate the information on a player, it became obvious that no one could judge the 300th player as objectively as he had the first."

Sessions between coaches, scouts, and computer personnel produced the guidelines for the make-up of a good football player. A list of 300 variables that figured into the judging of talent and everything that was not physically possible to measure (speed, height, weight, etc.) was reduced to five dimensions: (1) character, (2) quickness and body control, (3) competitiveness, (4) mental alertness, and (5) strength and explosiveness. To reduce the problems of semantics, to be sure that scouts and coaches all meant the same thing when they analyzed a player, key words were agreed upon.

"We even evaluate the evaluators," says Brandt. "We found that some people are high raters and some are low raters. It was necessary to program that into the system."

The fielding of a Dallas Cowboys team, whether it is for the first day of summer training camp or on a regular season Sunday, is a high-tech proposition.

*While players go through a myriad of conditioning drills and instruction, scouts like John Wooten and Red Hickey watch closely for signs that indicate a player has NFL abilities.*

# An Interview With Gil Brandt

One of the first things Tex Schramm did after assuming the role of general manager, as mentioned earlier, was hire Gil Brandt to serve as director of player personnel. To the more casual observer, it was something of a strange choice.

Brandt's background as a player scout was limited to some part-time work he had done for the Los Angeles Rams. It was, he admits today, more hobby than profession. In fact, he earned his living as a baby photographer.

His interest in football began as a high school quarterback of marginal talent. And while the game itself intrigued him, the most fascinating aspect of the sport was the determination of just what physical elements went into the makeup of a top-notch player. He began writing various colleges, telling them he was a high school coach, requesting films of standout players. In time he graduted to college films and by the mid-fifties was compiling his own list of the top college players in the nation. From that he grew into the part-time job as a scout for the Rams.

Then came the call from Schramm. "The first time I called him," Tex recalls, "I gave him the names of three or four free-agent players we were interested in. In two days he had all of them signed. He was amazing. It was obvious he was a person who put no limit on the time or energy necessary to get the job done."

Today, Brandt is generally regarded as one of the most inventive and successful men in his profession.

*In the early days of the Dallas Cowboys you and your staff broke new ground in the scouting area, signing players from small, little-known schools and athletes who had earned their reputations in sports other than football. Was it difficult to sell the rest of the organization on such a revolutionary philosophy?*

There was no problem selling Tex Schramm or Tom Landry, but I think some of the assistant coaches had their doubts. But we were in a position where we had to do something out of the ordinary. Having come into the league without benefit of a college player draft, we had to find as many ways as possible to improve our team as quickly as possible. We went to the small schools and found people like Jethro Pugh and Rayfield Wright and Cliff Harris. In the case of athletes who had excelled in other sports, patience was the big thing. We went after basketball players, track athletes — anyone with potential to develop into a pro football player. In time, our coaches began to recognize that potential and took the time to develop it.

*Were there moments, in those early days, when you wondered if the Cowboys' master plan was working?*

I was always convinced that we had a good plan. It just required some patience on all our parts. We were fortunate that we had an owner, a general manager, and a head coach who gave it time to work. In any successful business, I think, you are going to find that stability is a key ingredient. The Cowboys have enjoyed that and, quite frankly, have been doing things much the same year after year.

But, sure, there were times when everyone got a little impatient. We started so far down back in 1960, having to open the season with whatever players we could find. And there was no time to even evaluate those we found. We just suited them up and played. Then, in 1963, we were lulled into a false sense of success, probably thinking we'd arrived ahead of schedule. What it really amounted to was the fact we had finally managed to get together a team of players who at least made us look good in the hotel lobby. But there was still too many missing ingredients for it to be a solid team.

*When you were approached about becoming the player personnel director of the Cowboys did you have any reservations at all?*

None at all. I was young and thought it was the greatest opportunity in the world. But I didn't have any idea what a mountain we were going to have to try and climb back then. The only thing that kept us headed in the right direction year after year was the fact everyone in the organization was pulling as hard as he could in the same direction. Everyone knew there were a lot of other teams out there trying to accomplish the same goals we were, and I think that awareness made everyone work just that much harder.

*How would you describe your relationship with the Cowboys players, past and present?*

I'm proud of every player we've had here. It has given me a special feeling to see them succeed, as athletes, then in private life after getting out of the game. And, understand, I'm not taking credit for signing every great player we've had. For instance, I wasn't the one who signed Cliff Harris out of Ouachita, but he's one of my favorite people. I liked him as a player, and I'm delighted he's done so well in business since he retired. We've stayed in touch. I signed Calvin Hill and we became very close. I hear from him on a regular basis. I try to stay in touch with all our ex-players as much as possible. Every week or so, I'll get on the phone and call a few up who I haven't heard from in a while. You know, it is difficult for some to adjust when they leave a team. Too often the organization forgets about them. The Cowboys have made a special effort not to do that.

*In recent years, however, the press has been filled with stories of player vs. management stories. Has it become more difficult to maintain a one-on-one relationship with a player?*

The advent of the agent has helped deteriorate the relationship between player and management in recent years. The agent, who is trying to justify his 10 to 15 percent cut of a player's earnings, has placed management on the bad side of what has developed into a business triangle. Today, salaries are public knowledge; so I question the need for an agent. What it has done is make the whole business of negotiation very complicated. And I think there is a selfish interest on the part of an agent. Rather than ask for a fair salary, one in line with other players at similar positions who have been drafted in similar rounds, some guys shoot for the moon. It gets very unreasonable. To the agent, it is all business: the more money he gets for his client, the bigger his cut

is going to be. What you get into is a one-upmanship kind of thing that is sometimes very hard to deal with.

*In a quarter century of evaluating talent, what changes have you undergone? Are you looking for a different kind of player today than you did 10 or 15 years ago?*

Trends constantly change. Some of the characteristics we were once so impressed by have become less important. In a sense, I think maybe you don't need as good an athlete today. You are looking more for players with special abilities. For instance, the coaches tell us they're looking for offensive linemen with long arms so they can hold off the pass rush. They're looking for running backs who can also catch the football. They want wide receivers who can catch the ball over the middle and not be intimidated by linebackers. Naturally, you're still looking for outstanding athletic ability, but there are occasions when that ability needs to be focused in certain closely defined areas.

*Would you consider the changes dramatic?*

I read in the *Harvard Business Review* recently where it said that for a person to just stay even today he has to be five times more intelligent than he was 10 years ago. I think that whole learning curve thing is taking place in every area of professional football,

from coaching to scouting to actual on-the-field performance. Today, we scouts have to know more about a player simply because the competition is going to be trying to learn more than we are. That's why you test them every way conceivable.

The greatest difference between the seventies and eighties, however, won't be intelligence or ability. In the seventies, the teams that won were those who had the best organization. In the eighties, the successful teams are going to be the ones with the most money — to sign players, to keep up with the modern techniques of training and conditioning, things of that nature.

*Today it is standard procedure for football players, from the high school to the professional level, to be timed in the 40-yard dash to evaluate speed. Wasn't that your idea?*

There was a time when everyone timed a player at 50 yards or maybe 100 yards. And, if a kid ran a 10.4 in the 100, one scout would say he was slow while another might say he was fast. The distance just wasn't a proper one to determine football speed. You always want the fastest player you can find, so we began looking for another way to evaluate speed. I felt 40 yards was an ideal distance to check a player's speed. At that distance you could determine how fast he started, how quickly he built his speed, and how well he maintained it.

The first player who was ever timed at the 40, to the best of my knowledge, was a University of Georgia tight end named Mickey Babb.

*In recent years, you and your staff have come under some criticism for not coming up with the superstar, No. 1 draft selections as you did on a pretty regular basis in the past. Do you feel it is justified?*

I think you have to look at and evaluate the performances of everyone in the league before you say anyone has been successful or failed. It's true we haven't maintained the level of success we had years ago, but I wonder if the other teams have. Still, because our successes were pretty noteworthy in the past, we're watched pretty closely. But you don't see the media saying other teams have had bad drafts when, in fact, some of them have from time to time. And, you have to remember, it has become more and more difficult for a rookie to make this club. Just look around the league at players who didn't make it with the Cowboys but are doing good jobs for other teams. Criticism is a part of life, however, and you just deal with it, then go on trying to do the best job you can do.

*If you could go into the draft with the opportunity to select the ideal professional football player, what would you come away with?*

First, you would want a guy who is a great competitor, someone who, with 35 seconds to go, the ball on your own 20, and no time-outs left, was certain there was some way you could come from behind and win the ball game. Then, of course, you would look for different things at different positions. You would want linemen who were 6-4 to 6-6, who could run the 40 under five seconds, and could bench press 450 pounds. In a quarterback, you want someone with a strong arm and excellent accuracy. In a wide receiver, you want someone who is going to be able to jump well and come down with the ball at the end of the game, getting you that necessary first down or touchdown. A running back should have great quickness so he can avoid that first wave of contact and the speed to go all the way. And he needs the strength to get the tough two or three yards on third down. And, regardless of the position, you are always looking for a great competitor. That, in my opinion, is the thing which separates the greats from the near-greats.

# Training Camp

It began in Forest Grove, Oregon, on the campus of Pacific University. There, in the summer of 1960, what had to be an NFL record 193 players reported to the first Dallas Cowboys' training camp in hopes of gaining a spot on the roster of pro football's newest team. So crowded were the conditions that players took their meals in shifts and were forced to use both the men's and women's physical education facilities for dressing.

"It was like a revolving door," remembers linebacker Jerry Tubbs. "There were new faces at every practice. It seemed there was always one busload of guys leaving and another coming in. It was a madhouse."

It was also a less than ideal site for which to prepare a team. So, during the middle of the pre-season schedule, the team changed addresses, moving to the campus of St. John's Military Academy in Delafield, Wisconsin. "That place," Tubbs says, "had everyting but a moat. It was like a medieval castle. And in the middle of nowhere. The nearest movie was seven miles away and nobody had any transportation. The place was one Gil Brandt had found. He was hanged in effigy twice while we were staying there."

The next season the Cowboys would move again, this time to St. Olaf's College in Northfield, Minnesota. Then, in 1962, they resided at Northern Michigan College on the banks of Lake Superior. When it snowed during one afternoon practice, Tex Schramm conceded that it wasn't the ideal place for summer conditioning.

It was prior to the 1963 season that Schramm received a call from former Army running back Glenn Davis, suggesting that Dallas serve as the Los Angeles Rams' annual opponent in the pre-season *Los Angeles Times* Charity game. Schramm liked the idea but indicated his team would need a place somewhere in Southern California to train. Davis advised him of a locale that might be ideal for training camp. Located in the Conejo Valley, just 45 minutes north of Los Angeles, Thousand Oaks offered a cool ocean breeze, a quiet college campus, and friendly people. Schramm, desperate to find a permanent home away from home for his team, paid a visit to the campus of California Lutheran, talked with officials, who expressed great enthusiasm for the idea of housing the Dallas Cowboys, and decided it would be ideal.

Cal Lutheran and "The Oaks," as most veteran players now call it, has been the summer home of the Cowboys ever since.

And, while it is unlikely that players would embrace even the Hawaiian beaches as a site for the six weeks of two-a-day practices, team meetings, curfews, and dormitory living, Thousand Oaks is about as good as training camp gets.

"I was like everyone else at first," says former defensive lineman Larry Cole. "The idea of training camp really turned me off. The whole idea of being away from home, locked into a 24-hour-a-day football atmosphere wasn't what any sane adult looks forward to. In time, though, I came to look forward to it. There was work to do, of course, but it

was nice to get away from the telephone at my business. The weather was pleasant and the people out there were great. I made a lot of friends in Thousand Oaks over the years. They really adopted us as their team. I doubt you're ever going to find a pro football player who will say he honestly enjoys the idea of training camp. But, it is one of the game's necessary evils. And going through it in Thousand Oaks probably made it easier than it is for guys on some teams."

In the 22 years the Cowboys have been making their annual trek to the Cal Lutheran campus they have witnessed the tremendous growth of the community. Where once there was nothing more than a few residential areas, a bowling alley, and the college, there now are shopping malls, movie theaters, a welcome selection of fine restaurants and a population which has grown from 10,000 to 100,000.

And there are people like Fred Wright, manager of a quiet, dimly lit neighborhood bar and restaurant, who offers weary players sanctuary from the rigors of practices and meetings. His Pub & Grub is hidden away in the corner of a Thousand Oaks shopping center located near the Cal Lutheran campus. "The guys need a place to kick back and unwind for an hour or so before their curfew," Wright says, "and we try to provide them a quiet, friendly atmosphere in which to do so."

For many of the players, in fact, a visit to Wright's establishment offers a touch of reality. In the Pub & Grub, they're removed from the military-school mentality of training camp, even if for just a few minutes each evening.

"You do everything you can think of to get your mind off things when you're out there," says longtime camp veteran Drew Pearson.

"Actually, you go a little crazy out there every year. You fight against it, but you can't help it. The same routine, same food, same faces every day gets tough. But it is part of the game. Aside from losing, it's probably the worst part."

*The picturesque campus of St. Olaf's was one of the early day pre-season training sites of the Cowboys (above). And picture day (below) was conducted in something of a circus atmosphere as famed sports photographer Jim Laughead (in hat) urged the players to growl for the camera.*

# Conditioning & Equipment

In a time when high-tech has become a way of life, when biomechanics and computerized tests to judge strength, fatigue, speed, and durability have become commonplace in the athletic arena, the Dallas Cowboys have worked to stay one step ahead in the area of conditioning their players.

Standing watch over the manner in which the Cowboys prepare themselves physically for each new season is Dr. Bob Ward, a one-time college track coach who goes out of his way to seek out new and inventive ways to develop a conditioning program. Sometimes, in fact, it would seem the more futuristic and far-out it is, the better Ward likes it.

In addition to providing the players with suggested diets, weight-lifting programs, flexibility training routines, running, and a battery of tests to determine everything from the amount of excess body fat one is carrying to the hand-eye coordination he has, the Cowboys conditioning coach is ever on the look-out for new routines which might be beneficial.

Recently, for instance, he introduced those who engaged in the off-season program at the Cowboys' training facility to the martial arts. By using everything from yoga to Bruce Lee's *jeet kune* to the Filipino *escrima* and *Kali*, Ward developed a program which he felt certain would improve his students' football skills.

"I'm a physical educator by profession and academic training," he says, "so consequently, and hopefully, I have a good understanding of how a ballplayer must be able to move to be effective. I saw where the martial arts provided a way I could explain the body movements and their importance to the players."

"The martial arts are multi-faceted and an excellent resource in training all elements of the body. Moving to your left, moving to your right, the use of the hands in football can be accentuated through the martial arts. I think one would have to be blind not to see that."

While some of his suggestions occasionally draw smiles and/or rolled eyes from the players he supervises, they test his methods nonetheless. When he brought a couple of aerobic dance instructors to the practice field to put them through some dance routines, everyone fell into place. When, recently, he invited an expert in wholistic science and the Chinese martial arts to training camp to demonstrate something called Dragon Dancing, several players were interested to learn what he had to say.

The visiting instructor described how the movements of Dragon Dancing could be used to stretch muscles of the body, strengthen and tone, and even improve cardiovascular fitness, and Ward busily took notes.

Then, a few seasons back, there was the sensory deprivation tank, something that looked as if it had been borrowed from a science fiction movie. In it, a player would float on his back, buoyed in salt water that was kept at a normal external skin temperature

of 93.5 degrees. What he was there to achieve was the "alpha state," in which the brain waves slowed from seven to 12 cycles per second. Research, Ward explained, has shown that when one's body and mind are in such a receptive state, the learning process could be multiplied ten-fold. "By relaxing," he said, "a player can absorb more information — learn the game plan more quickly, things like that."

Which is to say Ward and the Cowboys are ever on the lookout for new ways to improve the minds and bodies of players.

And, while they don't always understand them, they give them a try.

It was Jackie Smith, the former St. Louis Cardinals tight end who joined the Cowboys for one final NFL season in 1978, who came up with one of the most interesting responses to Ward's myriad of tests. Having put the new Cowboy through a battery of exams that determined everything from explosiveness to body fat, Ward presented Smith with a bound computer print-out filled with charts and numbers.

Smith looked it over, then turned his attention to Ward who stood, awaiting some reaction. Jackie shook his head. "Bob," he said, "I can't read any of this. Can't you just tell me whether I'm alive or dead and let it go at that?"

*When the new crop of rookies first arrive their strength is immediately tested during a weight-lifting session (above). Few, however, come close to the efforts of veteran Randy White (right), who is the club record-holder.*

Training camp is a variety of things: regular meetings (top left), long hours in the weight cage near the practice fields (bottom left), and exercise drills. Young Mike Hagen (bottom right) is now a member of the Cowboys staff.

You probably don't remember ol' Muddy Wallace, former quarterback of the Dallas Cowboys; a guy whose flame burned brightly for a brief period of time before bad knees and booze took their toll. The same Muddy Wallace who occasionally drops in to shoot a few games of pool at the Pub & Grub near the Cal Lutheran campus in Thousand Oaks.

The reason you don't remember Muddy is because he exists only in the imagination of Fred Wright, manager of the quiet little bar which has, over the years, been a favorite late-night stop of Cowboys players.

"A few years ago," Wright explains, "some people came in, hoping to see some of the players. On that particular night there wasn't a single player in the place and you could see the disappointment on the visitors' faces. I felt liked I needed to do something to lift their spirits. We've got this big, athletic-looking guy who is a regular, and he was in the back, wearing a football jersey, playing pool.

"So I made up this story about Muddy Wallace. As soon as the people approached him for his autograph he looked over at me and I gave him a wink. He went along with the whole story; even began adding a few stories of his own. He told them how he likes to come around every year when the Cowboys are in town, just to see some of his old teammates and relive old memories.

"One night this was going on and Billy Joe DuPree came in and sat down at the bar. I said something like, 'Hey, Muddy, you remember your old tight end, don't you?' Damned if Billy Joe didn't get in on the act, too. They started trading stories about big games they'd played together. It was a riot."

# The Coaches

There are few coaches in the National Football League who can make the following statement; even fewer who, truth be known, would feel comfortable with such a public stance. Yet with Tom Landry, head coach of the Dallas Cowboys, it has, in the last dozen or so years, been paraphrased with near boring regularity. It goes something like this: "I feel strongly that this can be an outstanding football team, one capable of going to the Super Bowl if the players are willing to do the amount of work necessary."

It is the latter part of the oft-repeated statement which most deserves attention. Hidden beneath that challenge to the players is the confidence Landry feels in himself and his system. What he is saying is that he can, and will, provide the plan. For the ultimate success to be achieved, however, the players must uphold their end.

Such is the philosophy which has carried Thomas Wade Landry to one of the most remarkable coaching careers in professional football history. He's done it all: five trips to the Super Bowl, two world championships, winning season after winning season, citations honoring him with everything from the Horatio Alger Award for his inspirational rise to prominence, to the Order of the Leather Helmet for his distinguished service to the game.

Only George Halas now deceased, has claimed more career victories. Since Halas coached 40 years, that record will likely never be topped.

What, then, is there left to achieve; what is the carrot that is now dangled in the face of the man generally judged as the most successful and innovative in the professional game today?

"What a guy like Tom does," says assistant coach Dick Nolan, "is go out and achieve goals, then once they're achieved he sets new ones. We never talked about it, but you can be sure he has new goals in mind. No doubt he would like to win another Super Bowl, but I think it's more than that. What exactly, I'm not sure I can tell you. But he knows. Believe me, he knows."

*"What a guy like Tom does is go out and achieve goals, then once they're achieved he sets new ones."*

*Neill Armstrong and wife Jane.*

*Dick Nolan*

*Jim Myers*

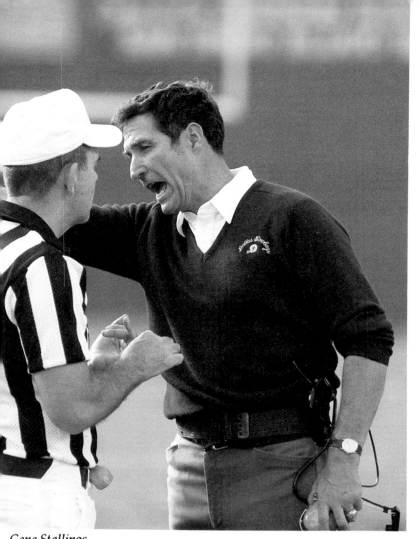

*Gene Stallings*

*Ernie Stautner*

*Ermal Allen*

*Alan Lowry*

*Ben Agajanian*

*Jim Shofner*

*Al Lavan*

*Jerry Tubbs*

*Bob Ward and wife Joyce.*

# An Interview With Tom Landry

*You've managed to enjoy stability in a profession long known as one which offers very little. Did you ever think you would spend your entire head coaching career with the same team?*

In the first place, I had decided that I didn't really want to coach at about the time I was approached by Clint Murchison. I'd been an assistant with the [New York] Giants and could have had the head job there. Jim Lee Howell was stepping down and Vince Lombardi, his top assistant, was leaving. If I had seiously thought I wanted to pursue a coaching career, I'd have stayed there in New York. But I had decided to work my way out of football. If anyone but Dallas had tried to hire me, I probably wouldn't have seriously considered the offer. But since we were living here, I decided to give it a shot for a while and just see how things worked out.

*Those early years were quite a struggle and the fans weren't exactly fascinated by the record you had accomplished. Did you feel the pressure to build an instant winner in those first seasons?*

I really never recognized the fact the fans were getting impatient with us. With me. It has always been my nature not to concern myself with things I have no control over. I was just doing the best I knew how to build our team into a winner. Truthfully, I never worried about being fired for the simple reason I didn't want to coach all that badly. I had approached it as a short-term thing. I fully expected to be fired at some point, knowing that it would probably take longer to build the team than most felt it would take. My attitude was simply to do the best I could until it was decided someone else should get a shot at it.

I really stopped and took stock of things after Clint gave me that 10-year contract in 1965. It wasn't so much the fact that I was looking for job security at the time. Rather, I saw it as a sign that I should stay in coaching. I didn't rush out and start working any harder than I'd already been doing, but I think I began to look at what I was doing on a more long-range basis.

*Did your priorities undergo any changes after you signed that long-term contract?*

Not dramatically. I felt at that time in my life I had my priorities pretty well in line. I had made a personal commitment to God and therefore my number one priority was His service. Being in football, I decided, provided me an excellent platform from which to witness. Second, I've always enjoyed the challenge the game offers, bringing a team back into contention, specifically. It hasn't been the Super Bowls that have been the most gratifying, really. What I've enjoyed most was initially building the team to a point where it was a championship contender, then bringing it back after we've won and been down again. Watching new players progress and gain confidence in themselves and each other has always been very rewarding. And, third, I've enjoyed the association with the players who have played for me. It makes me feel great to see how well so many of them have done after they've left the game.

*There are those who say much of your success is related to the fact you've been able to change with the times, to make adjustments and continue to innovate as the game and people who play it change. Would you agree with that evaluation?*

I've always been fascinated by the social changes that are constantly taking place. And professional football players have changed right along with every other part of society. In the late fifites, we saw the first of the postwar kids reach the age of pro football. Generally speaking, they were a much more independent group, seeking a kind of freedom young men of my generation hadn't even considered. In the fifties everyone was looking for material success. But that wasn't as true in the new generation. Their needs were more personal, more individual. So, I had to learn to deal with them as individuals.

It was something different for me since it had always been my personal nature to pay the price for every bit of success or material reward I'd gained. When I was playing football, everyone was treated equally. That was the basic philosophy of coaching. One rule for all. And that's the philosophy I started with for the simple reason I felt it was the most fair. It was the philosophy I had played under in high

school, college, and as a professional. But, eventually I learned that it doesn't work today. The players today want to be treated as individuals. And, I like to think I've learned that lesson and have matured to a point where I can still keep the team concept intact while dealing with players on more of a one-on-one basis at the same time. But, quite honestly, there are still times when it is a little difficult for me.

*How would you describe today's player?*

He's basically a product of the society we now live in. There's a lot being said of the ambiton, greed, and constant search for pleasure on the part of today's athlete, but I think all that's overrated. I still believe a football player is a football player; he has a love for the game and a willingness to make the sacrifices necessary to achieve the success he is after.

The thing that has changed him is the constant pressure he's under. We're in a money market society today and with all the agents and unions and publicity about salaries, he's pressured to go after bigger and bigger contracts just to prove to himself and everyone else he's one of the best. But I believe if a player feels he's being compensated properly he'll do everything possible to get his job done. By the same token, a mediocre player is never going to become a great one just because you've paid him a lot of money. The basic pride of performance is still there. When the game starts on Sunday, no one's out on the field thinking about what he's making or how much the guy across the line from him is making. He just wants to prove that he's a good athlete and that his team is better than the one he's playing against.

Another thing is the fact he's so visible today because of the tremendous television exposure and popularity of the game he plays. That visibility attracts all sorts of people, many who have get-rich-quick propositions for him. Today's athlete, at least the pro football player, has become over-enterprising because of all the business opportunities which come his way. In a lot of instances, the business involvements become a distraction which affects his performance.

*Speaking of pressure, do you feel the overwhelming
popularity of the Cowboys — "America's Team" — has
placed you and your team at a disadvantage?*

I think there was far more pressure placed on the
Cowboys prior to our winning our first Super Bowl.
In fact, I doubt any championship-caliber team dealt
with more pressure. We had gained a great deal of
popularity and had a large following, but we hadn't,
as they were saying, won the big one. Then, there
were those who didn't care for us because we were
getting so much publicity and all. When we fell
short so many times, it placed a great deal of pressure
on us. It really got bad in 1970 after we lost so badly
to St. Louis [38-0] in the regular season. To see our
team come back and go to the Super Bowl against
Baltimore was the most satisfying experience of my
career. It was a great tribute to the spirit of that team.
Then, the next year when we went to the Super bowl
again, and won — that was the most *rewarding*. We
had finally done everything you can do in a season
and everyone felt a great sense of relief along with
the satisfaction.

*Is there any particular thing about that first Super Bowl
title that serves as a touchstone for you today?*

The year we won it was a really amazing one. That,
you'll recall, was the season (running back) Duane
Thomas got so much publicity for not talking and all.
It is a great tribute to the players on that team that
they were able to accept two standards. Duane was
operating under one set of rules while everyone else
was operating under another. It was a unique
situation. But, I think the players realized that Duane
had problems and that I was trying as best I knew
how to help him. In fact, by not making an issue of
the manner in which I was dealing with Duane,
everyone on the team was trying to help him.

*What dangers do you see ahead for the game?*

Again, I have to go back to money. Players were
being overpaid and the owners seem willing to
continue spending great amounts of money in
something of a one-upmanship kind of game. Thus
far, the NFL has generally managed to hold the line
on salaries and remain stable. Pro basketball,
meanwhile, almost destroyed itself with all the
multi-million dollar contracts it was giving out. This
is a danger every team in pro sports has to be aware
of. If we aren't careful, we're all going to spend our
way out of a stable, comfortable position.

At present, football is America's game. The
popularity is at such a high level that I have to
wonder how it can get any more popular. The only
thing that will enhance the game more is the
information age we live in. The media continues to
place more and more importance on it and, in doing
so, continues to make more people aware of it. I'd say
that if we don't destroy ourselves, we're going to
enjoy tremendous popularity for some time to come.

*Certainly, this is not a new question, but have you given
any consideration to how much longer you'll stay in
coaching? You talk to some and they say you're getting
very near retirement, then others say you'll stay around
until they drag you, kicking and screaming, from the
sidelines.*

I don't think anyone's going to have to drag me
away, telling me it is time for me to call it quits. It's
only natural for someone who has been coaching as
long as I have to give some thought to retirement.
So, yes, I've thought about it more in the last few
years. Probably because I've been asked about it so
often, though. My answer right now is still the same:
as long as it remains enjoyable and challenging, I'll
continue to coach. Right now, I have no more
definitive answer than that.

Walt Garrison, rodeo

Billy Joe DuPree, basketball

Wade Manning, baseball

Bob Hayes, track

Richmond Flowers, track

# Cowboys in Other Sports

In addition to those pictured here, there have been several other Cowboys who have performed well in sports other than football.

All-Pro cornerback *Cornell Green* was an All-American basketball player at Utah State.

Punter *Ron Widby* played basketball professionally in the American Basketball Association while with the Cowboys. Then, following his NFL career, he established himself as a club golf professional.

Running back *Preston Pearson* was a standout member of the University of Illinois basketball team.

Tight end *Billy Joe DuPree* was a member of the basketball team at Michigan State University.

Defensive back *Mike Gaechter* was a standout sprinter on the University of Oregon track and field team.

Kicker *Rafael Septien* played soccer in his Mexico homeland.

Former kicker *Efren Herrera* was also an outstanding soccer player in Mexico.

Defensive end *Ed Jones* left the Cowboys in 1979 to pursue a career as a professional boxer and won six consecutive fights before returning to football. At Tennessee State he was also a member of the basketball team.

While at the Naval Academy, *Roger Staubach* was an outstanding centerfielder on the baseball team.

Long before making his reputation as one of the NFL's most outstanding receivers, Florida A&M's *Bob Hayes* was the world record holder for the 100-yard dash and had won the 100 meters in the Tokyo Olympic Games.

As a high schooler, *Mel Renfro* was voted the top schoolboy track and field performer in the nation. Then, at the University of Oregon he was an outstanding hurdler, sprinter, and long jumper.

At Michigan State, *Pete Gent* was an outstanding performer on the basketball team but never seriously considered going out for football.

Quarterback *Danny White* played the infield well enough at Arizona State to get several offers to play baseball professionally.

Before ever signing a contract to play cornerback for the Cowboys, *Wade Manning* excelled as a member of the Ohio State baseball team.

Before graduating from the University of Tennessee, *Richmond Flowers* had established an international reputation for himself as a hurdler on the Vols track team.

107

Roger Staubach, baseball

Pete Gent, basketball

Mel Renfro, track

Danny White, baseball

Ed Jones, boxing

Cornell Green, basketball

# Big Plays in Cowboys History

*Many times the great games are best remembered for one or two great plays. This is a record of some of them.*

Selection of the most memorable plays in Dallas Cowboys' history is a task no individual is totally qualified to do. Even head coach Tom Landry, the man who has stood on the sidelines calling them throughout the quarter-century life of the team, is reluctant to compile a list, claiming faulty memory on such matters. In truth, it is likely that he views the assignment much like a father asked to announce which of his children is prettiest.

Thus the following compilation has been done with the help of a variety of people who have participated in and observed the unfolding of the franchise's history. Players, coaches, administrators, scouts, and members of the media who were there have been asked to pick the cream of a bountiful crop, taking into consideration the importance of the play not only as it affected one game but the entire history of the team as well.

To place them in 1-2-3 order, however, would be much like isolating the most perfect snowflake. Because all are different — different times, different situations, different people — a rating system has not been applied. That's your job.

Drew Pearson takes the final step into the
end zone at the end of the Hail Mary
touchdown against the Minnesota Vikings
in 1975.

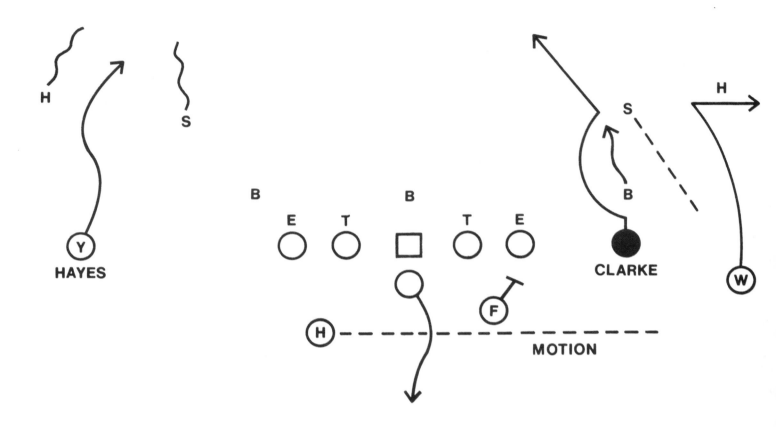

*January 1, 1967*
*NFL Championship Game*
*Dallas, Texas*

Just over four minutes remained in a game that saw the Green Bay Packers, the dominant figure in pro football, leading by 14 points. The Packers had jumped to a quick 14-point lead early in the game, Dallas rallied to tie, then Green Bay surged back in front by 14.

But, on third-and-20 from his own 32-yard line, quarterback Don Meredith sent wide receiver turned tight end Frank Clarke deep. Clarke surprised the Green Bay secondary with his post pattern and was wide open when the ball reached his hands. The result was a 68-yard touchdown, which put the Cowboys in a position to send the game into overtime if the defense could hold and another score could be accomplished.

The defense did its job and with 2:19 remaining, the Cowboys offense took over at the Packers 47-yard line. A pass to Clarke over the middle moved Dallas to the 26. Then Meredith went to Clark again and, while the pass fell incomplete, an official signaled interference on Packer Tom Brown.

Dallas faced a first-and-goal situation at the two-yard line with 1:52 remaining. Fullback Don Perkins went off-tackle to the one before Meredith decided to go to the air again. Receiver Pettis Norman dropped the ball in the endzone, bringing a thunder of groans from the Cotton Bowl stands. Those groans would grow even louder when it was realized that a

five-yard penalty had been assessed tackle Jim Boeke for moving before the snap. Dallas was moved back to the six-yard line. A flair pass to Dan Reeves was incomplete, then a badly underthrown pass to Pettis Norman, was caught at the two.

On the fourth down Meredith called a roll-out pass — Fire 90 Quarterback Roll Right — and never had a chance. Linebacker Dave Robinson charged the Dallas quarterback, obscuring his view of his receivers. As the big Green Bay defender wrapped his arm around him, Meredith threw toward where he hoped one of his white-jerseyed teammates would be. Instead, it was Tom Brown, wearing the green and gold of the Packers, who caught the ball.

There the dreams of a miracle ended. The Packers went on to face AFL champion Kansas City in the first Super Bowl while the Cowboys, exciting and dramatic but just a few plays short, began to deal with the suggestion they couldn't win the big one.

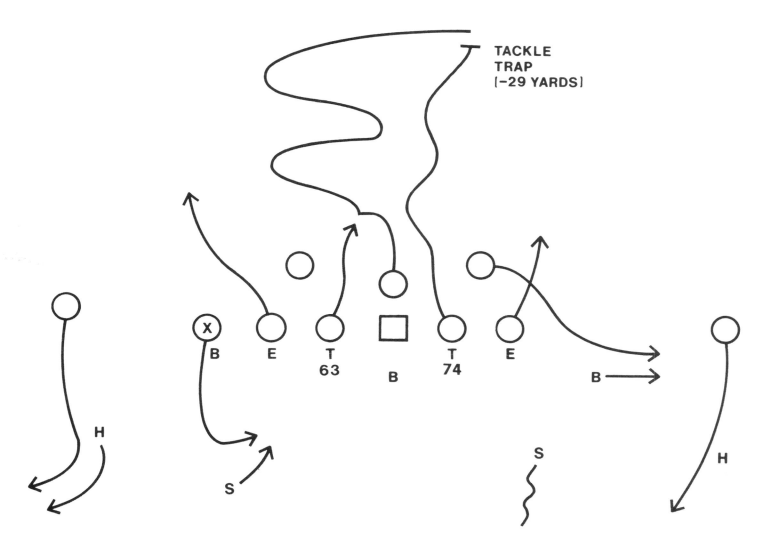

TACKLE
TRAP
(-29 YARDS)

X
B
E
T
63
B
T
74
E
B
H
S
S
S
H

*January, 1972*
*Super Bowl VI*
*New Orleans, Louisiana*

It was the final play of the first quarter and the Miami Dophins, playing in their first-ever Super Bowl, appeared to be gathering offensive momentum. But, as he dropped back to throw on a crucial third down, quarterback Bob Griese found himself in trouble even as he attempted to retreat to the safety of the pocket.

Cowboys defenders Bob Lilly and Larry Cole broke through, forcing the Dolphins quarterback to scramble. Cole got a hand on Griese just a couple of yards behind the line of scrimmage but wasn't able to hold on. The chase continued until, finally, Lilly brought the frustrated Miami quarterback down from behind for a staggering 29-yard loss.

It was a set-back of such proportions that the steam was taken from the Dolphins offense.

Thereafter it was all Dallas as the famed Doomsday Defense completely shut down the Miami offense, and the Cowboys went on to register a decisive 24-3 victory. On that clear, sunny afternoon, Dallas outrushed the Dolphins, 252 yards to just 80.

Clint Murchison, Jr., enjoying his team's first world championship, stood in the dressing room, smiling. "This," he said, "is a very successful culmination of our 12-year plan."

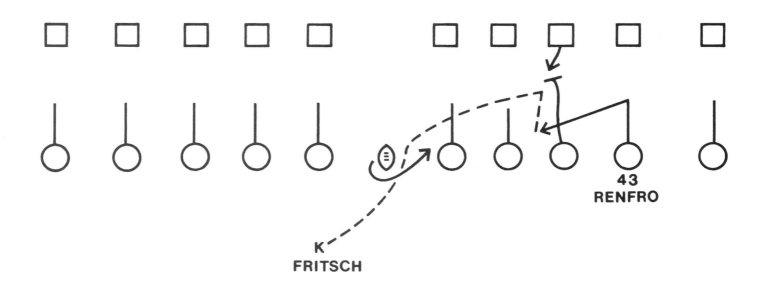

S

K
FRITSCH

43
RENFRO

## 1972
## Divisional Playoffs
## Dallas vs. San Francisco
## San Francisco, California

Less than two minutes remained in the 1972 Divisional Playoffs in Candlestick Park and the host San Francisco 49ers owned a 12-point advantage over the struggling Dallas Cowboys. It had been an afternoon filled with frustration and mistakes for the visitors and, as the final seconds ticked away, 49ers linebacker Dave Wilcox delighted in the situation. "How does it feel to lose a game like this?" he shouted to the Dallas offense.

Already Cowboys coach Tom Landry had done everything he could to spark some life into his team's attack. He had called starting quarterback Craig Morton to the bench in the third period, substituting Roger Staubach. But the young Naval Academy graduate had little success getting back on track. Until late in the game.

With 1:30 remaining, a hurry-up offense underway, he connected with Billy Parks for a touchdown that narrowed the San Francisco margin to 28-23. The 49ers fans expressed little concern, however, since in all likelihood the remaining time on the clock could be whittled away by the San Francisco offense following the Dallas kickoff.

Anticipating an on-side kick, San Francisco coach Dick Nolan placed his best receivers up on the line to field the ball Toni Fritsch would kick.

A one-time soccer standout in Austria, Fritsch approached the ball, appearing to run past it. Then, kicking one foot behind him, he sliced the ball on a sharp diagonal course across the field.

San Francisco wide receiver Preston Riley grabbed at the crazily bouncing ball but before he could gain control of it, Dallas rookie Ralph Coleman hit him. The ball trickled away — and into the hands of Mel Renfro. Dallas would get one more chance.

Staubach went to work, racing against the clock. He ran for a 21-yard gain, then hit Parks for 19 more, moving the ball to the 49ers' 10. Then, with a San Francisco blitz in his face, he lofted a touchdown pass to Ron Sellers, bringing the Cowboys to a 30-28 victory.

"The kick Toni made gave us the chance we needed," Staubach would say later. "It was unbelievable. You have to wonder if he could do it again, even if he had a million chances."

On that day, one was all it took.

114

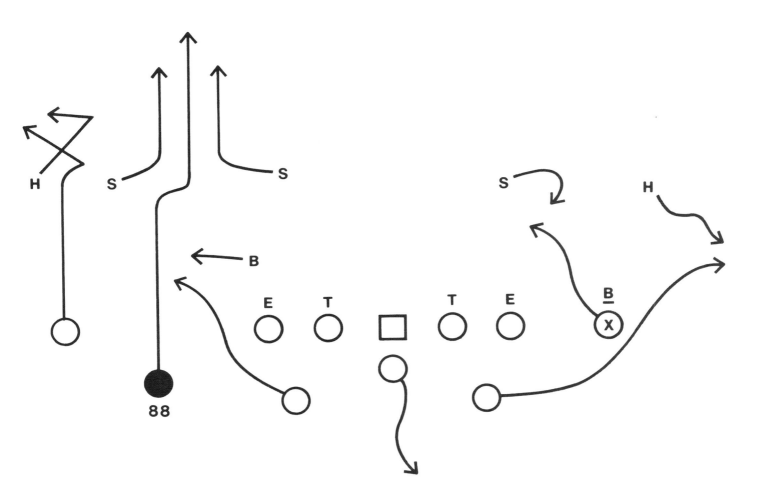

## 1973
### Divisional Playoffs
### Dallas vs. Los Angeles
### Texas Stadium

He was a free-agent out of the University of Tulsa; small, almost frail-looking. But by mid-season of his 1973 rookie year Drew Pearson had earned himself a spot in the Dallas Cowboys starting lineup.

Untested in playoff situations, he knew little about the pressure to be faced when the Cowboys hosted the NFC West champion Los Angeles Rams in the Divisional Playoffs. In the early going, however, there appeared to be little pressure to deal with. Taking advantage of Rams turnovers, the Cowboys had bolted to a 17-0 lead before the first quarter was completed. One of the touchdowns had come on a routine four-yard pass from Roger Staubach to Pearson.

Then, however, the Cowboys went flat and the Rams, 12-2 during the regular season, settled into a methodical brand of football, which saw them draw to within one point of the Cowboys in the fourth quarter.

Few in Texas Stadium were convinced that Los Angeles was finished for the day. The Rams defense, in fact, bottled Dallas in its own end of the field, forcing it into a third-and-14 at the 17-yard-line.

Staubach dropped back all the way to his own goal line, then fired a long, go-for-broke pass in the direction of Pearson who was crossing over the middle at the 50-yard line. Surrounded by two Rams defenders, the young rookie went up for the ball,

made the catch, and raced goalward as the 64,291 on hand cheered. The cheers had turned to a roar by the time Pearson ran into the endzone, completing the 83-yard touchdown play.

Dallas would go on to pad its margin with a late field goal, but it was clearly Pearson's circus catch — the first of many he would make over the course of his career — that turned the tide and lifted the Cowboys to the NFC Championship Game.

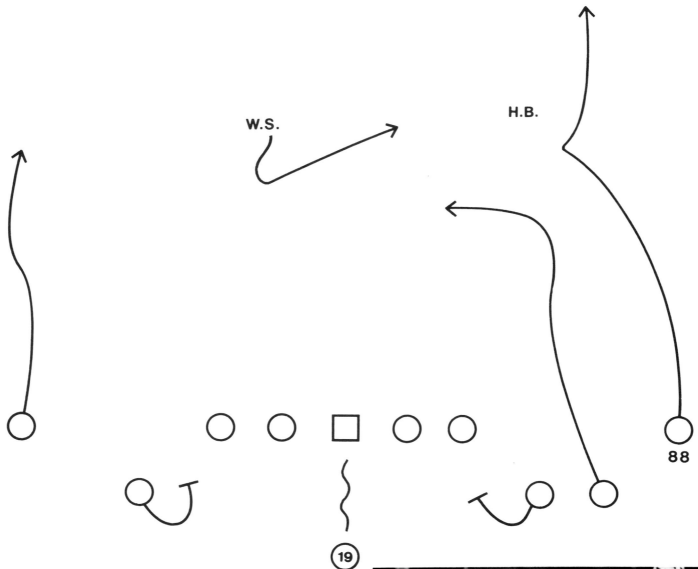

## 1974
### Regular Season
### Dallas vs. Washington
### Texas Stadium

He was considered something of a rebel, a strong-armed young quarterback whose off-the-field activities included hunting rattlesnakes. Clint Longley, a college record-setter while playing for Abilene Christian, had seen precious little action until a Thanksgiving Day afternoon in Texas Stadium in 1974.

The opposition was the Washington Redskins and at halftime they led 9-3. Starting quarterback Roger Staubach, having enjoyed little success in the first two quarters, found the going even rougher in the third. Finally, his futility would end when he was led off the field, dazed by a crushing Redskins tackle.

Longley came on with his team trailing by nine points and quickly surprised the sellout Texas Stadium crowd by marching Dallas to a touchdown. A 34-yard toss to tight end Billy Joe DuPree put the Cowboys within striking-distance. Then a one-yard TD plunge by Walt Garrison gave Dallas the lead.

But as the fourth quarter got underway, a name from the past came back to haunt Dallas. Duane Thomas, wearing a Redskins uniform, broke for a 19-yard touchdown which lifted the visitors back into the lead.

The Cowboys offense returned to the field with 1:45 left and Longley quickly moved the ball to midfield. Time, however, was becoming his major adversary. Thirty-five seconds remained and Dallas had no time-outs left.

As Longley called for wide receiver Drew Pearson to go deep down the sidelines, Washington went into a prevent defense, inserting seven defensive backs into the game. Ignoring the probabilities of completing a long pass, Longley dropped back and lofted a high spiral, which Pearson gathered in at the four-yard line, then danced into the end zone. Efren Herrera then came on to kick the extra point which provided Dallas with yet another "miracle" win over the Redskins.

Afterwards, lineman Blaine Nye, marveling at the performance of the youthful Longley, remarked, "It was a triumph of the uncluttered mind."

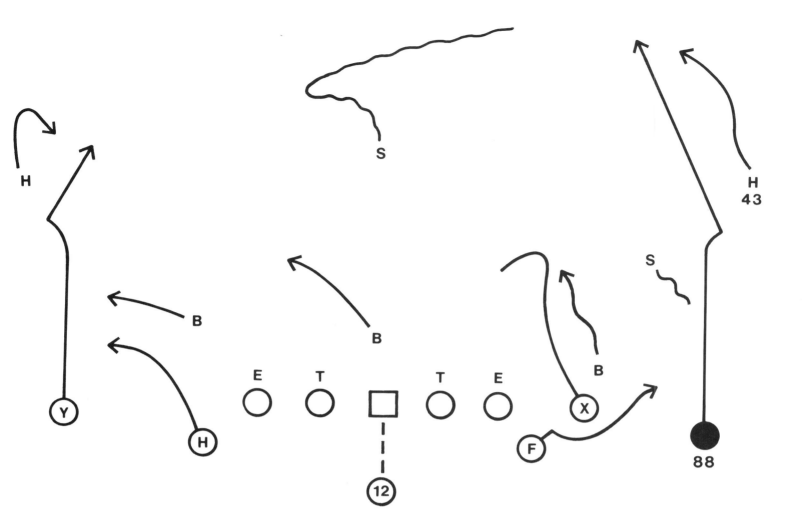

## 1975
## Divisional Playoff
## Bloomington, Minnesota

In the frozen gloom of Metropolitan Stadium, the favored Minnesota Vikings had entered the Divisional Playoff game with the Cowboys as an eight-point favorite. And, as the fourth quarter was winding down, Coach Bud Grant's team, led by league-leading passer Fran Tarkenton, held a 14-10 advantage.

Dallas, having suffered offensive problems throughout the dismal afternoon, would have one final chance as just two minutes remained. Working from deep in their own end of the field, that chance was a long-shot. Quarterback Roger Staubach did, however, manage to move his team out of the hole. But, with just 44 seconds remaining, the Vikings defense had put the Cowboys in a fourth-and-16 situation. With good protection, Staubach stood in the pocket until wide receiver Drew Pearson broke into the open on the right sidelines, then fired a perfect strike. Pearson was pushed out of bounds as he dove for the ball at the 50-yard line. Dallas had new life and 24 seconds to work with.

Working out of the shotgun formation, Staubach waited as Pearson, lined up on the right side, made a move to the inside, then broke straight upfield, engaged in a footrace with defender Nate Wright.

Staubach launched a high, arching pass — a Hail

Mary, as Staubach called it — that began its downward spiral just as Pearson and Wright seemed to collide. Wright fell but Pearson remained on his feet.

The ball reached Pearson's hands, then appeared to slip to his hip. It was there the remarkable receiver clutched it with one hand just a couple of steps before reaching the end zone. By the time he reached the goal the ball was secure and the official was signaling a Dallas touchdown.

That play, the Hail Mary Pass, would provide the Cowboys with a 17-14 upset win over the Vikings and a trip to the NFC Championship game.

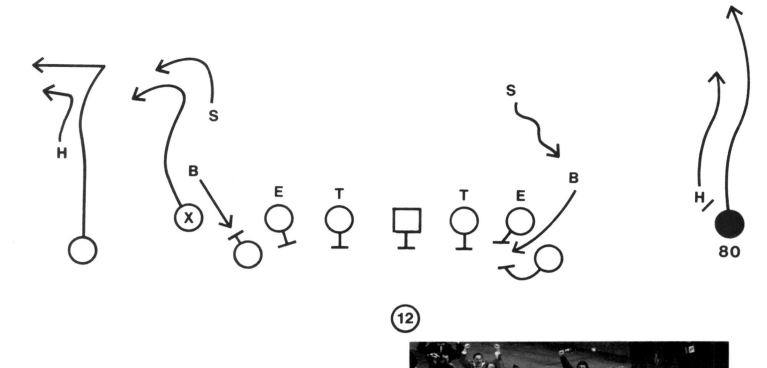

*1979*
*Regular Season*
*Dallas vs. Washington*
*Texas Stadium*

It was a game tailor-made for high drama. The Dallas Cowboys, playing at home, could clinch the NFC East title and avenge an earlier season loss to the Washington Redskins with a victory. For the visitors, the stakes were equally high. A second straight win over Dallas would give them the division title. A loss, however, would completely eliminate them from the playoff picture.

Quarterback Joe Theismann directed the Redskins into a 17-0 lead early in the second period, but rival Roger Staubach had piloted Dallas into the lead in the third. Then, however, Washington came back to life and mounted a 34-21 lead as just four minutes remained in the final period. It appeared the Cowboys would have to settle for a wild card playoff berth.

Free safety Cliff Harris, however, breathed new life into the situation when he forced a Washington fumble, which teammate Randy White fell on. Quickly Staubach fired a 26-yard touchdown pass to running back Ron Springs and the gap narrowed to 34-28.

But, with just two minutes remaining the Redskins had the ball and faced a third-and-two situation. One more first down, and they would be able to run the clock out. Powerful running back John Riggins, who had rushed for 150 yards during the see-saw afternoon, took the handoff from Theismann — and

was immediately hit by Dallas lineman Larry Cole for a 2-yard loss. Instead of managing the much-needed first down, Washington was forced to punt the ball away to the inspired Cowboys.

A minute and 46 seconds remained as Dallas' offense got underway at its own 25-yard line. Staubach, working the clock masterfully, connected with Tony Hill and then specialty back Preston Pearson to move the ball to the Washington eight-yard line with but 45 seconds remaining.

He then called a pass play that had tight end Billy Joe DuPree as the primary receiver. But, just before breaking the huddle, he told wide receiver Tony Hill to be ready. If the Redskins blitz was overwhelming, he would alley-oop the ball to the right corner of the end zone.

Washington did blitz, providing Staubach precious little time to get the ball off. Never even looking toward DuPree, he lofted an arching pass to Hill in the right corner. It sailed over the head of Redskins defender Lamar Parrish, into the waiting hands of Hill. Rafael Septien's conversion did the final bit of damage and the Cowboys managed a 35-34 triumph in Staubach's final regular season game.

"It was," said president and general manager Tex Schramm afterwards, "our greatest comeback ever."

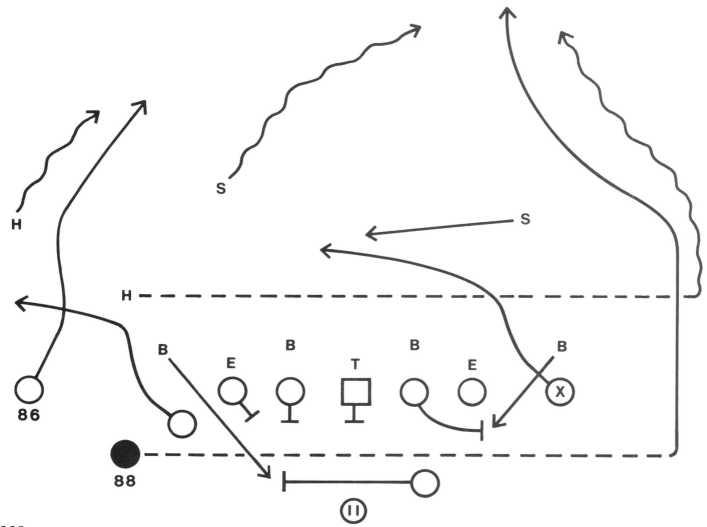

## 1980
### Divisional Championship
### Atlanta, Georgia

Danny White had inherited the quarterback job from a man who had made the last-minute escape a trademark. And, now, as the final period of the 1980 Divisional Playoff game with the Atlanta Falcons wound down in Fulton County Stadium, White had his chance to prove he, too, could come up with the miracle finish.

As the final period opened, Atlanta, champions of the NFC West, enjoyed a 24-10 advantage. Even when Cowboys fullback Robert Newhouse crashed in to score, narrowing the margin to seven, there was little visible concern that the momentum had changed. The Falcons, in fact, added a field goal soon thereafter.

White suddenly was facing two adversaries, the enthusiastic Falcons and the scoreboard clock. He launched a passing assault that resulted in a 14-yard touchdown to wide receiver Drew Pearson who made a remarkable catch in the end zone with 3:40 remaining in the game.

Then it was the defense's turn to contribute. It did, turning the ball back to the offense at its own 29-yard line with 1:48 left to play. Despite the prevent defense put up by the Falcons, White connected with wide receiver Butch Johnson at midfield. Then a pass to Preston Pearson advanced the ball to the 36. A screen to Tony Dorsett moved the ball to the 24.

Only 49 seconds remained when White sent Drew Pearson deep toward the end zone. With a defender on each side of him, Drew made the catch. Septien's extra point missed, but nobody cared. The Cowboys had 30-27 victory, which advanced them to the NFC Championship game.

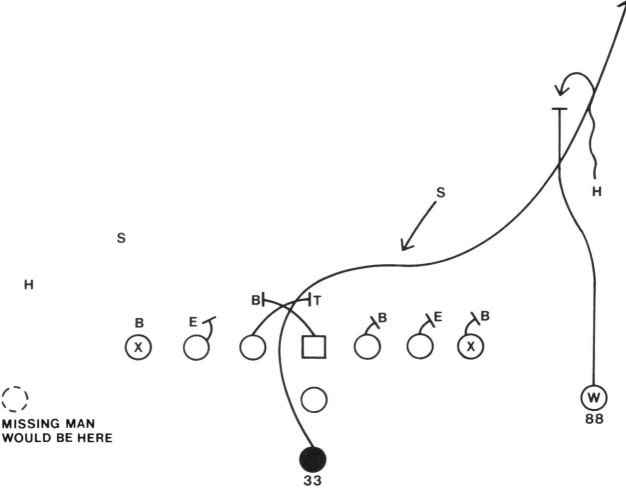

S

H

B
E T
B E B

B
X
E
X

MISSING MAN
WOULD BE HERE

S

H

W
88

33

*1982*
*Regular Season*
*Dallas vs. Minnesota*
*Bloomington, Minnesota*

It was one of those evenings of lackluster performances and the Dallas Cowboys, already assured of a spot in the playoffs, were having precious little success against the Minnesota Vikings. When the final gun sounded, in fact, the Cowboys had been beaten, 31-27.

In years to come, however, the score will not be remembered nearly as well as the moment when Cowboys running back Tony Dorsett established a NFL record that will never be broken.

Dallas, having struggled offensively throughout the game, was backed to its own one-yard line and quarterback Danny White, hoping to manage some operating room, called a play known as H 31 Fold. By design, center and guard, Tom Raferty and Herb Scott, were to block the Vikings right tackle and linebacker, creating a lane for Dorsett.

The play had all the earmarks of failure even before it got underway. Fullback Ron Springs, hearing the formation called in the huddle, suddenly decided he was not supposed to be on the field and ran to the sidelines, leaving Dallas with just 10 offensive players.

Still, things went like clockwork. Rafferty and Scott blocked their men from Dorsett's path and right guard Steve Wright prevented a pursuit defender from filling the hole. Dorsett, putting his 9.5 speed to the best of use, broke through the

opening, cut back to his right, and raced 99 yards for a touchdown — the longest run in league history.

Afterwards, Dorsett had but one regret. In the exciting aftermath of the achievement, he failed to get the ball he had carried into pro football history. It would have made a nice additon to his trophy case.

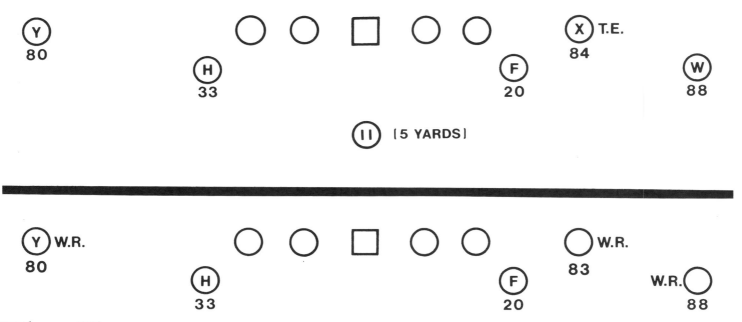

Y 80    O O □ O O    X T.E. 84

H 33    F 20    W 88

(II) [5 YARDS]

Y W.R. 80    O O □ O O    83 W.R.

H 33    F 20    W.R. 88

# The Shotgun

(II) [5 YARDS]

The year was 1974 and the Dallas Cowboys, a dynasty in the making, had suddenly fallen on hard times. After a string of eight straight playoff appearances, their remarkable offensive machine had run off the track. Not only did they miss the playoffs, but they finished a distant third in their division with an 8-6 record.

Head coach Tom Landry thought it best to go back to the drawing board. A drastic change, one which would eventually alter the game as the National Football League knew it, was brewing.

Defenses, he realized, had begun to change, bringing in an extra back on obvious passing downs. They would rush only three linemen and stop the third down pass with greater regularity. Offensive productivity was dramatically down, not only in Dallas, but throughout the league. It was time, Landry determined, to provide the defense with something new to worry about.

What the man who was already recognized as a coaching innovator came up with was far from new. Instead, he dug back into the dusty playbook pages of another coach, one who had dared ten years earlier to defy tradition and try something out of the ordinary.

The Cowboys coach would call it the Spread. The media would call it the Shotgun. And Red Hickey, the former San Francisco 49ers coach, would call it justification.

It would become the Cowboy's standard formation on third down passing situations and in their famed two-minute offense. With the quarterback stationed ten yards deep, taking a direct snap from center, the Shotgun became one of Dallas' most lethal weapons, and since that 1974 disappointment the Cowboys have regularly been in the playoffs.

"I never understood," says Landry, "why a quarterback has to take the ball from center, turn, and run back ten yards when everybody in the stadium knows full well he's going to have to pass on a particular down."

In truth, it is not a question only he began asking

during that mid-seventies redesign of the Cowboys offense. The Shotgun had been in his playbook since he took over the newborn Cowboys in 1960. But in those early days the quality of the offensive line wasn't good enough to allow the formation to work. Too, his quarterback, Don Meredith, made it clear he was not the least comfortable with the formation.

"It is one of those things which works only if your players have confidence in it," notes Landry. "Meredith was never comfortable with it. On the other hand, Roger Staubach loved it. And Danny White has done well with it.

"On a passing down nothing else makes as much sense. When the quarterback is standing in the backfield to get the snap, he can immediately see the entire field and all his receivers."

It was a lack of confidence in the formation, designed for the San Francisco 49ers by then-head coach Red Hickey in the early sixties, which caused it to return to mothballs for so long.

Hickey, who would later serve as a coach and a scout for the Cowboys, had designed the Shotgun in 1960 in an attempt to transform his downtrodden 49ers offense into a competitive attack. Initially, it was a roaring success, at one point lifting San Francisco to a 7-2 record. During that nine-game stretch opponents were outscored, 254-109. So confident was Hickey in the formation that he turned to the Shotgun exclusively.

All went well until an afternoon in 1962 when the Chicago Bears came up with a defense that stopped the 49ers attack. Thereafter there would be four consecutive losses and players began to lose confidence in the strange offensive philosophy.

"Once the players lost confidence in what I was trying to do," recalls Hickey, "it was all over. There was no way we were going to win when I was the only person around who felt it would work.

"But, it makes me feel good to see that teams like the Cowboys have gone to it and made it work. Back when I was trying to run it, it cost me my job. Now, I'm considered a genius."

# The Image

It has been suggested that during their tenure in the National Football League, the Dallas Cowboys have taken the brawling, macho image of professional sports and put it in an attache case. "Cowboy Cool," *Newsweek* magazine has called it. Today they are seldom measured against other teams in the league which is the practice long accepted by those seeking to judge the best of the best. Rather, they are weighed against their super-power corporate neighbors like Texas Instruments and Neiman-Marcus.

So exceptional have been the organizational methods of the Cowboys that even the United States Army dispatched observers to their training camp in Thousand Oaks a few years ago, seeking input from key members of the franchise.

And while their peers may begrudge the Cowboys their "America's Team" title, there is proof positive that they have been generally admired and emulated by virtually every other team in the NFL. At last count, no less than 14 other teams in the league had adopted some form of the Shotgun offense after head coach Tom Landry proved it a successful weapon. After the Cowboys employed computers to evaluate draft prospects and devise game plans, others quickly followed suit. When they sprinkled sex appeal on the sidelines by revolutionizing the image of pro sports cheerleaders, most other teams jumped on the bandwagon. When Dallas began publishing a successful weekly newspaper, others were attempted.

New franchises, like the Seattle Seahawks, made little effort to hide the fact they used the Dallas blueprint in their own efforts to launch football dynasties. And men with Cowboys backgrounds can be found in front offices and on the sidelines throughout the NFL. Former quarterback Eddie LeBaron is president of the Atlanta Falcons, while Tom Braatz, a former Cowboys player and scout, serves as general manager. Such former players as Dick Nolan, Jack Patera, Forrest Gregg, Dan Reeves, Monte Clark, and Mike Ditka have risen to head coaching jobs in the NFL.

"It all adds to the Cowboys' mystique," says St. Louis Cardinals owner and general manager Billy Bidwill. "No matter whether the rest of us like it or not, the Cowboys have managed to capture the fancy and imagination of professional football's vast following. And it all starts with their organization and the image it has.

"The continuity of personnel at the top level — Tex Schramm, Gil Brandt, and Tom Landry — has provided them with the cornerstone upon which they've built their success. They are smart enough to put together a strong organization at the very beginning and have stayed with it. And the results speak for themselves. Equally important, they've used winning to their best advantage. Over the years, as the Cowboys have emerged as one of the league's most highly regarded teams, they have carefully cultivated their image, that mystique. They're constantly looking for new and inventive ways to make the public aware of the Dallas Cowboys. They are one of the most promotion-minded organizations in the league."

The parade of stars who have traveled through the Cowboys organization was dramatically emphasized during this halftime show celebrating the Cowboys 20th Anniversary in 1979.

Cowboys 25th anniversary festivities included the Silver Soiree at the Dallas Registry Hotel attended by more than 1,200 fans, media, veteran players, celebrities and guests. Moderators Pat Sumrall and Frank Gifford introduced the Cowboys All-Time Team as well as speakers such as All Pro Tackle Bob Lilly (above). At half time of the November 4 Giants game, the All-Time Offensive Team (right) and Defensive Team (below) were introduced to the Texas Stadium crowd.

It was former Chicago Bears general manager Jim Finks who pointed out that the Cowboys were the first to realize that it is necesary to provide the fans with a show along with the game itself. "You walk into Texas Stadium and you immediately feel class," he said. "You feel it from the structure itself, from the private skyboxes, the painted field, the people who are there, uniformed and ready to help you find your seat. And it goes right down to the field. The Cowboys squad has always been very presentable. You don't see any over-weight players — or coaches. It's a catching thing, really. I've told several people before that I honestly believe that when a player becomes a member of the Dallas Cowboys he immediately begins playing better than he's actually capable of. It's a little like putting on the New York Yankees' pinstripes."

There are, however, criticisms. All the hype that has become such a visible part of the Cowboys organization has not been greeted enthusiastically on all fronts.

"The Cowboys," said outspoken ABC-TV sportscaster Howard Cosell, "are the most overrated, over-hyped team in professional sports. I need not say more."

A spokesman for the highly successful Pittsburgh Steelers chose his words a bit more carefully. "We've been a pretty successful franchise," points out public relations director Joe Gordon, "and we've never had cheerleaders or a lot of hype and promotion that did not directly involve the team. The Cowboys seem to really be hung up on image, whereas the Steelers are far more concerned with the end results — which is winning. But, you can use different roads to reach that same destination. It's just that we feel ours is the most direct."

"I agree that it all starts with winning," says president and general manager Schramm. "Without that, nothing of a successful nature would be possible. But, I feel it is important that we cultivate our image as we go. I want everyone in the world to know about the Dallas Cowboys and what they stand for."

The proof of what the franchise stands for is in the record books: the Cowboys hold television audience rating records for games shown on Sunday, Monday, Thursday and Saturday. They also can boast of rating records for the pre-season Hall of Fame game and playoffs.

"The two most important people to CBS," said former network TV spokesman Beano Cook, "are J. R. Ewing and Tom Landry. We have a rule we go by when planning NFL telecasts. Give people the best game possible. And when in doubt give them the Cowboys. Generally, when our ratings are up, there's only one reason: the Dallas Cowboys."

With hookups in almost 200 stations in fourteen states, the Dallas Cowboys also have the largest radio network of any team in professional sports, as well as the NFL's first foreign language network, sixteen Spanish-speaking stations in seven states carrying their games on a weekly basis.

NFL Properties, the licensing agency and clearinghouse for all the league-endorsed souveniers available in the nation's marketplace — hats, gloves, T-shirts, pennants, etc. — reports that the Cowboys account for almost thirty percent of their sales, making Dallas the hands-down leader in that area of commerce. Dallas Cowboys Cheerleaders-related

items, in fact, outsell all *teams* in the league with the exception of the Steelers, Wshington Redskins, and, of course, the Cowboys.

Then there is the *Dallas Cowboys Weekly*, a tabloid publication begun nine years ago to better spread the gospel about the team. At present it is enjoying a paid circulation of 100,000, with subscribers in every state in the U.S. and several foreign countries. A Spanish edition has a circulation of 300,000 in Mexico.

In truth, the Cowboys see themselves as something more than a team. They are, in the truest business sense, a product — and are marketed as such better than any other professional sports franchise. And Schramm, for one, is working hard on that.

*The original design for the Cowboy Joe logo (top) and the finished product (bottom).*

A man with a strong sense of history, he is admittedly concerned about how the Cowboys will be remembered in years to come. "I'd like for people to remember us as they do the great Yankees teams of the twenties, thirties, and forties," he says. "Now there was an organization for you — one you could use as a perfect example to follow. The great players would come and go and so would the managers and coaches. But they maintained their status because the Yankees organization maintained its excellence.

"We've been able to maintain a high level of performance while going through the rebuilding process," says Schramm. "Teams like the New York Giants, Baltimore, and Green Bay had their moments at the top, but when their players got old, they crumbled. We've fought hard to keep that from happening to the Cowboys."

If, in fact, the Cowboys are legitimate claimants to the title of "America's Team," at what point did they gain that distinction? When did that image begin to take roots?

"It's probably the sum total of a lot of things," Schramm says. "I think it all started back in the sixties when we played the Green Bay Packers in those two NFL Championship games and narrowly lost. To most people then, we were still just a growing expansion team, the scrappy little kids from down the block who took on the big, bad Packers and gave them a run for their money. We were the underdogs then, and people identified with us because of it.

"Then, there are other things: we have great-looking uniforms, for instance. We have a very distinctive emblem (the star on the helmet). And we have a reputation for doing things first, then having others follow. Too, there has been the All-American image of people like Roger Staubach and, of course, Landry."

Which is the way he likes it. High profile, maximum visibility, class, and flair. It's the Cowboys' way.

*Trophies, rings, and other symbols of the NFL are very much a part of the Cowboys tradition.*

*No other team in professional sports history has had a commercial airliner done up in team colors and logo except the Dallas Cowboys. Braniff Airlines came up with the idea when it was serving as the charter for the team.*

On December 18, 1981
Braniff dedicated this
aircraft N457BN to the

DALLAS COWBOYS FOOTBALL CLUB

This aircraft is dedicated to a remarkable football team and an outstanding organization. Since the Cowboys' first season in 1960 Braniff has been their official airline. During these 22 years together we have been to the playoffs 15 times and to the Super Bowl 5 times seeing the Cowboys become Super Bowl Champions twice.

This aircraft will be used for team charters in the years ahead and in regularly scheduled service throughout the United States when not being used by the team.

At Braniff we felt a 22 year relationship warranted much more than applause. Thus, this flying salute to the players, coaches and management of the DALLAS COWBOYS.

*Braniff*

BOB LILLY
DALLAS COWBOYS | DEFENSIVE TACKLE

*1984 Silver Season Tickets*

# The Dallas Cowboys Cheerleaders

The Cheerleaders began as the creation of one man: Texas E. Schramm, President and General Manager of the famous Dallas Cowboys. Schramm is a man who knows how to make dreams come true. Together with Tom Landry, a brilliant coach and strategist, he dared to pit his young NFL expansion club against the greatest teams in football. The Cowboys, classic underdogs, battled their way into NFL record books and captured the imagination of a nation.

But Schramm dared to do even more. Bucking traditions and risking criticism, he dared to bring a new dimension to the nation's favorite sport. It was Schramm's idea to put young women on the football field — pretty young women who could dance. And dance they did — straight into the hearts of America and the world. "When we introduced the 'new' Dallas Cowboys Cheerleaders at Texas Stadium in 1972, we wanted to have a bright new look on the playing field and add another form of entertainment for the football fan. Little did we know that we were starting something that one day would become what is now considered an American phenomenon."

In truth, the Cowboys have had cheerleaders as long as they've been in the pro football business. No sooner had the franchise begun to function than a group of male and female cheerleaders from the various Dallas high schools were organized, outfitted in traditional cheerleader uniforms, and were called the Belles and Beaux. As the number of Dallas schools increased and interest in serving as Sunday cheerleaders grew, open tryouts were held for several years to select the dozen local teenagers who would perform in the Cotton Bowl, going virtually unnoticed as they tried to persuade the crowd to do the traditional "two-bits, four-bits" kind of cheers. Such would be the format until 1972.

But there is also an element of circumstance and timing in the Cheerleaders' story. From the start, they were coached by one of the most talented dancers in America, Texie Waterman, the first choreographer in history to bring New York style jazz dancing to the 50-yard line.

It was an untried idea, and at first Texie wasn't sure it would work. She told the Cowboys so. "When they told me they wanted dancing Cheerleaders, I told them they were crazy," Texie says. But she gave it a try, and the rest is now a legend, but the debut of the "new" Dallas Cowboys Cheerleaders drew applause. For every one who morally objected to beautiful young women dancing to the vibrant music being piped through the stadium, there were thousands who cheered their arrival on the sports scene. Network TV cameramen, on hand for Cowboys home games, found focusing on the girls a good way to pass the idle moments created by time-

outs. The love affair had begun.

If Texie Waterman was one vital ingredient in the Cheerleaders' phenomenal rise to success, there was still another. When, under Texie's coaching, the "new" Dallas Cowboys Cheerleaders took the field in 1972, they were wearing new uniforms: white shorts, a royal blue halter blouse with long sleeves, a fringed, star-spangled vest and belt, and white boots. The uniforms were controversial — and they were smashing.

The games were often televised, and occasionally, so were the Cheerleaders. When one of the girls was caught by the eye of a camera, the others were quick to hug and congratulate her. But the networks were still far more interested in the action on the football field, and those camera shots were rare.

That was all to change in January, 1976, when the Cowboys met the Pittsburgh Steelers head-on for Super Bowl X in Miami. When a network cameraman caught the eye of one of the young women in blue and white, she smiled, winked, and suddenly 75 million Americans watching that telecast fell in love.

It was three months after that Miami Super Bowl, and Tex Schramm had a problem. The Cheerleaders were a roaring success, but with success came dozens of responsibilities — auditions, rehearsals, special appearances, meetings and all of the preparations needed to put the group in top form on the football field.

Schramm looked glumly at the memos and phone messages that littered his desk. Texie Waterman was doing a heck of a job, he told himself, but she couldn't possibly coach, choreograph *and* manage the Cheerleading squad.

Something had to be done. Schramm called his secretary into his office. "Look, Suzanne," he said, "no one's handling the Cheerleaders. Why don't you manage them in your spare time?"

If the Miami Super Bowl was one major milestone for the Dallas Cowboys Cheerleaders, then Suzanne Mitchell, who took the helm that same historic year, was the other. In the years to follow, Suzanne was to pilot the organization to worldwide renown, steering the Cheerleaders through hundreds of personal appearances, Hollywood movies and television specials, charity shows and U.S. Department of Defense/USO tours overseas. She'd keep a weather eye out when storms of controversy brewed, defending the Cheerleaders against the critics and preserving their dignity from anyone who tried to malign it.

Suzanne's devotion to the Cheerleaders is total, and her energy is overwhelming. She puts in 16-hour days, works through lunch, attends legal meetings with attorneys, goes to rehearsals, and

travels everywhere with the squad. She screens requests for appearances, arranges trips, judges at auditions, handles all merchandising and makes absolutely certain that the girls who become Cheerleaders look and act their best. She is business manager, drill sergeant and mother figure all rolled into one. She can be their worst enemy and their best friend. "I feel a deep responsibility," she says, her fist clenched across her desk, her blue eyes wide and direct. "It's difficult for them. They're really not individuals any longer. They become members of a team who overnight have assumed a 'corporate' identity. I try to teach them how to deal with that new identity but at the same time not lose their 'real' self."

The Dallas Cowboys Cheerleaders squad as in the past represent almost every phase of the American woman: teachers, secretaries, company executives, homemakers, nurses, students, medical technicians, fashion coordinators, accountants, models, sales persons, file clerks, receptionists, advertising representatives, cashiers, dental hygienists, flight attendants, etc. Some are single, some are married — several have children.

There is perhaps a uniqueness about the Dallas Cowboys Cheerleaders in that each young lady is so different. The concept is that each person in the stadium and the television audience has a mental picture of their ideal girl. The Dallas Cowboys Cheerleaders offer someone for everyone to identify with, as they are individuals in their own right. These young ladies are all bright, energetic, and intelligent contributors to society.

For the girls themselves, Cheerleading is the culmination of a dream. They come to the squad from all backgrounds and all walks of life to form a unique sisterhood. Together, they practice long into the night, polishing their dancing to perfection. Together, they share their hopes and fears, learning from one another. Together, they share that magic moment on the football field when the crowd rises to its feet in unanimous acclaim. And when they leave the Cheerleading squad, they go on to fulfill other dreams: as doctors and mothers, lawyers and secretaries, models and dancers.

They are a phenomenon, one that, as Tex Schramm says, "has not been restricted to Texas Stadium and the television eye that has carried their image across the country. Armed Forces in remote outposts throughout the world, children and veterans in hospital wards plus state fair and college audiences have all experienced a part of this dream. Because of their freshness and smiles, their beauty and talent, these young women bring a little touch of happiness to everyone they meet."

*Suzanne Mitchell, Director (1976 — present)*

*Texie Waterman, Choreographer (1972-1980)*

*Shannon Werthman, Choreographer (1981 — present)*

*Judy Trammell, Asst. Choreographer (1984)*

*Celebrity status has followed the Dallas Cowboys Cheerleaders since they first appeared on the sidelines. Now, through civic benefits, film and network TV appearances with stars such as Bob Hope and the Oak Ridge Boys (above), or on their USO tours worldwide, the Cheerleaders have attained an international reputation.*

# The Fans

In Yonkers, New York, Mike Mooney, a business manager for Macy's advertising department, always answers his phone the same way: "Hello, this is Randy White."

He is not an imposter. Rather, it is simply the way he has chosen to let any and everyone who might call know that he is (a) the "world's biggest Cowboys fan," and (b) a personal, first-name basis friend of the Cowboys' All-Pro defensive tackle. Mike's wife, Joyce, does not see her husband's behavior as odd. In fact, she was the one who suggested a couple of years ago that they send out personalized Christmas cards featuring a photo of Mike and her posing with Randy.

In San Francisco, a school teacher, Irene Carnazola, has, since the mid-seventies, been arranging her weekend schedule so that she might be in the stands on Sundays when the Cowboys play, regardless of the game site. Over the years she has become such a familiar face in the crowd of Cowboys fandom that Dallas officials regularly offer her a ride on one of the team's charter buses going to the airport following out-of-town games so she might be sure to make her usually tight flight schedule and get back home in time to be in the classroom on Monday morning.

"When people ask why I started following the Cowboys," she says, "I don't have a real good answer for them. I have no family connections in Dallas and no friends on the team or anything. I just admire the way they play, the way the organization is run, and the class they show. It didn't take me long to get hooked. Now, I guess I'll follow them from now on."

It is a feeling which has spread nationwide. In Albuquerque, New Mexico, stock car race driver Scott Horner drives a blue and silver "Dallas Cowboys Special," with Ed (Too Tall) Jones' number 72 painted on the door. A Pittsburgh truck driver who delivers bundles of newspapers to streetcorner vendors ignores the wrath of Steelers fans who constantly give him a hard time about the Cowboys insignias painted on the side of his truck. In West Orange, Texas, painter-stenciler Bobby Orta designed the interior of his young son's room to resemble the interior of Texas Stadium. And when Dallas independent oilman John John's first well came in out in West Texas, the silver storage tank that was erected near the drilling site featured a Cowboys helmet painted on the side. In Fort Worth, Dan Allen insists he has the most complete collection of Cowboys memorabilia in existence and has his house painted in Cowboys blue with gray-silver trim. "There is no place in my house that you can't see signs of the Cowboys everywhere," he says. That includes a garage filled with game programs, posters, etc., and a bedroom done in what he calls "modern Cowboy."

There's a fan in Florida who, on rare occasions when he's unable to get the Cowboys on television, calls a friend in Dallas who places the phone near a radio carrying the play-by-play. Marian Dillon, who works for Texas instruments in Dallas, traditionally paints her fingernails blue and silver as soon as the Cowboys report to Thousands Oaks, California for

*Tony Wargo was always there when the Dallas Cowboys played. Home or away, he was on hand, waiting outside the locker room to offer his congratulations. For those who had played exceptionally well there was a special handshake, one that included the discreet passage of a silver dollar. That was his trademark. Tony Wargo silver dollars they were called, and they became trophies, not payoffs, to those who received them.*

*John Fitzgerald still has his; so does Tony Dorsett. Same for Billy Joe DuPree and Drew Pearson. They've kept them because Wargo, a resident of Coaldale, Pa., was a special person. More than a fan, he was a friend.*

*He had, in effect, followed Roger Staubach from the Naval Academy to the Cowboys, never missing a game. But, in 1981, prior to his planned attendance at a Dallas-Rams game in Los Angeles, he died of a heart attack at age 62.*

*"He was a unique individual," Staubach says. "Tony was a giver, a man who delighted in doing something for others. If you tried to do something for him, it would embarrass him. When I was at the Naval Academy he started this tradition of giving out silver dollars to players who had good games. He did it up until my senior year when some of the people in the athletic department asked him not to. I've still got 17 of them, each representing a touchdown or a touchdown pass I was involved in at Navy. They're special to me, prized possessions. Tony Wargo was special to me."*

*Wargo stood out in a sea of faces which would greet the Cowboys as they checked into hotels on the road. Quiet and friendly, he struck up a strong friendship with many members of the team.*

*"He would come around the room on Saturday night," remembers Fitzgerald, "and tell everyone how their college team had done that day and just sit and chat for a few minutes. He was a delightful man, a friend to everyone."*

*When the Cowboys arrived for a game in San Francisco several years ago and failed to see Tony, several of the players began checking around and found he was in the hospital.*

*"He was a diabetic and had circulatory problems," Staubach says, "and had become ill after arriving in San Francisco. Everyone on the team was concerned about him."*

*Staubach and Drew Pearson paid him a visit in the hospital.*

*"He was Catholic," Roger says, "and always attended our team Mass. He would hand out the booklets and keep an eye out for the priest. Everyone who knew the man loved him."*

*To get a Tony Wargo silver dollar, then, was special. Those who have them now, treasure them.*

training camp. And in Odessa, Texas, O. E. Cumbie, another who travels faithfully to wherever the Cowboys might be playing, hands out business cards with the following message printed on them: "Peace on Earth and Goodwill Toward All Cowboys Fans. O. E. Cumbie, Cowboys' No. 1 Fan."

And, mail arrives at the Cowboys' front offices from foreign countries on a regular basis. Mexico has a remarkable percentage of its population that follows the Cowboys, and in Great Britain recently a poll was conducted and Dallas was far and away the most popular American football team of fans there.

Hotels housing the Cowboys on the road routinely brace for a rush of Cowboys fans to the lobby. Corridors leading to elevators often get so jammed with well-wishers that getting on and off is a near impossbility. At the Meadowlands Hilton, where the Cowboys have stayed prior to games with the New York Giants, the management finally had to rule that anyone who did not have a room key would have to remain outside the hotel entrance. Dan Williams, manager of the Marriott Pavilion in St. Louis, books numerous sports teams into his hotel, he says, but none attract the following the Cowboys do. "Nothing compares to the enthusiasm people show for the Cowboys. A week before the game we get calls from people wanting to know when they're going to arrive. It's incredible." Such is the case at virtually every stop Dallas makes during the season.

"When you get right down to it," says president and general manager Tex Schramm, "we've always got at least a taste of the home-field advantage. There's no stadium we play in that you don't find a sizeable pocket of Cowboys fans cheering, waving pennants."

"You know," says, St. Louis Cardinals vice president Curt Mosher, a former Cowboys public relations director, "even the die-hard fans of the local teams have a strong interest in Dallas when it comes to town."

And, of course, there are the supporters in the Dallas-Fort Worth area. They have been, on occasion, accused of being spoiled by the Cowboys' success, seldom lapsing into the frenzy of game day enthusiasm familiar to stadiums in Philadelphia and Washington. "The rap against our fans," says Schramm, "isn't at all fair. I wouldn't trade them for any others in the world. There is no team in professional sports that has enjoyed the loyalty we have from our fans for so many years."

Perhaps no Cowboys fan in history has gained more attention than did Dallas nightclub performer Bubbles Cash when she made her regular appearances at the Cotton Bowl on Sundays. Former players and their wives, like Charlie Waters (top right), are also among the enthusiastic crowds of Cowboys fans.

# The Media

## BOOKS WRITTEN ABOUT THE DALLAS COWBOYS

*Next Year's Champions*, by Steve Perkins (World).
*Winning The Big One*, by Steve Perkins (Grossett and Dunlap).
*Landry . . . The Man Inside*, by Bob St. John (World).
*We Love You, Cowboys*, by Bob St. John (Sport Magazine Press).
*The Dallas Cowboys*, by Bob St. John (Prentice-Hall).
*Dallas Cowboys: Pro or Con*, by Sam Blair (Doubleday).
*The Dallas Cowboys and The NFL*, by Donald Chipman, Randolph Campbell, and Robert Calvert (University of Oklahoma Press).
*Staubach: Third Down and Lifetime to Go*, by Roger Staubach with Bob St.John and Sam Blair (Word).
*The Dallas Cowboys Super Wives*, by Bobbi Field (Shoal Creek Press).
*Roger Staubach of the Dallas Cowboys*, by Joe Gergen (Scholastic Press).
*Dallas Cowboys: Great Teams, Great Years*, by Jeff Meyers (McMillian).
*The Crunch*, by Pat Toomay (Norton).
*When All The Laughter Turned to Sorrow*, by Lance Rentzel (Harper's Magazine Press).
*Drive to Win*, by Steve Perkins, paperback version of *Winning the Big One* (Tempo).
*Tony Dorsett, Sports Star*, by Sue Burchard (Harcourt Brace Jovanovich).
*The Dallas Cowboys, Super Bowl Champions*, by Julian May (Creative Education, Inc.).
*Tony Dorsett*, by Marcia McKenna Biddle (Julian Messner).
*The Kicking Game*, by Ben Agajanian with Paul Owens (Celestial Arts).
*The Tony Dorsett Story*, by Phil Musick (Enslow).
*Tony Dorsett: From Heisman to Super Bowl in One Year*, by Dick Conrad (Children's Press).
*The Courage to Believe*, by Craig Morton with Robert Burger (Prentice-Hall).
*Roger Staubach: Sports Hero*, by Marshall and Sue Burchard (G. P. Putnam).
*The Dallas Cowboys, An Illustrated History*, by Richard Whittingham (Harper & Row).
*Journey to Triumph*, by Carlton Stowers (Taylor).
*Decade of Dreams*, by Mary Candace Evans (Taylor).
*Dallas Cowboys Bluebook I*, by Steve Perkins and Greg Aiello (Taylor).
*Dallas Cowboys Bluebook II*, by Steve Perkins and Greg Aiello (Taylor).
*Dallas Cowboys Bluebook III*, by Steve Perkins, Carlton Stowers and Greg Aiello (Taylor).
*Dallas Cowboys Bluebook IV*, by Carlton Stowers and Greg Aiello (Taylor).
*Dallas Cowboys Bluebook V*, by Steve Perkins and Greg Aiello (Taylor).
*Cowboys/Raiders: Football's Special Teams*, by Ken Rappoport (Ace Tempo).
*Speed King: Bob Hayes of the Dallas Cowboys*, by David Lipman (G. P. Putnam).
*Roger Staubach: Time Enough to Win*, by Roger Staubach with Frank Luksa (Word).
*Bob Lilly's All-Pro Football Fundamentals*, edited by Tom Matts (Sports Underwriters, Inc.).
*Cowboys an' Indians*, by Tim Panaccio (Leisure Press).
*Bear Bryant on Winning Football*, revised and updated by Gene Stallings (Reward Books).
*Bob Lilly: Reflections*, by Bob Lilly with Sam Blair (Taylor).
*The Dallas Cowboys: The First 25 Years*, by Carlton Stowers (Taylor).

## COWBOYS AUTHORS

Pat Toomay: *The Crunch; On Any Given Sunday.*
Pete Gent: *North Dallas Forty; Celebrity Turkey Trot; The Franchise.*
Lance Rentzel: *When All The Laughter Died in Sorrow.*
Roger Staubach: *Third Down, Lifetime to Go; Time Enough to Win; Winning Strategies in Selling.*
Craig Morgon: *Courage to Believe.*
Bob Lilly: *Reflections.*

## SINGING COWBOYS

Don Meredith: "Them That Ain't Got It Can't Lose," and "Travelin' Man," 45 rpm.
Buddy Dial: "Baby, Baby," 45 rpm, and an album of religious music for Word Records.
Danny White: "I'm Just a Country Boy," album.
Ed Jones: "Funkin' on the Radio"/"Doing the Dip," 45 rpm.
Bob Breunig: "Jesus Loves The Little Children," album.

## TEN BEST COMMERCIALS DONE BY COWBOYS

1. Tom Landry, *American Express.*
2. Ernie Stautner, *Lite Beer.*
3. Don Meredith, *Lipton Tea.*
4. Walt Garrison, *American Tobacco.*
5. Clint Murchison, Jr., *Haverty's Furniture.*
6. Bob Lilly, *Black & Decker.*
7. Billy Joe DuPree, *United Way.*
8. Randy White, *Dannon Yogurt.*
9. Ed Jones, *Atari.*
10. Charlie Waters and D. D. Lewis, *Lite Beer.*

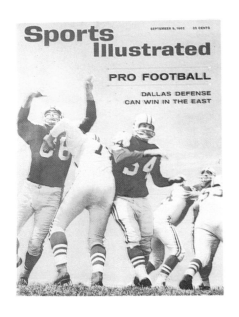

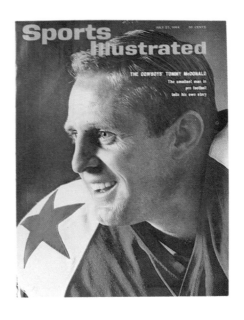

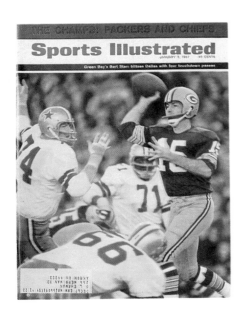

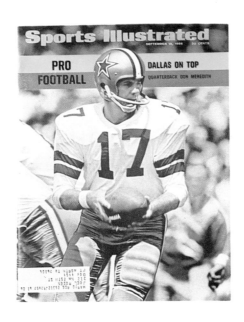

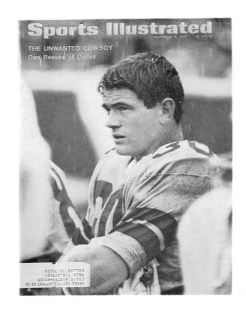

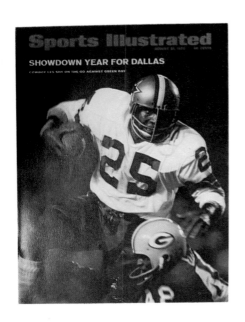

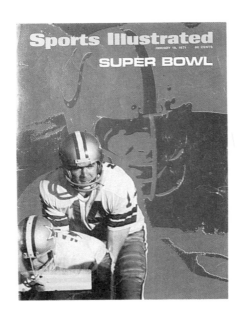

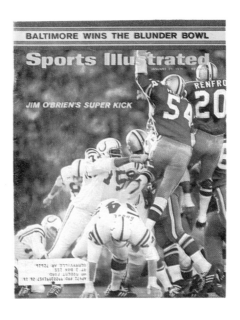

144

**Sports Illustrated**

DALLAS OVERWHELMS LOS ANGELES

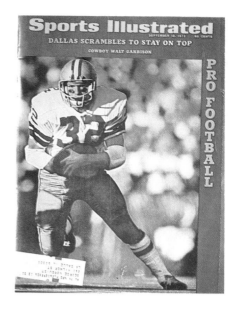

**Sports Illustrated**

SUPER DAY FOR DALLAS
The Sphinx They Couldn't Stop

**Sports Illustrated**

DALLAS SCRAMBLES TO STAY ON TOP
COWBOY WALT GARRISON

PRO FOOTBALL

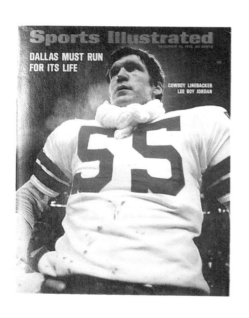

**Sports Illustrated**

DALLAS MUST RUN
FOR ITS LIFE

Cowboy Linebacker
Lee Roy Jordan

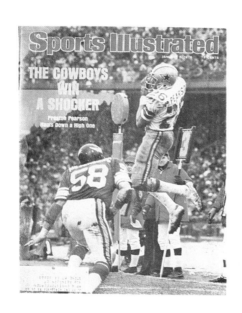

**Sports Illustrated**

THE COWBOYS
WIN
A SHOCKER
Preston Pearson
Hauls Down a High One

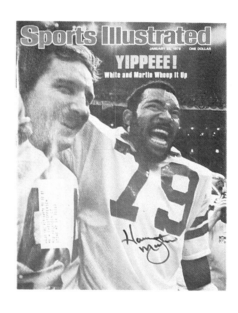

**Sports Illustrated**

YIPPEEE!
White and Martin Whoop It Up

PENN STATE DOES A NUMBER ON NO. 1 PITT
THE TERRIBLE ORDEAL OF THE ATLANTA HAWKS' EDDIE JOHNSON
BEAR BRYANT GETS THE RECORD AS 'BAMA BEATS AUBURN

**Sports Illustrated**

MAN
ON THE
RUN

Tony Dorsett
Of the
Dallas Cowboys

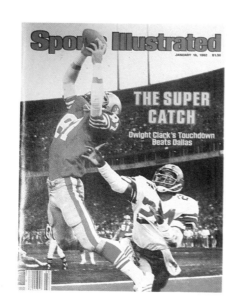

**Sports Illustrated**

THE SUPER
CATCH
Dwight Clark's Touchdown
Beats Dallas

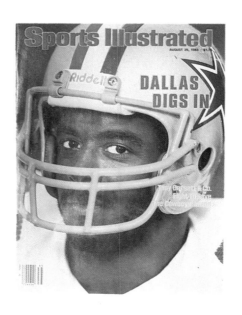

**Sports Illustrated**

DALLAS
DIGS IN

145

## Cowboys in the Press

Few teams in sports history have captured the imagination of the national media as have the Dallas Cowboys during their 25 years of existence. It was in 1963 that *Sports Illustrated* first called attention to the growing power in Texas when it proclaimed on its cover that the Cowboys could win the Eastern Conference. Since that time magazine editors have featured the Cowboys — individually or collectively — on a wide range of publications, from *Time* to *Life* to *Sport.* Clearly the Cowboys are a favorite of the magazine-buying population.

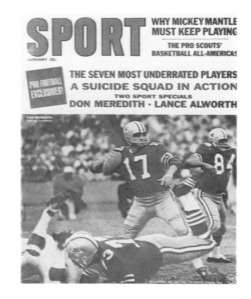

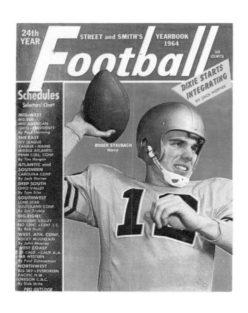

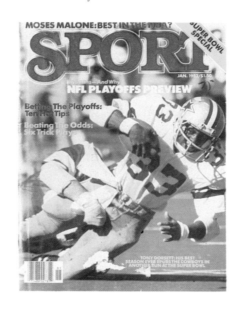

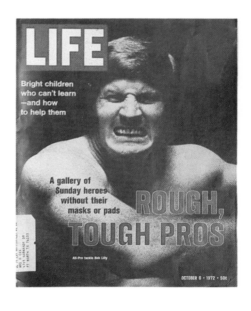

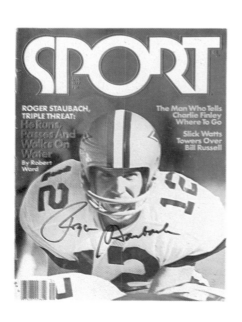

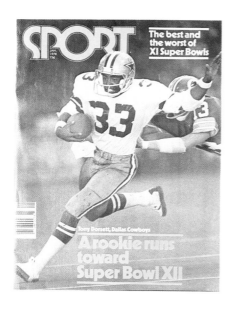

SPORT

The best and
the worst of
XI Super Bowls

Tony Dorsett, Dallas Cowboys

A rookie runs
toward
Super Bowl XII

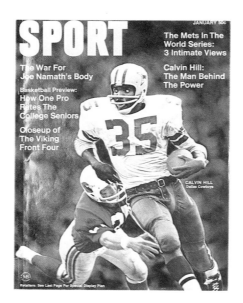

JANUARY 50c

SPORT

The Mets In The
World Series:
3 Intimate Views

The War For
Joe Namath's Body

Calvin Hill:
The Man Behind
The Power

Basketball Preview:
How One Pro
Rates The
College Seniors

Closeup of
The Viking
Front Four

CALVIN HILL
Dallas Cowboys

Retailers: See Last Page For Special Display Plan

INSIDE
SPORTS

BEST LITTLE
BODY PARTS
IN TEXAS
How America's
Team Gets
A Leg Up
On The NFL

What Makes
Gastineau Jump?

Boston's Ultimate Fan

Arguello-Pryor

Too Tall Jones

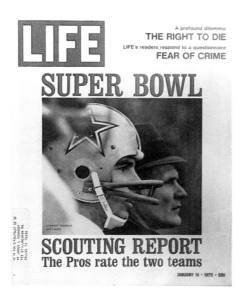

LIFE

A profound dilemma:
THE RIGHT TO DIE

LIFE's readers respond to a questionnaire
FEAR OF CRIME

SUPER BOWL

SCOUTING REPORT
The Pros rate the two teams

JANUARY 14 · 1972 · 50¢

SPORT

The SPORT interview:
Howard Cosell

The shocking inequities
and hypocrisy of the NCAA

Behind the Cowboy
struggle to reach
Super Bowl XIII

College football playoffs?
The players sound off!

Sonny Werblin, sport's
wiliest wheeler-dealer

NFL centers:
The stars nobody knows

Cowboy Harvey Martin
sacking Cardinal Jim Hart

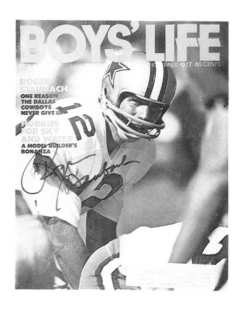

BOYS' LIFE

NOVEMBER 1977 60 CENTS

ROGER
STAUBACH
ONE REASON
THE DALLAS
COWBOYS
NEVER GIVE UP

HOBBIES
FOR SKY
AND WATER
A MODEL BUILDER'S
BONANZA

the DALLAS
COWBOYS

1967
OUTLOOK

$1.00

17

A NATIONAL COLUMNIST
AND THE AUTHOR OF
"PRO QUARTERBACK"
SIZES UP THE COWBOYS

QUARTERBACK DON MEREDITH
What To Do, Fast

High Priest of Football. By Gary Cartwright.
Houston's Super Law Firms: Invisible Empires.
Austin: New Capital of Country Rock.
Cops as Junkies.

NOVEMBER 1979

TexasMonthly

Tom Landry

78
55

"In Landry's presence
you do not feel the plastic and
computers you might expect.
You feel something
more visceral.
You feel fear."

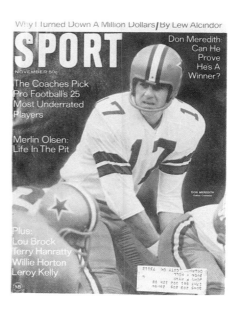

Why I Turned Down A Million Dollars / By Lew Alcindor

SPORT

Don Meredith:
Can He
Prove
He's A
Winner?

NOVEMBER 50c

The Coaches Pick
Pro Football's 25
Most Underrated
Players

Merlin Olsen:
Life In The Pit

Plus:
Lou Brock
Terry Hanratty
Willie Horton
Leroy Kelly

DON MEREDITH
Dallas Cowboys

*Cast as bikers and bad guys, Cowboys Ed (Too Tall) Jones, Drew Pearson, Jay Saldi and Thomas (Hollywood) Henderson starred in "Squeezze Play."*

148

## COWBOYS IN MOVIE ROLES

Don Meredith: Numerous made-for-TV movies and guest appearances on such series as "Police Story."

Ed Jones: "Double McGuffin," "Squeezze Play," "Semi-Tough," and TV series, "Different Strokes."

Jay Saldi: "Squeezze Play."

Drew Pearson: "Squeezze Play."

Thomas Henderson: "Squeezze Play," "Semi-Tough."

Harvey Martin: "Mean Joe Green and the Pittsburgh Kid."

John Niland: "Horror High."

D. D. Lewis: "Horror High."

Craig Morton: "Horror High."

Jim Boeke: "North Dallas Forty," "Heaven Can Wait," and numerous bit parts in TV movies and series.

## TITLES OF COWBOYS HIGHLIGHT FILMS

1963 — The Dallas Cowboys in Action
1965 — Where The Action Is
1967 — Appointment With Destiny
1968 — The Elusive Throne
1970 — The Decline and Rise of the Dallas Cowboys
1972 — Season of Challenge
1973 — Something Old, Something New
1974 — A Champion in Waiting
1975 — Against All Odds
1976 — Wild and Wooly
1977 — The Year the Clock Struck XII
1978 — America's Team
1979 — Team on a Tightrope
1980 — Like a Mighty River . . .
1981 — Star-Spangled Cowboys
1982 — Great Expectations
1983 — Shoot for the Stars — 25 Years of the Dallas Cowboys

## NEWSPAPER BEAT WRITERS

*Dallas Morning News*
Charlie Burton
Sam Blair
Gary Cartwright
Bob St. John
Carlton Stowers
Gary Myers

*Dallas Times Herald*
Bud Shrake
Charlie Holmes
Steve Perkins
Frank Luksa
Jim Dent

*Fort Worth Star-Telegram*
Paul Brookshire

Frank Luksa
Roger Kaye
Jim Dent
Ken Murray
Steve Pate
Richard Justice
Paul Hagen
Gil LeBreton
Ken Sins

*Associated Press*
Harold Ratliff
Denne Freeman

*United Press International*
Ed Fite
Mike Rabun

It's Super Time For Cowboys

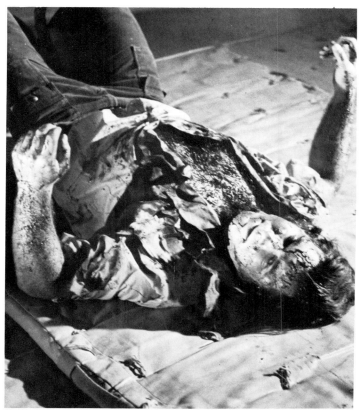

Former quarterback Roger Staubach worked with Frank Glieber (top) during CBS telecasts of NFL games. That's All-Pro John Niland looking rather bloody and battered in a scene from "Horror High."

# Cowboys Trivia

*Q: In the 1980 season there were four key members of the Dallas Cowboys who were, at one time, enrolled at the University of Houston during their collegiate careers. Who were they?*

A: Fullback Robert Newhouse and linebacker Guy Brown both played for the University of Houston Cougars throughout their collegiate careers. Linebacker Anthony Dickerson attended classes at Houston between the time he left SMU and went to Canada to play professionally. And tackle Larry Cole briefly enrolled there after leaving the Air Force Academy but later transferred to Hawaii to complete his college eligibility.

*Q: What current member of the Dallas Cowboys organization was once a member of the Brooklyn Dodgers baseball organization?*

A: Equipment manager Tom (Buck) Buchannan signed with the Dodgers as a catcher in 1951 at the age of 17. Following graduation from Ballinger (Tex.) High School he played for a year in the Concho Basin League before attending a Dodgers tryout camp in Fort Worth. He was signed, went to spring training but developed arm trouble and was released.

*Q: What former Cowboys player was once penalized for knocking an official unconscious during a game?*

A: The unfortunate "accident" occured when tight end Lee Folkins, who was with the Cowboys from 1962-64, was angered during the 1960 College All-Star game. Involved in a skirmish with another player, Folkins removed his helmet and swung it in the direction of the other player. The player ducked and Folkins' helmet struck the official squarely in the back of the head. Folkins was ejected.

*Q: It is generally believed that the Cowboys have had only three starting middle linebackers in their history — Jerry Tubbs, Lee Roy Jordan, and Bob Breunig. Actually, there have been four. Who started at the position in the team's first regular season game in 1960?*

A: Jack Patera (until recently the head coach of the Seattle Seahawks) opened at middle linebacker for the Cowboys but was ultimately moved to the outside, giving way to Tubbs, who had come to the Cowboys from the San Francisco 49ers.

## HOW THEY BECAME THE COWBOYS

When Clint Murchison, Jr., finally got word in January of 1960 that he and Dallas would be allowed to field an NFL franchise, he already had the name for his team picked. Feeling the need for something that would fit with the Southwest lore and locale, he had decided on Rangers.

By March of the same year, however, problems with the name developed. A Dallas minor league baseball team playing in the Texas League already had the name. But the word had been that it was either going to go out of business or move to another city. After another two months had passed and time neared for the inaugural season, Murchison and his general manager, Tex Schramm, decided it was unwise to stick with a name that might have their team confused with a baseball team.

It was Schramm who first suggested the name Cowboys, pointing out that it captured the same elements of the region and its history as did Rangers. Murchison agreed. And the team went off to training camp as the Dallas Cowboys.

*The first Cowboys sign and logo were a proud sight for
early players like Guy "Sonny" Gibbs, above.*

## THE FIRST COWBOYS

Since the 1960 Cowboys would be forced to field a team without the benefit of participation in the annual college player draft, each of the 12 NFL teams were forced to give up three veteran players to the Dallas franchise. They were allowed to freeze 25 of the 36 players on their roster, leaving 11 from which the Cowboys would choose the three they wanted.

Here are those players who were picked:

*CHICAGO BEARS:* Don Healy, DT; Jack Johnson, DG; Pete Johnson, DB.

*SAN FRANCISCO 49ers:* Fred Dugan, WR; John Gonzaga, DE; Jerry Tubbs, LB.

*LOS ANGELES RAMS:* Tom Franckhauser, DB; Bob Fry, OT; Duane Putnam, G.

*GREEN BAY PACKERS:* Nate Borden, DE; Bill Butler, DB; Don McIlhenny, RB.

*DETROIT LIONS:* Charlie Ane, OT; Gene Cronin, DE; Jim Doran, WR.

*BALTIMORE COLTS:* L.G. Dupre, RB; Ray Krouse, DT; Dave Sherer, P.

*WASHINGTON REDSKINS:* Tom Braatz, LB; Joe Nicely, G; Doyle Nix, DB.

*PITTSBURGH STEELERS:* Ray Fisher, DT; Bobby Luna, DB; Ray Matthews, WR.

*PHILADELPHIA EAGLES:* Dick Bielski, TE; Jerry DeLucca, T; Bill Striegel, G.

*NEW YORK GIANTS:* Al Barry, G; Don Heinrich, QB; Buzz Guy, G.

*CLEVELAND BROWNS:* Leroy Bolden, RB; Frank Clarke, WR; Ed Modzelewski, FB.

*ST. LOUIS CARDINALS:* Ed Hussman, DT; Bob Cross, OT; Jack Patera, LB.

Of the 36 players selected, 22 made the 1960 roster: Healy, Tubbs, Gonzaga, Dugan, Putnam, Fry, Franckhauser, McIlhenny, Butler, Borden, Cronin, Sherer, Dupre, Braatz, Matthews, Bielski, Guy, Heinrich, Clarke, Patera, and Hussmann.

### FIRST COWBOYS ON GUM TRADING CARDS

In 1960, the first year the Cowboys were a member of the NFL, the following players appeared on the bubble gum trading cards distributed by Topps:

Don Heinrich, QB
Fred Cone, FB
L. G. DuPre, RB
Dick Bielski, E
Charley Ane, C
Jerry Tubbs, LB
Ray Krouse, DT
Ed Modzelewski, FB
Doyle Nix, DB

### OAK FARMS DAIRIES 'FAVORITE COWBOY' CONTEST WINNERS

1968 — Bob Lilly
1969 — Calvin Hill
1970 — Craig Morton
1971 — Roger Staubach
1972 — Craig Morton
1973 — Lee Roy Jordan
1974 — Roger Staubach
1975 — Roger Staubach
1976 — Roger Staubach
1977 — Roger Staubach
1978 — Charlie Waters
1979 — Roger Staubach
1980 — Charlie Waters
1981 — D. D. Lewis
1982 — Danny White
1983 — Jim Cooper

### COWBOYS ON SPORTS ILLUSTRATED COVERS

Walt Garrison
Preston Pearson
Roger Staubach
Tony Dorsett
Randy White
Harvey Martin
Dan Reeves
Don Meredith
Lee Roy Jordan
Duane Thomas
Calvin Hill
Craig Morton
Les Shy
Chuck Howley
Mel Renfro
Everson Walls
Richard Flowers

### COWBOYS ON TIME COVERS

Roger Staubach

### COWBOYS ON NEWSWEEK COVERS

Thomas Henderson

### COWBOYS ON LIFE COVERS

Bob Lilly

### COWBOYS PICTURED ON CEREAL BOXES

Danny White, Corn Flakes

## AMERICA'S TEAM

Bob Ryan, editor-in-chief of NFL Films, had just put the finishing touches on the 1978 Dallas Cowboys highlights film and — frankly — was having some difficulty finding anything unique about the year the team had recently completed.

The year before it had been easy. Dallas had won its second Super Bowl and the focus of the film had been easy. But the Lombardi Trophy had gone to the Pittsburgh Steelers in '78. Highlight films about those who finish second, Ryan was fast deciding, weren't easy.

"What I was looking for," he recalls, "was something that would serve as a hook to build the highlights around, something a little different. Then I noticed that in all the research that had been done, all the games I'd been to and in all the films I'd seen, the kids across the league were wearing Roger Staubach and Dallas Cowboys jerseys.

"Dallas was on Monday Night Football all the time and the second game of just about every Sunday doubleheader. I think during the 16-game schedule that year they were on national TV 12 times. Obviously they were popular nationwide.

"I decided they were like the Montreal Canadiens in hockey and Notre Dame in college football. They were, in truth, a national team. So, I began playing around with a title along those lines. First, I thought of something like 'The Dallas Cowboys — National Team.' That lacked the ring I wanted, though. Then, I thought about 'America's Team,' and decided that was what it should be."

Thus was born the most famous highlight film title in sports history; one which would add a new name to the Dallas franchise. While players would, in days to come, insist the designation was a heavy burden, it would stick.

"I don't think the Cowboys were happy with it the first year because a lot of newspapers and teams used it as a motivational tool against them. And it stands to reason that anyone would be jealous if they heard some team other than their own being called 'America's Team.' But, the title fit for that particular year.

"Frankly, I think I've come up with some more catchy titles during my career with NFL Films, but I suppose that's the one that will be my epitaph. I'll go to the grave known as the guy who came up with 'America's Team.'"

## COWBOYS WHO HAVE PARTICIPATED IN NFL-USO TOURS

1967 — Don Meredith
1968 — Lance Alworth
1969 — Dan Reeves
1971 — Bob Lilly
1973 — Cliff Harris
1976 — D. D. Lewis

*Charlie Waters (far left) was cited as the Oak Farms Favorite Cowboy in 1980.*

## RADIO PLAY-BY-PLAY AND COLOR ANNOUNCERS FOR COWBOYS

1960 — Bud Sherman and Frank Glieber, KBOX
1961 — Frank Glieber and Don Buehler, KBOX
1962 — Charles Boland and Bill Meek, KLIF
1963 — Rick Weaver and Gary DeLaune, KLIF
1964 — Jay Randolph and Gary DeLaune, KLIF
1965 — Jay Randolph and Bill Mercer, KLIF
*1966 — Bill Mercer, KRLD
*1967 — Bill Mercer, KRLD
*1968 — Bill Mercer, KRLD
1969 — Bill Mercer, Blackie Sherrod, and Verne Lundquist, KLIF and KFJZ
1970 — Mercer and Lundquist, KLIF and KFJZ
1971 — Mercer and Lundquist, KLIF and KFJZ
1972 — Lundquist, Wisk, and Glieber, KRLD
1973 — Lundquist, Wisk, and Glieber, KRLD
1974 — Lundquist, Wisk, and Glieber, KRLD
1975 — Lundquist, Wisk, and Glieber, KRLD
1976 — Verne Lundquist and Bob Lilly did home games and Lundquist and Chris Needham did road games for first half of the season; then Brad Sham replaced Needham as color analyst, KRLD
1977 — Verne Lundquist and Brad Sham, KRLD
1978 — Verne Lundquist and Brad Sham, KRLD
1979 — Verne Lundquist and Brad Sham, KRLD
1980 — Verne Lundquist and Brad Sham, KRLD
1981 — Verne Lundquist and Brad Sham, KRLD
1982 — Verne Lundquist and Brad Sham, KRLD
1983 — Verne Lundquist and Brad Sham, KRLD

*Mercer worked with various staff announcers at home games and commentators from the home cities on road games.

*Signed in 1965, wide receiver Bob Hayes made a quick transition from Olympic sprint champion to standout pro football player.*

## COWBOYS ALL-ROOKIE TEAM

Throughout the history of the Dallas Cowboys the general rule has been that first-year players spend most of their time on Sunday afternoons watching from the sidelines and dreaming of the day they will be elevated to the starting lineup. There have, however, been exceptions. Fan Michael Walsh, a follower of the Cowboys since the 1960 season, has come up with the All-Time Dallas Cowboys Rookie Team.

The rules for making his imaginary team included (1) a player should have had no previous experience with any other NFL team; (2) could not have been on any kind of "reserve" list prior to being selected to the active roster, and (3) had to be a starter in his first years, at least for a major portion of the season.

With that criteria, Walsh selected the following All-Rookie team:

### OFFENSE

| Pos. | Name | Season |
|------|------|--------|
| QB | Don Meredith | 1960 |
| RB | Tony Dorsett | 1977 |
| RB | Calvin Hill | 1969 |
| C | Mike Connelly | 1960 |
| G | Burton Lawless | 1975 |
| G | Tom Rafferty | 1976 |
| T | Ralph Neely | 1965 |
| T | Tony Liscio | 1963 |
| WR | Drew Pearson | 1973 |
| WR | Bob Hayes | 1965 |
| TE | Billy Joe DuPree | 1973 |
| K | Toni Fritsch | 1971 |

### DEFENSE

| Pos. | Name | Season |
|------|------|--------|
| MLB | Lee Roy Jordan | 1963 |
| OLB | Dave Edwards | 1963 |
| OLB | Bob Breunig | 1975 |
| DE | Bob Lilly | 1961 |
| DE | Ed Jones | 1974 |
| DT | Guy Reese | 1962 |
| DT | Larry Cole | 1968 |
| CB | Everson Walls | 1981 |
| CB | Cornell Green | 1962 |
| S | Mel Renfro | 1964 |
| S | Michael Downs | 1981 |
| P | Ron Widby | 1968 |

## THEY FINALLY SIGN A CANNON

Officially, there was still no NFL team in Dallas, and Tex Schramm, the man who would serve as general manager if and when the city did get the franchise everyone expected it would, was still living in Connecticut. Still, he was very much on the job. Aware the team he would watch over would not be permitted the benefit of a college player draft, Schramm had gone after collegiate talent in another manner. He had signed Southern Methodist quarterback Don Meredith and University of New Mexico running back Don Perkins to personal service contracts.

Encouraged by his early successes, Schramm decided to go for the man everyone was after. It was in December of 1959 and he received word that LSU's Billy Cannon, winner of the Heisman Trophy, was in New York to attend a televised All-America function.

"He was regarded as the best running back in the country," Schramm remembers, "so naturally I wanted him. I gave him a call and asked if he might be interested in playing for Dallas. He indicated to me that he was, so we began talking money."

"I think we were pretty close to a deal on the phone, but I told him I'd come to New York, then we could finalize everything. My plan was to take one of the personal services contracts with me and get him signed while he was in New York."

Before Schramm could get to New York, however, a call came from Pete Rozelle, who was then General Manager of the Los Angeles Rams. Rozelle made it clear that his team was also very interested in Cannon.

"He was pretty upset over the idea of my signing another player to a personal services contract," Schramm recalls. "In fact, he told me I had already taken two excellent college players out of circulation and that if I signed Cannon I couldn't be too sure the Rams would vote favorably for Dallas being awarded a franchise at the league meeting. That was clear enough for me. I didn't bother catching the train to New York."

And Cannon would wind up signing with both the Rams of the NFL and the Houston Oilers of the AFL. (A judge would later rule he was the property of the Oilers.)

It would be 1984 before the Cowboys got another shot at a Cannon. And that one, linebacker Billy Cannon, Jr., a first round draft selection from Texas A&M, was signed with NFL Commissioner Pete Rozelle's full blessing.

*Rookie linebacker Billy Cannon, Jr.*

## COWBOYS IN COACHING

The following list is a sampling of the football coaching jobs former members of the Dallas Cowboys went into once their playing days were over:

*Jerry Tubbs, LB (1960-1967)* — current linebacker coach of the Dallas Cowboys.

*Obert Logan, DB (1965-1966)* — former coach of the semi-professional San Antonio Toros.

*Jim Doran, WR (1960-1961)* — receiver coach of the Pittsburgh Steelers, 1964-65.

*Gene Babb, LB-RB (1960-1961)* — former assistant coach at Ranger Junior College, Austin College, SMU, Oklahoma State.

*John Wilbur, T (1966-1969)* — part-time coach at University of Hawaii.

*Don Heinrich, QB (1960)* — former assistant coach for Los Angeles Rams, Pittsburgh Steelers, New Orleans Saints, and San Francisco 49ers.

*Fred Cone, K (1960)* — high school coach, Mobile, Alabama.

*Jim Ridlon, DB (1963-1964)* — defensive backfield coach at Syracuse for six years.

*Dale Memmellar, G (1962-1963)* — athletic director, Washingtonville (New York) High School.

*Dick Nolan, DB (1962)* — current Cowboys assistant coach who was previously head coach of San Francisco 49ers and New Orleans Saints.

*Mike Ditka, TE (1969-1973)* — current head coach of Chicago Bears.

*Dan Reeves, RB (1965-1972)* — former Cowboys assistant, now head coach of the Denver Broncos.

*Craig Morton, QB (1965-1974)* — former head coach of the Denver Gold of the United States Football League.

*Jack Patera, LB (1960-1961)* — former head coach of the Seattle Seahawks.

*Forrest Gregg, G-T (1971)* — former head coach of Cincinnati Bengals; now head coach of the Green Bay Packers.

*Monte Clark, T (1962)* — head coach of the Detroit Lions.

*Bob Fry, T (1960-1964)* — former assistant coach with the New York Jets.

## COWBOYS SUPERSTITIONS

Throughout the world of sports there are athletes who freely admit to certain superstitions that play a part in their competitive lives. Former Dallas Cowboys players Harvey Martin and Golden Richards are no exceptions.

Martin, the standout defensive end, would become frantic if he could not eat at least two hotdogs prior to a game. If the Cowboys trainer or lockerroom attendant was unable to provide Harvey with his required pre-game fare, he would seek out a stadium concession stand or a vendor in the stands and purchase his "good luck" hotdogs.

And wide receiver Golden Richards always felt it necessary to wear his right sock lower than his left. It was a tradition begun during his high school days and carried through his collegiate and professional careers.

Just how it helped him catch passes he never fully explained.

## COWBOYS AND THE HEISMAN

The Dallas Cowboys, as most everyone is aware, have had two players come to them after winning the Heisman Trophy, collegiate football's highest honor. Running back *Tony Dorsett* received the honor in 1976, his senior season at the University of Pittsburgh. And quarterback *Roger Staubach* was the 1963 honoree while at the Naval Academy.

While they are the only winners, a dozen others who wore (and wear) the Cowboys uniform finished in the top ten in past Heisman ballotings, dating back to 1949 when quarterback *Eddie LeBaron* of the College of the Pacific finished sixth. Then in 1952 another of the Cowboys' original quarterbacks, *Don Heinrich* of the University of Washington, was ninth. Running back *Dickie Maegle* of Rice, who played for Dallas in 1961, finished sixth in the 1954 voting.

The 1956 race saw wide receiver *Tommy McDonald* and linebacker *Jerry Tubbs*, both of the University of Oklahoma, finish third and fourth. Former quarterback *Don Meredith* of SMU was ninth in 1958 and moved up to third the following season. And in 1960, University of Pittsburgh tight end *Mike Ditka* was sixth. Linebacker *Lee Roy Jordan* of Alabama was fourth in 1962, the year before Staubach won the honor.

The following year two future Cowboys quarterbacks, Tulsa's *Jerry Rhome* and California's *Craig Morton*, finished second and seventh respectively. Then, in 1968, Florida State wide receiver *Ron Sellers* was tenth on the voters' list.

Current Cowboys quarterback *Danny White* was ninth in 1973, his senior year at Arizona State, finishing just one place ahead of Pitt freshman Dorsett. The following season Tony would finish thirteenth, trailing the likes of Maryland standout *Randy White*, who was ninth in the '74 balloting. Dorsett would climb to fourth as a junior in 1975 before leading the list in his senior year.

# DORSETT'S 1000 YARD SEASONS

During his 13-year football career, Dallas Cowboys' running back Tony Dorsett has compiled a remarkable record of 12 seasons in which he has gained 1,000 or more yards rushing, dating back to his junior year at Hopewell High School in Aliquippa, Pa. If, in fact, it had not been for the strike-shortened 1982 season in which just nine games were played, Dorsett no doubt could claim the unprecedented distinction of having never dipped below the 1,000-yard mark.

The first college back ever to string together four straight 1,000-yard seasons, he managed to duplicate the feat in his first four years in the NFL.

He has, in 13 years, rushed for 14,984 yards. Here's how:

### HOPEWELL HIGH SCHOOL

| Year | Att. | Yds. | Avg. | TDs |
|---|---|---|---|---|
| 1971 | 116 | 1,012 | 8.7 | 19 |
| 1972 | 139 | 1,034 | 7.4 | 23 |
| *Totals* | 255 | 2,046 | 8.0 | 42 |

### UNIVERSITY OF PITTSBURGH

| Year | Att. | Yds. | Avg. | TDs |
|---|---|---|---|---|
| 1973 | 288 | 1,586 | 5.5 | 12 |
| 1974 | 220 | 1,004 | 4.6 | 11 |
| 1975 | 228 | 1,544 | 6.8 | 14 |
| 1976 | 338 | 1,948 | 5.8 | 21 |
| *Totals* | 1,074 | 6,082 | 5.7 | 58 |

### DALLAS COWBOYS

| Year | Att. | Yds. | Avg. | TDs |
|---|---|---|---|---|
| 1977 | 208 | 1,007 | 4.8 | 12 |
| 1978 | 290 | 1,325 | 4.6 | 7 |
| 1979 | 250 | 1,107 | 4.4 | 6 |
| 1980 | 278 | 1,185 | 4.3 | 11 |
| 1981 | 342 | 1,646 | 4.8 | 4 |
| 1982 | 177 | 745 | 4.2 | 5 |
| 1983 | 289 | 1,321 | 4.6 | 8 |
| *Totals* | 1,834 | 8,336 | 4.5 | 53 |

# STAUBACH IS LANDLORD

In a sense, he ran the team for those ten years he was serving as quarterback for the Dallas Cowboys. Now, it seems, Roger Staubach is the team's landlord — at least for the time being.

Former team owner Clint Murchison, while in the process of selling the Cowboys' holdings he had owned since 1960, agreed to sell the land on which the team's practice field is located to Staubach's real estate firm.

Roger, in turn, leased the property back to the Cowboys for use until they make the move next year to their new facilities at The Valley Ranch.

Eventually, Staubach says, the Forest Lane practice field will be used for condominiums.

*Roger Staubach's Heisman Trophy was put to unusual use.*

M. Corning
BOB LILLY

# Bob Lilly

As his spectacular 14-year career with the Dallas Cowboys was winding to an end, drawing him closer to the day he would be summoned to Canton, Ohio, for induction in the National Football League Hall of Fame, Bob Lilly never wished for a return to times past. Rarely, in fact, did he ever speak nostalgically of the infant days of the Dallas franchise when he, the first No. 1 draft pick in the team's history, was the cornerstone upon which the Cowboys defense would eventually be built.

"When it was getting about time for me to retire," he remembers, "people would ask me if I ever wished I could start my career all over again. The question always amused me.

"In the latter stages of my career I was rarely hurt, for the simple reason I finally knew what I was doing. My first year in the league was a little different story. That [1961] season I broke five ribs, a wrist, a thumb, hurt my knee, and sprained both ankles."

The fact that he earned a spot on the All-Rookie team that season as a defensive end, a position at which he never felt comfortable, hardly overshadowed the pain and the frustration of those hardscrabble times.

Through those early, struggling years the big TCU All-American from Throckmorton, Texas, was the proof that there was hope for the future. Seven times an All-Pro defensive tackle, the first Dallas player inducted into Texas Stadium's Ring of Honor, and the first original Cowboy to be named to the Hall of Fame, he is still "Mr. Cowboy" to many who have witnessed the team's championship climb.

As Dallas gained power and prestige, he was there, leading the way. And when finally the Cowboys managed to win the big one, which many had doubted they could, it was Bob Lilly who celebrated most enthusiastically, understanding, perhaps better than any other member of the team, the significance of a world championship.

It is no surprise, then, that the game that remains most vivid in his mind is the one in which Dallas accomplished a goal it had been working toward for over a decade.

"I can think back to some pretty doggy days during those early expansion years," he says, "as well as some pretty high times, like winning our first Eastern Conference championship in 1966. There were some gripping disappointments even in that time frame, though; losing to a couple of great Green Bay teams in '66 and '67 and the sick feeling of losing to Baltimore in our first trip to the Super Bowl in 1970."

It was a time of a unique brand of frustration, a time when the Cowboys were winners but not champions. It was a time when a great deal of attention was dealt to the negative performances that were coming with far less regularity than they had years earlier. The Cowboys, the critics howled, were a team of great talent but simply weren't able to win the big one.

"And for that reason, if nothing else, the game I'll still be able to call to memory years and years from now will be our Super Bowl victory over the Miami Dolphins. On that day — January 16, 1972 — the Dallas Cowboys set to rest a lot of the conversation about our previous failures. That 24-3 victory was far more than a big payday and a diamond ring to me.

"I can't really describe the feeling that comes from winning the Super Bowl. It's something you can only share with the players and coaches on your own team. I can only say that it was the greatest thrill of my playing career. The Hall of Fame thing was nice, something I'll always cherish, but finally winning the championship after all we'd gone through for so many years. It made a lot of hard work worthwhile."

Lilly recalls that afternoon in New Orleans as one on which the Cowboys came as close to perfection as is possible in a game where the human element plays such a demanding role. "We were as prepared and ready to play as any team I've ever been on ever was. We arrived in New Orleans with a ten-game winning streak and were playing outstanding football. We felt that all we had to do was continue doing the things we'd been doing for weeks. There was such an atmosphere of confidence.

"Looking back, I'd say that on that given day we were almost flawless. I remember reporters coming up to me afterwards and asking me to single out players who had done exceptional jobs. Generally, I don't mind doing that sort of thing because in a lot of games there are certain individual performances that make the big difference. That wasn't the case in Super Bowl VI. It might sound a little trite, but that was a tremendous team effort, the kind of thing you feel proud to have been a part of."

For Lilly, it was a day that wiped away years of disappointment and it was a day when a man he regards highly received a just reward.

"After the game our dressing room was a mad house. Tom Landry's face was one big smile — and I don't have to tell you how unusual that is — and everyone was slapping each other on the back and yelling. Someone gave me a cigar and I lit up. I was happy for me, and I was happy for the guys on the team, but what I felt for Landry finally winning the Super Bowl — well, I can't tell you how I felt. But I'd been with him a long time and thought I knew him pretty well. And I think I had a pretty good idea what winning the Super Bowl, finally winning the big game, meant to him.

"Somehow, he had known way back in the early '60's that our day would come. Along the way there were a lot of us who wondered. That day he made believers of us all."

M. Corning

# Don Perkins

There was, in the formative days of the Dallas Cowboys, a training camp ritual referred to as the Landry Mile. It was the first-order-of-business test of endurance, stamina, and grit forced upon all who hoped to earn a spot on the team. Those unable to complete it in the prescribed time, word had it, could anticipate but small chance of gaining notice from head coach Tom Landry once practices formally began.

Don Perkins, a stocky running back with a superlative collegiate career at the University of New Mexico to his credit, was among the first to recognize the seriousness that Landry attached to the test. It was a hot July day in Forest Grove, Oregon, during the inaugural Dallas training camp, when Perkins' professional career flashed before his eyes, and all but ended before it even began.

He had reported 20 pounds over his college playing weight, confident in the belief that in pro ball bigger was better. The added weight and what he would later describe as a "biscuit and gravy" off-season training program resulted in a Grade A disaster.

President and general manager Tex Schramm, an eyewitness that July day in 1960, remembers it well: "He looked absolutely awful. Trying to run the mile, he would fall down, get up, try to run some more, and fall down again. He never finished it. We didn't know what to think. Usually, when a guy pulls something like that it tells you right away that he doesn't have much of what you're looking for — pride, courage, determination."

With precious few bonafide players on hand, the Cowboys immediately had cause to doubt their own good judgment. Here was an athlete who had wrecked school rushing records in Albuquerque; a 5-10, 200-pound powerhouse who had been selected to play in the annual College All-Star game, unable to pass the first test of camp. Touted by U.S. Senator Clinton Anderson of New Mexico, Perkins, they felt, was one of the few "can't miss" players they had. Clint Murchison, so eager to have him, had signed him to a personal services contract even before the Cowboys formally existed. It was even necessary to deal away a ninth round draft choice to the Baltimore Colts to be assured that he would remain Dallas property.

And there he was, struggling through, and not even completing, the Landry Mile.

Now, 24 years later, Perkins still finds little humor in that failure. It is, on the other hand, a moment in his life he still vividly remembers. Now a staff member of the New Mexico Governor's office where he oversees a statewide incentive work program, Perkins admits that he spent several anxious years as a pro wondering if he had been forgiven for his miserable showing. "The fact that Tom Landry gave me a second chance after that mile," he says, "is probably the thing that stands out in my mind when I look back on my career with the Cowboys. Without his patience and fairness, nothing I eventually accomplished would have been possible. He gave me a break and in return I gave him my best shot."

Landry's patience, of course, would come to pay high dividends. During an eight-year professional career Don Perkins represented the backbone of the still developing Dallas offense. He gained 6,217 yards rushing, earned All-Pro recognition and participated in no less than five Pro Bowls. When the Cowboys initiated a Ring of Honor in Texas Stadium, Perkins and former quarterback Don Meredith were the second and third players selected after Hall of Famer Bob Lilly had become the original inductee.

And he became the prototype of the Dallas Cowboys fullback. Though he lacked blazing speed, he could cover 10 yards faster than his Olympic sprinter teammate Bob Hayes. His blocking earned him remarkably high grades week in and week out, and, when short yardage was needed, he could deliver a blow that belied his size.

About the only man in Dallas who did not feel Don Perkins was among the best in the business was Don Perkins.

Even with the advantage of two decades of hindsight, he views his career with surprise and some measure of wonder. "The honest truth of the matter," he says from his Albuquerque office, "is that I never felt I was good enough to be playing at the professional level. I spent most of my career afraid someone would find me out, suddenly discover that I didn't have any business being where I was. I never even had aspirations of a pro career while I was in college. That was before the game was so much a part of the public consciousness, before the big money and overwhelming publicity. Even after I signed with the Cowboys it never occurred to me that I might be around for a long career.

"My lack of confidence or negative feelings about myself — I don't really know what to call it — made every play of every game a maximum challenge for me. I never felt comfortable that I could have a bad game, an off-day, and come back and still have my job. Maybe I'm just one of those underachievers, but the fact was I was always looking over my shoulder. That's the way it was from that first rookie camp until the last couple of years of my career."

Indeed, the failure in the Landry Mile was not the only difficulty Perkins had to deal with in the early going. In that same rookie season he suffered a broken bone in his foot during practice for the College All-Star game and, following an operation, returned to Albuquerque to await a second chance when camp opened prior to the '61 season. "It was," he recalls, "a year of anxious waiting. I wasn't sure the failure in that mile run had really been forgiven. But, I had signed a two-year contract, so I felt obligated to go back and give it a better try."

Though he would earn himself a spot on the roster with relative ease, training camp was far from an enjoyable experience. "At one point in practice I thought I had broken my foot again. And I didn't really think I had been doing that well. Things had just sort of built up. The usual agony and loneliness of camp had begun to get to me so I decided to tell them I'd had it. I had a no-cut contract but was willing to let them keep their money. All I wanted to do was go home. But, eventually, they talked me out of it."

A year later Don Perkins would be selected to Associated Press and NEA All-Pro teams. And throughout his career the honors would come in a steady flow.

# Don Meredith

Winter had fallen on Detroit like a sledgehammer. Snow swirled, the temperature had long since dipped well below the freezing mark and a 17 mile-per-hour wind was coming off the icy lake. All in all, it was an almost poetic setting for the end of the Dallas Cowboys' initial season in the National Football League. Yet on that dismal day in 1960 a crowd of 43,272 had braved the elements, probably because they were virtually assured of seeing their hometown Lions win over Dallas. Everyone else had. They built fires in the stands to keep warm as their coffee froze in their cups.

It was, to be sure, not Don Meredith's kind of day; yet even now, 24 years and a small fortune removed from his rookie season as a pro quarterback, he remembers it as if it were yesterday.

Sitting in an east coast motel recently, preparing for his regular chores on ABC's Monday Night Football, he put aside his studies of the game he was to work and began to laugh.

"There was," he remembers, "no way I was going to play against the Lions. Eddie [LeBaron] had been playing well and I was dead certain he would go all the way. So, the night before ol' Don decides to spend the entire evening introducing himself to the Motor City. That was the first time in my football career I had ever made a complete night of it. But, shoot, I wasn't worried. In fact, by the time the sun came up I wasn't even feeling the cold anymore."

If the truth were known, by the time he reported to the visitors dressing room and began preparation for the last hurrah of Dallas' 0-11-1 season — the worst in 18 years in the NFL — he was feeling very little of anything. Except for the need of eight or 10 hours of hard sleep. Only when coach Tom Landry informed him that he was going to be the starter that afternoon did the former SMU All-American begin to worry.

"I was sitting there," Meredith recalls, "with my pads on, my jersey, my socks and shoes, trying to figure how I was going to make it through the day when Nate Borden [the former Green Bay defensive end who had come to Dallas that first season] came up. He looked down at me and said, 'Boy, you are gonna need a lot of help today.' I told him, 'Hey, man, I'm ready.' Well, he started laughing his head off and then said, 'Maybe it would be a good idea, then, to put your pants on before we go out. Which I understand we're going to do in just a few minutes. It's a little cold today.' "

The cutting cold air in the stadium performed a minor miracle. Meredith quickly made a return to the living and, in fact, became more and more excited about the prospect of commanding the team. Then at the last minute Landry had a change of heart and informed his rookie field general that LeBaron would be starting. "But," the Cowboys coach said, "I want you to be warming up through the first quarter in case I decide to turn it over to you."

"I got tired of warming up," Don recalls, "and besides I was getting cold so I went over to the bench and bundled up. I was sitting next to Don Heinrich [who had come to Dallas by way of the New York Giants] and he always carried a pack of cigarettes on the field with him in his socks. I bummed one from him and had me a smoke while Eddie kept on quarterbacking."

Another sinking spell plagued him when the team returned to the warmth of the dressing room during halftime yet Meredith, the man who would one day become the leader of some of the Cowboys' finest hours, the eventual winner of such honors as the Bert Bell Award and a man who would earn himself a place in the hallowed Ring of Honor when all was said and done, wearily made his way back onto the field.

"It was even colder and snowing harder," he recalls, "but Tom told me to warm up and be ready. I did. And Eddie opened the second half. He got his hand stepped on and for a few minutes they thought something might be broken. But he stayed in and I kept warming up until the third quarter ended. Then I went over and sat down on the bench again. Late in the fourth quarter Tom said warm up again. I couldn't believe it. I told him I wouldn't do it. I was worn out from warming up and didn't see any reason to do it again with the game almost over."

Thus, it is that 23-14 loss at the hands of the Detroit Lions on that final day of the '60 season — a game in which he did not play so much as a single down — that "Dandy" Don Meredith, fun-loving, free-spirited, Emmy Award-winning man that he is, looks back on as one of his memorable moments in a Dallas uniform.

"I didn't play any football that day," he says, "but I learned a couple of things. First, I found out that all-night partying is okay if you don't have to play a football game the next day.

"And, it was on that afternoon that I first began to realize that Tom and I were going to really have a lot of fun together."

# Chuck Howley

It was, he remembers, a time of great confidence. And embarrassment. And, ultimately, overwhelming satisfaction. Chuck Howley, now sheltered from the violent world of professional football, a successful Dallas businessman, was reflecting on Super Bowl VI, January 1972.

Howley, the man Cowboy outside linebackers are now measured against, spoke in a savoring voice about that day — when the Cowboys demolished Miami, 24-3.

"You know, confidence is a funny thing," he pointed out. "It isn't something you can talk yourself into on the day of a game. It's something that builds, grows. With maturity. So, when I say we went into that game confident that we were going to win it, I don't mean to imply that we simply woke up that morning and said, 'Hey, we can win this thing.' It was something we had known, had felt for quite some time. Through most of the season, in fact. And it wasn't just a few of the guys on the team. It was a feeling shared by everyone. I know even Coach Landry has said he felt sure we were going to win."

And win they did, in one of the most decisive Super Bowl victories ever achieved.

While the defense was shutting down the Dolphins' attack, (powerful Bob Lilly once dropping Miami quarterback Bob Griese for a 27-yard loss) the offense, led by quarterback Roger Staubach, the game's Most Valuable Player, and running backs Duane Thomas, Walt Garrison, and Calvin Hill, was setting a Super Bowl rushing mark of 252 yards.

Kicker Mike Clark got Dallas on the board first with a nine-yard field goal. Then followed a brilliant 76-yard drive capped by a seven-yard Staubach-to-Lance Alworth scoring pass. The Dallas offense later upped the margin with a 71-yard, eight-play drive which saw the controversial Thomas sweep into the end zone from three yards out.

Early in the fourth period Miami faced a third-and-four situation at its own 49 and Griese dropped back to pass to running back Jim Kiick. Howley, a thorn in the Dolphins' side all afternoon, was knocked down, then bounced up to step in front of the intended receiver and intercept the ball. All that remained between him and a sure touchdown was a caravan of Dallas blockers. He began his run toward the goal, six points a certainty. But at about the 15 he began to stumble. At the nine, with no Dolphin player near him, he slipped, lost his footing, and fell and was downed by a Miami defender.

"Imagine," Howley laughs. "Nobody around me, blockers everywhere, and I just crash. Needless to say it was a little embarrassing. Lilly and [George] Andrie looked back and couldn't believe it. At that particular moment I was wishing it had been a very deep hole I had fallen into."

No damage was done, however, as Staubach later hit Mike Ditka with a seven-yard scoring toss to ice the victory.

A moment of embarrassment aside, however, it would ultimately rank as the most satisfying victory of Howley's career. It would even rank above the unprecedented achievement of having been cited as the MVP in the previous Super Bowl when a last second Baltimore field goal defeated Dallas, 16-13. "That was a nice feeling," he admits, "but the ball just didn't bounce right for us that day against the Colts. I thought we played well enough to win it, but it just wasn't to be."

"I think maybe we got a little caught up in all the hoopla of the game that year and weren't totally concentrating on what we had to do. The next year we did. We knew what Miami was going to do. Maybe against Baltimore there was some doubt that we could win. Maybe we were a little too nervous. None of those things got in our way as we prepared for the Dolphins. We were a mature team which went down there to get a job done. And we did."

By knowing that they were going to do so.

MEL RENFRO

# Mel Renfro

It would seem a difficult question to pose to a man who, over the course of a dynamic career, was five times named All-Pro, and played in 10 Pro Bowls and four Super Bowls. A player whose defensive efforts dominated historical playoff games, he established an arm-load of Dallas Cowboys records in his 14-year tenure with the NFL.

Yet former cornerback Mel Renfro is quick to answer. It is obvious that the task of selecting his most memorable game is not that difficult. His answer, while qualified a bit, is quick, precise — and his memory for details of the moment are such that one can't help but believe him.

"There are a lot of great victories that come to mind," he says. "There were the Super Bowls, several big playoff wins, some come-from-behind victories. All were satisfying and special for various reasons. And, yes, there were some big, big disappointments — the Ice Bowl in Green Bay and losing the first Super Bowl.

"But the individual performance I got the biggest kick out of? That's easy."

Bear in mind this is a man who did it all. Would he choose, for instance, the Washington game in 1964 when he set a club record for kickoff return yardage in a single game, carrying four returns back for 168 yards? Or maybe that 90 yard interception against St. Louis in 1967 for a touchdown? The entire '69 season wasn't too shabby inasmuch as he set a club record with ten interceptions. Maybe the 100-yard kickoff return against San Francisco in '65?

No, says Mel. The single-game performance he picks from a career which ran from 1964 to 1977 was not even a regular season game. The fact of the matter is, it came in a game he would have given his eye teeth not to have had to play in at all.

It was the 1971 Pro Bowl in Los Angeles.

"It was just after we had lost to Baltimore (16-13) in the Super Bowl and the last thing in the world I wanted to do was play another football game. I was really down after that loss. In fact, it was six full months before I got to the point where I wasn't sick inside every time I thought about that game.

"But I had been selected to play in the Pro Bowl — and it is quite an honor — so I went out to L.A. Generally, you take advantage of sight-seeing opportunities and go out to all the nice restaurants, sort of make a vacation out of it. But I was in no mood for that kind of thing and I just spent the week staying in my room when we weren't practicing. I knew that every time I went out people were going to ask me about our losing the Super Bowl. About that tipped pass that gave the Colts a freak touchdown and their late field goal to win it. I just wasn't up to it, so I stayed to myself.

"I was in good shape, but I never did get really excited about playing the game. The truth is, I really didn't want to be there. I just felt it was something I was obligated to do."

Obligation or no, he went out into the massive Coliseum and returned punts for 82 and 54 yards — both for touchdowns — and was as close to perfect defensively as a cornerback can ever hope to get. By the end of the afternoon quarterbacks like Daryl Lamonica had sent receivers like Paul Warfield and Warren Wells in Renfro's direction 14 times — and never was there a completion. The NFC won the game, 27-6, and Renfro was honored as the Most Valuable Player.

"That day," he says, "took some of the sting out of the disappointment of losing the Super Bowl. It got my chin up."

The fact of the matter is Renfro seemed always to perform well in the Pro Bowl, going back to his first appearance in his rookie year. "That was an exciting thing," he remembers, "because I was on the field with so many players I had heard so much about in high school and college. In fact, John Wooten (former Cleveland Browns lineman and current Cowboys scout) was in that one."

In that first Pro Bowl appearance Renfro intercepted a pass and returned it for a touchdown.

"There were a lot of good times," he says. "I had the good fortune to come to the Cowboys when they were developing into a solid football team that did nothing but get better as time went on. We had our hard times, of course, getting over that hump of winning the big one, but finally we passed that barrier and proved ourselves to the world by winning that first Super Bowl in '72. That, I'd have to say, was the greatest feeling I ever had as a member of the Cowboys. But that was a team thing, something we had all worked long and hard for.

"Being the MVP in the Pro Bowl that previous year was more of a personal thing."

# Roger Staubach

For thirty years he played the game, establishing milestones the way some people put up fence posts. For Roger Staubach, the highlights were not so much measured by games, even seasons, but by decades. Even as his final year of play wound down in that winter of 1979 he was hard pressed to point to that single moment of glory he would carry as a touchstone with him into retirement. There simply were too many from which to choose.

His involvement began with then-overwhelming excitement as he made the cut on a Cincinnati pee-wee team at age seven, and continued into all-star years as a schoolboy at Percell High School when winning a city co-championship was something special. Eventually, there was the Naval Academy and All-America honors, the Heisman Trophy, the cover of *Time* magazine, and the memorable Army-Navy games. And on to the professional ranks where, as a Cowboys quarterback for 10 years, the glories were numerous: Super Bowls, MVP honors, Pro Bowls, playoff victories, and an almost unbelievable record of having directed Dallas to come-from-behind wins on 23 different occasions.

As his career developed, so did a country's awareness of this athlete who came to be recognized not only for his uncanny abilities on the field, but his personal dedication to his Christian beliefs, his family, and American values. He disliked the fact some members of the nation's press referred to him as "Captain America," but the moniker fit. In an era of disappearing heroes, Roger Staubach stood firm as an example to young and old alike.

When he made final his intention to retire after the '79 season, his press conference attracted more members of the media than the governor of Texas had ever gathered. Local radio and television stations broadcast the announcement live. The networks would bid him farewell not on that segment of the evening news reserved for sports, but in that time slot used for things more vital, more important. A Dallas newspaper distributed a special retirement section; NFL Films hurried into production a documentary biography; and a song titled "Goodbye Roger" immediately climbed on the local charts.

"It was unbelievable," Staubach says in retrospect. "For a few days after announcing that I was retiring, I thought maybe I had died. The reaction was far more than I expected it to be."

It would, then, seem an unfair request to ask that he isolate a moment, a single game, from such a career and call it the most memorable, the high time of high times. Yet Staubach, true to his form as an athlete, did not even hesitate: "December 16, 1979," he says. "Dallas 35, Washington 34. Up to that point I felt sure the high point had already been reached somewhere in my career. But that one was like no other game I've ever been a part of. It was, to put it simply, the most thrilling 60 minutes I ever spent on the football field."

That it was a game matching the Cowboys and Redskins was enough, blood being bad between the two Eastern Division rivals, but on that particular chilly Sunday a great deal was at stake.

In the first meeting of the two teams the Redskins had soundly defeated Dallas, adding insult to injury by calling time out in the final seconds of play to kick a cinch field goal which upped the margin to 34-20. It was not a tactic easily dismissed. Thus despite the fact running back Tony Dorsett would sit the game out with a bruised shoulder and wide receiver Drew Pearson would be limited in his contribution due to a strained knee, enthusiasm was high.

It was difficult to detect in the early going, however, as the Cowboys offense went nowhere and gave up two fumbles which helped Washington jump out to a 17-0 advantage early in the second quarter.

"I've never been in a game with a stranger scoring pattern," Staubach says. "They scored the first 17, then we scored the next 21. Then they scored 17 more and we finally got the last 14. We finally got something going in the second quarter, moving 70 yards for a touchdown and then, with just nine seconds left before the half I threw a touchdown pass to Preston Pearson. We weren't in the greatest of positions at the time, either. We were facing third-and-20 at the Washington 26 when that one finally came.

Staubach best describes what took place from that point in his own book, "Time Enough to Win." A very appropriate title.

"I'll remember the first play of that series almost as long as the last because I sort of made it up. Instead of having [Tony] Hill run an inside route . . . I told him, 'Act like you're going to break inside, then go to the outside, . . . I threw the pass that somehow sailed between two defenders. How it did I'm still not sure because the ball wobbled all the way. It became a great pass only because it reached Hill who helped by making a great adjustment to be in the right place.

"The fact was we free-lanced our way 20 yards upfield with that one. Then Preston worked free for completions of 22 and 25 to put us on Washington's eight-yard line . . . In the huddle I told Hill, 'Be alert, because if they blitz I'm coming to you.' I think if I hadn't mentioned that to him he wouldn't have been looking for the ball because tight end Billy Joe DuPree was the hot receiver. The Redskins did blitz and frankly I never looked for DuPree. Instead I lobbed a semi-Alley Oop pass toward the end zone corner where Hill had gotten behind cornerback Lemar Parrish. Tony ran under it to make a touchdown catch with 39 seconds left.

For the day Staubach would complete 24 of 42 passing attempts for 336 yards, his second highest total as a pro. But on that day it was not the yardage which was important.

Days later a disappointed Washington coach Jack Pardee would offer the best summary of what had taken place that day: "I went through that film trying to find out what we did wrong so it would never happen again. My final conclusion was that Roger pulled off two or three plays that made the difference — with sheer athletic ability."

# PRO BOWL AND ALL-PRO PLAYERS

## PRO BOWL

1960 — Jim Doran, WR (1st appearance).

1961 — Dick Bielski, TE (1); Don Perkins, RB (1).

1962 — Don Bishop, CB (1); Eddie LeBaron, QB (1); Bob Lilly, DE (1); Don Perkins, RB (2); Jerry Tubbs, LB (1).

1963 — Sam Baker, K (1); Lee Folkins, TE (1); Don Perkins, RB (3).

1964 — Bob Lilly, DT (2); Mel Renfro, S (1).

1965 — Cornell Green, CB (1); Mel Renfro, S (2); Chuck Howley, LB (1); George Andrie, DE (1); Bob Lilly, DT (3); Bob Hayes, WR (1).

1966 — George Andrie, DE (2); Cornell Green, CB (2); Bob Hayes, WR (2); Chuck Howley, LB (2); Bob Lilly, DT (4); Dave Manders, C (1); Don Meredith, QB (1); Don Perkins, RB (4); Mel Renfro, S (3).

1967 — George Andrie, DE (3); Cornell Green, CB (3); Bob Hayes, WR (3); Chuck Howley, LB (3); Lee Roy Jordan, LB (1); Bob Lilly, DT (5); Ralph Neely, T (1); Don Perkins, RB (5); Mel Renfro, S (4).

1968 — George Andrie, DE (4); Chuck Howley, LB (4); Lee Roy Jordan, LB (2); Bob Lilly, DT (6); Don Meredith, QB (2); John Niland, G (1); Don Perkins, RB (6); Mel Renfro, S (5).

1969 — George Andrie, DE (5); Calvin Hill, RB (1); Chuck Howley, LB (5); Lee Roy Jordan, LB (3); Bob Lilly, DT (7); Ralph Neely, T (2); John Niland, G (2); Mel Renfro, S (6).

1970 — Bob Lilly, DT (8); John Niland, G (3); Mel Renfro, CB (7).

1971 — Bob Lilly, DT (9); John Niland, G (4); Mel Renfro, CB (8); Cornell Green, S (4); Rayfield Wright, T (1); Roger Staubach, QB (1); Ron Widby, P (1); Chuck Howley, LB (6); Duane Thomas (1, injured).

1972 — Bob Lilly, DT (10, injured); Mel Renfro, CB (9); Cornell Green, S (5); John Niland, G (5); Calvin Hill, RB (2); Rayfield Wright, T (2); Walt Garrison (1).

1973 — Mel Renfro, CB (10); John Niland, G (6); Rayfield Wright, T (3); Bob Lilly, DT (11, injured); Lee Roy Jordan, LB (4, injured); Calvin Hill, RB (3, injured).

1974 — Lee Roy Jordan, LB (5); Rayfield Wright, T (4); Calvin Hill, RB (4); Cliff Harris, S (1); Blaine Nye, G (1); Drew Pearson, WR (1).

1975 — Cliff Harris, S (2); Rayfield Wright, T (5).

1976 — Billy Joe DuPree, TE (1); Cliff Harris, S (3); Harvey Martin, DE (1); Blaine Nye, G (2); Drew Pearson, WR (2); Roger Staubach, QB (2); Charlie Waters, S (1); Rayfield Wright, T (6).

1977 — Billy Joe DuPree, TE (2); Cliff Harris, S (4); Efren Herrera, K (1); Harvey Martin, DE (2); Drew Pearson, WR (3); Roger Staubach, QB (3, injured); Charlie Waters, S (2); Randy White, DT (1).

1978 — Tony Dorsett, RB (1); Billy Joe DuPree, TE (3); Cliff Harris, S (5); Thomas Henderson, LB (1); Tony Hill, WR (1); Harvey Martin, DE (3, injured); Roger Staubach, QB (4); Charlie Waters, S (3); Randy White, DT (2, injured).

1979 — Bob Breunig, LB (1); Pat Donovan, T (1); Cliff Harris, S (6); Tony Hill, WR (2); Harvey Martin, DE (4); Herbert Scott, G (1); Roger Staubach, QB (5); Randy White, DT (3).

1980 — Bob Breunig, LB (2); Pat Donovan, T (2); Herbert Scott, G (2); Randy White, DT (4).

1981 — Tony Dorsett, RB (2); Pat Donovan, T (3); Ed Jones, DE (1); Herbert Scott, G (3); Rafael Septien, K (1); Everson Walls, CB (1); Randy White, DT (5).

1982 — Bob Breunig, LB (3); Pat Donovan, T (4); Tony Dorsett, RB (3); Ed Jones, DE (2); Everson Walls, CB (2); Danny White, QB (1); Randy White, DT (6).

1983 — Doug Cosbie, TE (1); Tony Dorsett, RB (4); Ed Jones, DE (3); Everson Walls, CB (3); Randy White, DT (7).

## ALL-PRO

1962—Don Perkins, RB (1), (AP, NEA); Jerry Tubbs, LB (1), (Sporting News).

1963—Chuck Howley, LB (1), (Sporting News).

1964—Frank Clarke, TE-WR (1), (AP); Bob Lilly, DT (1), (AP, UPI, NEA); Jim Ridlon, DB (1), (Sporting News).

1965—Bob Lilly, DT (2), (AP, UPI, NEA, Sporting News); Mel Renfro, S (1), (NEA, Sporting News); Bob Hayes, WR (1), (Sporting News)

1966—Bob Hayes, WR (2), (AP, UPI, NEA, Sporting News); Bob Lilly, DT (3), (AP, UPI, NEA, Sporting News); Chuck Howley, LB (2), (AP, UPI, NEA); Cornell Green, CB (1), (AP, NEA, Sporting News); Dan Reeves, RB (1), (Sporting News); Ralph Neely, T (1), (Sporting News); Lee Roy Jordan, LB (1), (Sporting News).

1967—George Andrie, DE (1), (Sporting News); Cornell Green, CB (2), (NEA, UPI, AP, Sporting News); Bob Hayes, WR (3), (Sporting News); Chuck Howley LB (3), (AP, Sporting News); Bob Lilly, DT (4), (NEA, UPI, AP, Sporting News); Ralph Neely, T (2), (UPI, AP, Sporting News); Mel Renfro, S (2), (Sporting News).

1968—Cornell Green, CB (3), (NEA); Bob Hayes, WR (4), (AP); Chuck Howley, LB (4), (AP, NEA); Bob Lilly, DT (5), (AP, UPI, NEA); Ralph Neely, T (3), (AP, UPI, NEA).

1969—Cornell Green, CB (4), (UPI); Calvin Hill, RB (1), (AP, UPI); Chuck Howley, LB (5), (AP, UPI, NEA); Bob Lilly, DT (6), (AP, NEA); Ralph Neely, T (4), (AP, UPI, NEA); John Niland, G (1), (AP); Mel Renfro, S (3), (NEA).

1970—Chuck Howley, LB (6), (PFWA, AP).

1971—Bob Lilly, DT (7), (AP, PFWA, NEA); Mel Renfro, CB (4), (NEA); John Niland, G (2), (AP, PFWA); Rayfield Wright, T (1), (AP, PFWA).

1972—Rayfield Wright, T (2), (PFWA, AP, UPI, NEA); John Niland, G (3), (AP); Blaine Nye, G (1), (NEA).

1973—Mel Renfro, CB (5), (NEA, PFWA); Rayfield Wright, T (3), (AP, PFWA); Lee Roy Jordan, LB (2), (NEA, PFWA); Calvin Hill, RB (2), (PFWA).

1974—Drew Pearson, WR (1), (AP, PFWA).

1975—Cliff Harris, S (1), (NEA); Rayfield Wright, T (4), (NEA).

1976—Cliff Harris, S (2), (AP, NEA, PFWA); Drew Pearson, WR (2), (AP, PFWA).

1977—Cliff Harris, S (3), (AP, NEA, PFWA); Efren Herrera, K (1), (AP, NEA, PFWA); Harvey Martin, DE (1), (AP, NEA, PFWA); Drew Pearson, WR (3), (AP, NEA, PFWA); Charlie Waters, S (1), (PFWA).

1978—Cliff Harris, S (4), (AP, PFWA); Charlie Waters, S (2), (NEA, PFWA); Randy White, DT (1), (AP, NEA, PFWA).

1979—Randy White, DT (2), (AP, NEA, PFWA).

1980—Herbert Scott, G (1), (AP, NEA); Randy White, DT (3), (NEA, PFWA).

1981—Tony Dorsett, RB (1), (AP, NEA, PFWA); Ed Jones, DT (1), (NEA); Herbert Scott, G (2), (AP); Rafael Septien, K (1), (AP, PFWA); Randy White, DT (4), (AP, NEA, PFWA).

1982—Ed Jones, DE (2), (AP); Everson Walls, CB (1), (PFWA); Randy White, DT (5), (AP, PFWA, NEA).

1983—Everson Walls, CB (2), (AP); Randy White, DT (6), (AP, PFWA).

Cowboys honorees have included Bob Lilly, Pro Football Hall of Fame; Roger Staubach, Super Bowl MVP; Chuck Howley, Super Bowl MVP; Harvey Martin, Super Bowl MVP; and Randy White, Super Bowl MVP.

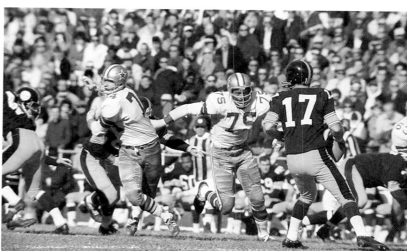

*Among those selected to All-Pro teams during their careers were Chuck Howley (top), and Harvey Martin (bottom). However, tackle Jethro Pugh (middle) may be the finest Cowboys player never to earn any kind of post-season honor during his impressive career.*

*Among those earning visits to the Pro Bowl were tackle Ralph Neely (below), cornerback Mel Renfro (right) and safety Charlie Waters (below).*

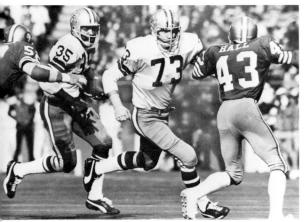

Middle linebacker Bob Breunig (above left) and tight end Doug Cosbie (above right) are two of the more recent Cowboys Pro Bowlers. Before them there were standouts like middle linebacker Lee Roy Jordan (left) and safety Cliff Harris (above).

# Who Wore the Number?

*"Number 17 in your program; number 1 in your heart . . ."*

— *Don Meredith, QB (1960-1968)*

## 1

Efren Herrera, K (1974, 1976-77)
Rafael Septien, K (1978-1984)

## 3

Jim Miller, P (1983)

## 5

John Warren, P (1983)

## 9

Mitch Hoopes, P (1975)

## 10

Ron Widby, P (1968-1971)
Duane Carrell, P (1974)

## 11

Don Heinrich, QB (1960)
Buddy Humphrey, QB (1961)
Guy Gibbs, QB (1963)
Danny Villanueva, (1965-1967)
Danny White, QB (1976-1984)

## 12

John Roach, QB (1964)
Roger Staubach, QB (1969-1979)

## 13

Jerry Rhome, QB (1965-1968)

## 14

Eddie LeBaron, QB (1960-1963)
Craig Morton, QB (1965-1974)
Gary Hogeboom, QB (1980-1984)

## 15

Toni Fritsch, K (1971-1973)
Brad Wright, QB (1982)

## 17

Don Meredith, QB (1960-1968)
Mike Clark, WR (1973)
Harold Carmichael, WR (1984)

## 18

Billy Lothridge, QB/K (1964)
Glenn Carano, QB (1977-1983)

## 19

Lance Rentzel, WR (1967-1970)
Lance Alworth, WR (1971-1972)
Clint Longley, QB (1974-1975)

## 20

Bob Bercich, DB (1960-1961)
Jerry Overton, RB (1963)
Mel Renfro, CB (1964-1977)
Ron Springs, RB (1979-1984)

## 21

Glynn Gregory, WR/DB (1961-1962)
Dick Daniels, DB (1966-1968)
Billy Parks, WR (1972)
Doug Dennison, RB (1974-1978)

## 22

Bill Butler, DB (1960)
Amos Bullocks, RB (1962-1964)
Bob Hayes, WR (1965-1974)
Wade Manning, DB (1979)
George Peoples, RB (1982-1984)

## 23

Woodley Lewis, WR (1960)
Mike Johnson, DB (1966-1969)
Margene Adkins, WR (1970-1971)
Mike Montgomery, RB/WR (1972-1973)
James Jones, RB (1980-1984)

## 24

Jim Mooty, DB (1960)
J. D. Smith, RB (1965-1966)
Dennis Homan, WR (1968-1970)
Alois Blackwell, RB (1978-1979)
Everson Walls, CB (1981-1982)

## 25

Ray Matthews, WR (1960)
Jerry Norton, DB (1962)
Dick Nolan, DB (1962)
Tommy McDonald, WR (1964)
Obert Logan, DB (1965-1966)
Les Shy, RB (1966-1969)
Aaron Kyle, DB (1976-1979)
Rod Hill, DB (1982-1984)

## 26

Buddy Dial, WR (1964-1966)
Herb Adderley, DB (1970-1972)
Preston Pearson, RB (1975-1980)
Michael Downs, DB (1981-1984)

## 27

Mike Gaechter, DB (1962-1969)
Ron Fellows, RB (1981-1984)

## 30

Mike Dowdle, LB (1961-1962)
Dick Van Rapphorst, K (1964)
Dan Reeves, RB (1965-1972)
Charles Young, RB (1974-1975)
Timmy Newsome, RB (1980-1984)

## 31

Fred Cone, K (1960)
Amos Marsh, RB (1961-1964)
Sim Stokes, WR (1967)
Otto Brown, DB (1969)
Gloster Richardson, WR (1971)
Benny Barnes, DB (1972-1982)
Gary Allen, RB (1983)

## 32

Tom Franckhouser, DB (1960-1961)
Walt Garrison, RB (1966-1974)
Dennis Thurman, DB (1978-1984)

## 33

Gene Babb, RB (1960-61)
Wendell Hayes, RB (1963)
Russell Wyat, LB (1965)
Duane Thomas, RB (1970-1971)
Cyril Pender, RB (1973)
Tony Dorsett, RB (1977-1984)

## 34

Fred Doelling, DB (1960)
Merrill Douglas, RB (1961)
Cornell Green, DB (1962-1974)
Aaron Mitchell, DB (1979-1980)
Monte Hunter, DB (1982)

## 35

Walt Kowalczyk, RB (1960)
J.W. Lockett, RB (1961-1962)
Pete Gent, WR (1964-1968)
Calvin Hill, RB (1969-1974)
Scott Laidlaw, RB (1975-1979)
Chuck McSwain, RB (1983)

## 36

Dick Bielski, TE (1960-1961)
Jimmy Sidle, RB (1962)
Joe Williams, RB (1971)
Bill Thomas, RB (1972)
Larry Brinson, RB (1977-1979)

## 37

Perry Lee Dunn, DB (1960-1961)
Phil Clark, DB (1967-1969)
Ike Thomas, DB (1971)
Dennis Morgan, RB (1974)
Jim Jensen, RB (1976)

## 38

Sam Baker, K (1962-1963)

## 40

Jim Harris, DB (1961)
James Stiger, RB (1963-1965)
Bobby Joe Conrad, WR (1969)
Les Strayhorn, RB (1973-1974)
Eric Hurt, DB (1980)
Bill Bates, DB (1983-1984)

## 41

Warren Livingston, DB (1961-1966)
Charlie Waters, DB (1970-1978, 1980-1981)

## 42

Don McIlhenny, RB (1960-1961)
Jim Ridlon, DB (1963-1964)
A. D. Whitfield, RB (1965)
Claxton Welch, RB (1969-1971)
Randy Hughes, DB (1975-1980)

## 43

Don Perkins, RB (1961-1968)
Cliff Harris, DB (1970-1979)

## 44

Don Bishop, DB (1960-1965)
Obert Logan, WR (1965-1966)
Robert Newhouse, RB (1972-1983)

## 45

L. G. Dupre, RB (1960-1961)
Dick Daniels, DB (1966-1968)
Richmond Flowers, WR (1969-1971)
Larry Robinson, RB (1973)
Roland Woolsey, DB (1975)
Steve Wilson, DB (1979-1981)

## 46

Les Shy, RB/DB (1966-1969)
Craig Baynham, RB (1967-1969)
Mark Washington, DB (1970-1978)
Roland Soloman, DB (1980)

## 47

Dickie Moegle, DB (1961)
Dick Daniels, DB (1966-1968)
Dextor Clinkscale, DB (1980, 1982-1984)

## 50

Jerry Tubbs, LB (1960-1967)
D. D. Lewis, LB (1968-1981)
Jeff Rohrer, LB (1982-1984)

## 51

Tom Braatz, LB (1960)
Lynn Hoyem, C (1962-1963)
Dave Manders, C (1964-1966, 1968-1974)
Anthony Dickerson, LB (1980-1984)

## 52

Wayne Hansen, LB (1960)
Dave Edwards, LB (1963-1975)
Robert Shaw, C (1979-1981)
Scott McLean, LB (1983)

## 53

Mike Connelly, C (1960-1967)
Dave Simmons, LB (1968)
Fred Whittington, LB (1969)
John Babinecz, LB (1972-1973)
Bob Breunig, LB (1975-1984)

## 54

Chuck Howley, LB (1961-1973)
Randy White, DT (1975-1984)

## 55

Lee Roy Jordan, LB (1963-1976)
Danny Spradlin, LB (1981-1982)
Bruce Huther, LB (1983)

## 56

Jack Patera, LB (1960-1961)
Bob Long, LB (1962)
Harold Hays, LB (1963-1967)
Tom Stincic, LB (1969-1971)
Rodrigo Barnes, LB (1973-1974)
Thomas Henderson, LB (1975-1979)
Bill Roe, LB (1980-1984)

## 57

Malcolm Walker, C/LB (1966-1969)
Mike Keller, LB (1972)
Louie Walker, LB (1974)
Kyle Davis, C (1975)
Bruce Huther, LB (1977-1980, 1983)
Angelo King, LB (1981-1984)

## 58

Calvin Peterson, LB (1974-1975)
Mike Hegman, LB (1976-1984)

## 59

Ken Hutcherson, LB (1974)
Warren Capone, LB (1975)
Guy Brown, LB (1977-1982)
Mike Walter, LB (1983)

## 60

Buzz Guy, G (1960)
Joe Bob Isbell, G (1962-1965)
Jackie Burkett, LB (1968-1969)
Steve Kiner, LB (1970)
Lee Roy Caffey, LB (1971)
Gene Killian, G (1974)
Tom Randall, G (1978)
Don Smerek, DT (1981-1984)

## 61

Duane Putnam, C (1960)
Allen Green, K (1961)
Blaine Nye, G (1968-1976)
Jim Cooper, G (1977-1984)

## 62

Don Healy, DT (1960-1961)
Andy Cvercko, G (1961-1962)
Lance Poimbeouf, K (1963)
Leon Donohue, G (1965-1967)
John Fitzgerald, C (1971-1980)
Brian Baldinger, G (1982-1984)

## 63

Mike Falls, G (1960-1961)
Larry Cole, DE/DT (1968-1980)
Glen Titensor, C/G (1981-1984)

## 64

Bob Grottkau, G (1961)
Jim Ray Smith, G (1963-1964)
Mitch Johnson, G/T (1965)
Halvor Hagen, C/G (1969-1970)
Jim Arneson, G (1973-1974)
Tom Rafferty, G/C (1976-1984)

## 65

Ray Schoenke, T (1963-1964)
John Wilbur, DE/DT (1966-1969)
Dave Stalls, DT (1977-1979)
Kurt Petersen, G (1980-1984)

## 66

Ed Husmann, DT (1960)
George Andrie, DE (1962-1972)
Burton Lawless, G (1975-1979)
Norm Wells, T (1980)
Chris Schultz, T (1983)

## 67

John Houser, C (1960-1961)
Jake Kupp, G (1964-1965)
Pat Toomay, DE (1970-1974)
Pat Donovan, T (1975-1983)

## 68

Guy Reese, DT (1962-1963)
Jim Boeke, T (1964-1967)
Herb Scott, G (1975-1984)

## 70

Bob McCreary, T (1961)
Dale Memmelaar, G (1962-1963)
Bill Sandeman, DT (1966)
Rayfield Wright, T (1967-1979)
Howard Richards, G/T (1981-1984)

## 71

Paul Dickson, T (1960)
Charlie Granger, T (1961)
Don Talbert, T (1962, 1965, 1971)
Willie Townes, DT (1966-1968)
Rodney Wallace, T (1971-1973)
Andy Frederick, T (1977-1981)
Mark Tuinei, DT (1983)

## 72

Bill Herchman, DT (1960-1961)
Tony Liscio, T (1966-1971)
Don Talbert, T (1962, 1965, 1971)
Ed Jones, DE (1974-1978, 1980-1984)

## 73

Ralph Neely, T (1965-1977)
Steve Wright, T (1981-1983)

## 74

Bob Lilly, DE/DT (1961-1974)

## 75

Bob Fry, T (1960-1964)
Jethro Pugh, T (1965-1978)
Phil Pozderac, T (1982-1984)

## 76

John Gonzaga, DE (1960)
Ed Nutting, T (1963)
Bill Frank, T (1964)
John Niland, G (1966-1974)
Jim Eidson, T (1976)
Larry Bethea, DT/DE (1978-1983)

## 77

Byron Bradfute, T (1960-1961)
Clyde Brock, T (1962-1963)
Larry Stephens, DE (1963-1967)
Jim Colvin, DT (1964-1966)
Bill Gregory, DE/DT (1971-1977)
Bruce Thornton, DE/DT (1979-1981)
Jim Jeffcoat, DE (1983-1984)

## 78

Don Healy, DT (1960-1961)
John Meyers, DT (1962-1963)
Maury Youmans, DE (1964-1965)
Bob Asher, T (1970)
Bruce Walton, G/T (1973-1975)
Greg Schaum, DT (1976)
John Dutton, DT (1979-1984)

## 79

Dick Klein, T (1960)
Ken Frost, DT (1961-1962)
Larry Stephens, DE (1963-1967)
Ron East, DT (1967-1970)
Forrest Gregg, G/T (1971)
Harvey Martin, DE (1973-1984)

## 80

Ola Lee Murchison, WR (1961)
Lee Folkins, WR (1962-1964)
David McDaniels, WR (1968)
Tony Hill, WR (1977-1984)

## 81

Bill Howton, WR (1960-1963)
Marv Bateman, P (1972-1974)
Percy Howard, WR (1975)
Jackie Smith, TE (1978)
Steve Wilson, WR/DB (1979-1981)

## 82

Frank Clarke, TE/WR (1960-1967)
Otto Stowe, WR (1973)
Beasley Reece, DB (1976)
Robert Steele, WR (1978)
Cleo Simmons, TE (1983-1984)

## 83

Jim Doran, WR (1960-1961)
Lee Folkins, WR (1962-1964)
Harold Deters, K (1967)
Mike Clark, K (1968-1971, 1973)
Golden Richards, WR (1973-1978)
Doug Donley, WR (1981-1984)

## 84

Gary Wisener, WR/DB (1960)
Pettis Norman, WR (1962-1970)
Jean Fugett, TE (1972-1975)
Doug Cosbie, TE (1979-1984)

## 85

Gene Cronin, LB (1960)
Rayfield Wright, TE/T (1967-1979)
Tody Smith, DE (1971-1972)

## 86

Dave Sherer, P (1960)
Garry Porterfield, DE (1965)
Ralph Coleman, LB (1972)
Bill Houston, WR (1974)
Butch Johnson, WR (1976-1983)

## 87

Nate Borden, DE (1960-1961)
Andy Stynchula, DE (1968)
Bill Truax, TE (1971-1973)
Ron Howard, TE (1974-1975)
Jay Saldi, TE (1976-1982)

## 88

A. A. Davis, LB (1961)
Colin Ridgeway, K (1965)
Sonny Randle, WR (1968)
Reggie Rucker, WR (1970-1971)
Ron Sellers, WR (1972)
Drew Pearson, WR (1973-1984)

## 89

Fred Dugan, WR (1960)
Donnie Davis, WR (1962)
Mike Ditka, TE (1969-1972)
Billy Joe DuPree, TE (1973-1983)

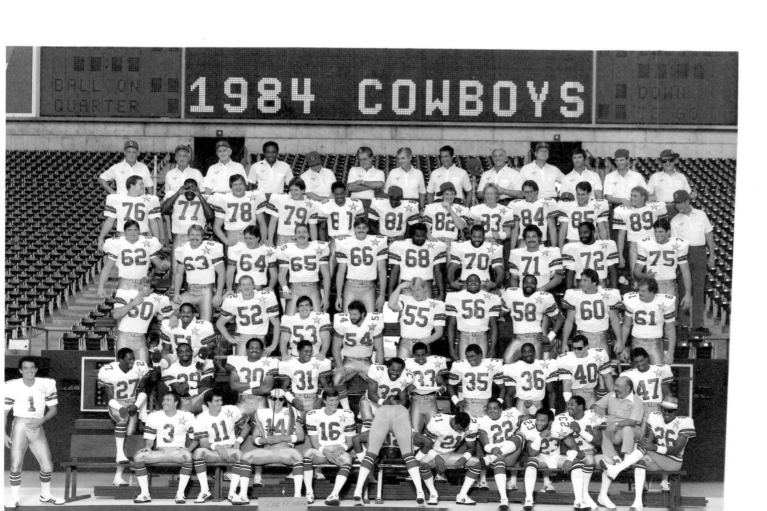

# Cowboys Humor

The Dallas Cowboys were still a team struggling for respectability during the 1962 season and more than a few of the veteran players had adopted a somewhat casual approach to the game. After all, they surmised, if the new franchise did ever get off the ground it would no doubt be long after they were gone and forgotten.

And there was more than a little grumbling about the new offense and defense head coach Tom Landry was teaching. Aware of the problem, Landry called a meeting and delivered a rather stern lecture of the need for more harmony if the Cowboys were to hope to accomplish anything.

From the back row, kicker Sam Baker, something of a free spirit, chose the moment after Landry's plea for harmony to issue a loud, resonate, "Hummmmm . . ."

The coach was the only one not laughing.

"There was another time," Baker remembers, "when Tom was talking to us about his philosophy of team dedication. He said 'If I thought it would help this team in some way, I'd climb on top of this building and sing Glory to God.' Billy Howton was sitting next to me and yelled out, 'Hallelujah!' I immediately started laughing. Landry, of course, turned just in time to see me crack up and obviously thought I was laughing at him.''

It was Baker who dealt Landry the greatest of misery during the early days. Sam still owns the distinction of establishing a rather lofty record for fines when he was assessed a $1,000 penalty for missing a team plane back to training camp after an exhibition game in Cleveland.

To his everlasting credit, he did manage to catch a later flight which got him back in the wee hours of the morning. Gil Brandt picked him up at the airport. "Coach Landry wants to see you," Gil Said. "Figured he would," said Baker.

So, wearing a suit very much in need of attention from the cleaners and holding a folded copy of the New York Times under one arm, Baker knocked on Landry's door at 4 a.m. When the awakened coach answered, his kicker snapped to attention, clicked his heels and reeled off a snappy salute. "Baker reporting for duty, Sir," he said.

Landry did not crack a smile. "That will cost you $1,000," he said, then shut the door and went back to bed.

Several years later, after Baker had moved on to another team and Landry had been selected to coach in the Pro Bowl, he was asking special assistant Ermal Allen who the best place kicker in the National Football Conference was. Allen, something of a walking statistical machine, immediately began detailing the accomplishments of Sam Baker.

Landry listened patiently, waited for Allen to finish, then asked another question: "Ermal, who is the second best kicker in the NFC?"

Quarterback Don Meredith stood at one end of the practice field, engaged in a drill which called for him to throw passes through an automobile tire which was hanging from a rope. Enjoying very little success, he reacted to one off-target throw by saying, "Well, I'll be an SOB."

Walking past just as Meredith spoke, head coach Tom Landry didn't even break stride but offered an observation as he passed: "Don, I seriously doubt that would make you any better quarterback."

It was the inaugural season for the Dallas Cowboys and owner Clint Murchison, Jr., felt something out of the ordinary was in order. After all, in that 1960 season, the NFL's oldest team, the Chicago Bears, were hosting the newest, Dallas, for the first time.

Thus Murchison instructed public relations director Larry Karl to have a trained bear waiting in the lobby when the Cowboys arrived in Chicago. Karl, fairly new to the PR business and not knowing where in the yellow pages one looked for such a rental, found one nonetheless. So it was that when the Cowboys arrived, they and hotel guests were witness to a scene in the lobby which included a mock battle between the bear and a man dressed in boots, ten-gallon hat, and fake six-guns.

So successful was the event that an obviously pleased Murchison invited the bear and his trainer to the

Cowboys' hospitality room afterwards. Fitting into the crowd easily, the trainer and the bear soon were drinking beer with the others on hand to celebrate the team's first trip to Chicago. In time, however, the trainer, having enjoyed himself a bit too much, staggered off into the night, leaving his bear behind.

Few noticed until the morning's wee hours when only the most hearty remained — including the beer-drinking bear.

Eventually, the problem of what to do with the bear arose just as the sun was coming over the Chicago skyline.

Murchison, realizing it was time to send the animal on his way, escorted him to the elevator, patted him on the back, pushed the "Lobby" button, and ushered him in. As the doors closed, Murchison waved goodbye.

The bear was never seen again.

The Cowboys were playing the New York Giants in Yankee Stadium in 1973 when there was a bomb scare in the press box. Following the game, Bob St. John of the Dallas Morning News advised Landry of the situation and asked what he might have done had there been a tragedy.

Landry considered the question for a minute, then said, "We would have observed thirty seconds of silence and then continued the game with great enthusiasm."

It was 1968, the rookie season of Dallas linebacker D. D. Lewis, and the team plane was circling to land in St. Louis. Looking out the window, Lewis saw the famed golden arch and remarked in his best Tennessee drawl: "Dadgum, I didn't know St. Louis was the national headquarters of McDonald's."

Wide receiver Pete Gent, something of a free spirit during his playing days with the Cowboys, swears he once hid himself inside a metal equipment locker during halftime to escape facing Landry's wrath after playing particularly poorly in the first half.

Then, on another occasion, he saw a young rookie studying the Cowboys playbook with great concentration. Pete walked over, placed a hand on the rookie's shoulder, and offered his special brand of advise: "Don't bother to read it, kid. Everybody gets killed in the end."

The Many
Faces of
Tom Landry
by
Bob Taylor

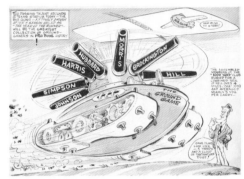

*The cartoons shown here, provided by* **Dallas Times Herald** *cartoonist Bob Taylor, represent some of the classic moments in Cowboys' humor.*

# Smile, Please . . .

*In recent years it has become tradition for the official team picture to be preceded by a squad photo in which each member of the team is allowed to ham it up for the camera. Here are the results.*

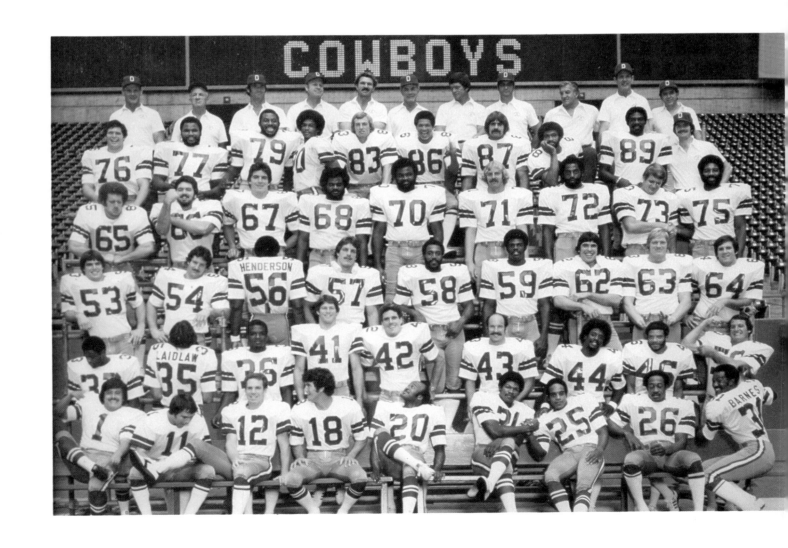

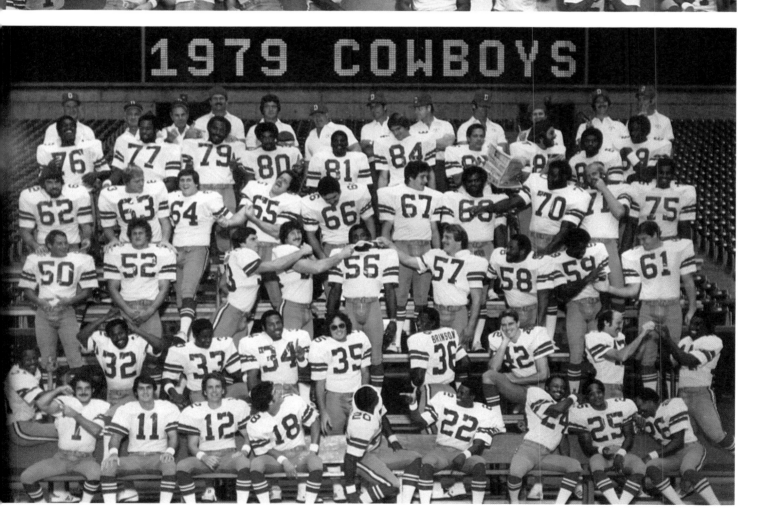

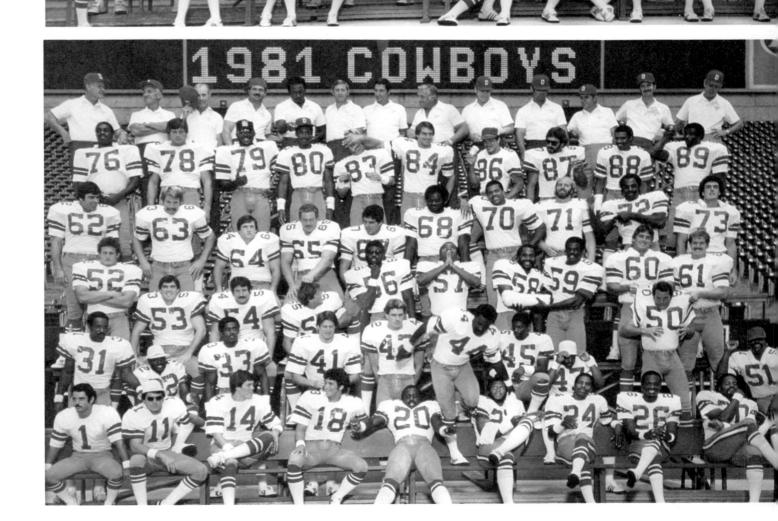

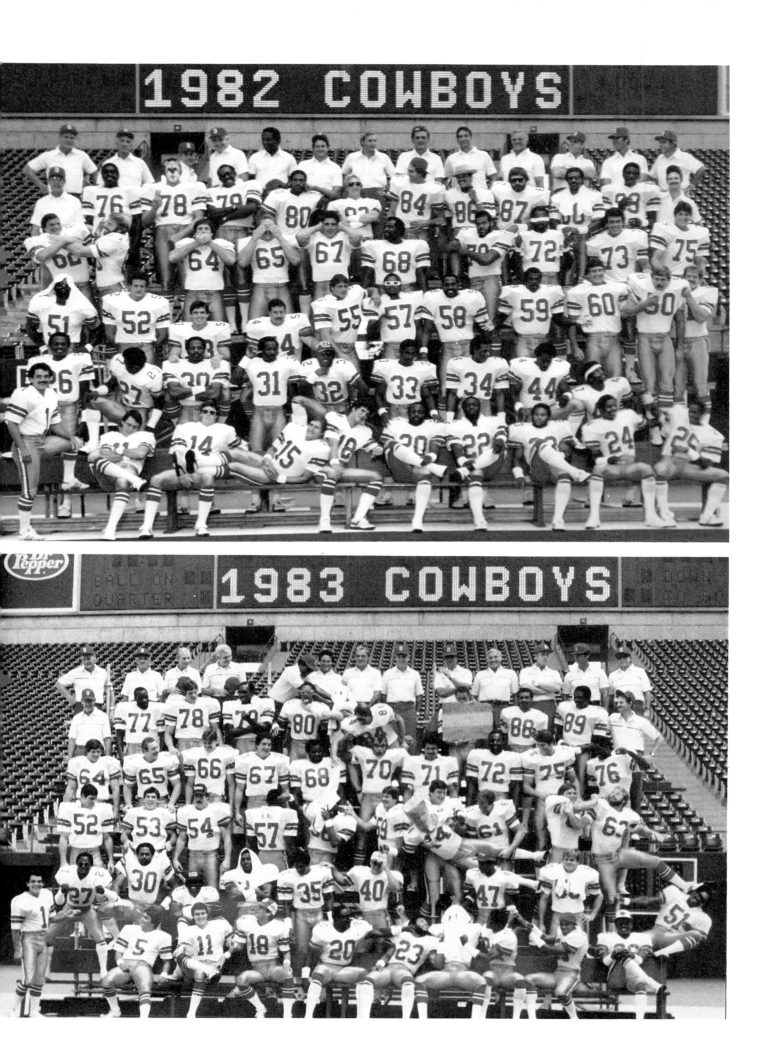

*That's Ken Curtis of "Gunsmoke" fame following along during a training camp drill.*

*Tackle Ed Husmann doesn't seem too thrilled at the idea of giving quarterback Eddie LeBaron a ride for a promotional photo.*

*Linebacker Jerry Tubbs (left) and quarterback Eddie LeBaron play the roles of real cowboys during a break in practice at Thousand Oaks.*

Surely you don't believe that 5-5 receiver Cleveland (Pussyfoot) Jones is actually lifting his teammates.

Yep, that's Roger Staubach astride a camel during a movie promotion during the off-season.

President and general manager Tex Schramm gives head coach Tom Landry a new hat for his collection during ceremonies at Cal Lutheran College. Tom never wore it again.

*That's Smokey the Bear, a training camp visitor, on the left. You'll have to guess who the coach on the right is.*

## ★ 1960 ★
### DALLAS COWBOYS

Clint Houey-Trainer, 81 Bill Howton, 22 Bill Butler, 32 Tom Franckhauser, 34 Fred Doelling, 14 Eddie LeBaron, 24 Jim Mooty, 45 L. G. Dupre, Jack Eskridge-Eqpt. Mgr.

61 Duane Putnam, 86 Dave Sherer, 67 John Houser, 44 Don Bishop, 42 Don McIlhenny, 83 Jim Doran, 50 Jerry Tubbs, 88 Fred Dugan, 63 Mike Falls, 20 Bob Bercich, 30 Mike Dowdle, 11 Don Heinrich, 85 Gene Cronin

87 Nate Borden, 17 Don Meredith, 75 Bob Fry, 56 Jack Patera, 82 Frank Clarke, 36 Dick Bielski, 72 Bill Herchman, 41 Fred Cone, 45 Ray Mathews, 79 Dick Klein, 23 Woodley Lewis, 51 Tom Braatz

52 Wayne Hansen, 73 Ray Fisher, 62 Don Healey, 71 Paul Dickson, 77 Byron Bradfute, 35 Walt Kowalczyk, 84 Gary Wisener, 33 Gene Babb, 54 Mike Connelly, 60 Buzz Guy, 65 Ed Husmann, 76 John Gonzaga

## ★ 1961 ★
### DALLAS COWBOYS

14 Eddie LeBaron, 17 Don Meredith, 20 Bob Bercich, 21 Glynn Gregory, 30 Mike Dowdle, 31 Amos Marsh, 32 Tom Franckhauser, 33 Gene Babb, 34 Fred Doelling

Trainer-Clint Houy, 35 J. W. Lockett, 36 Dick Bielski, 40 Jim Harris, 41 Warren Livingston, 43 Don Perkins, 44 Don Bishop, 45 L. G. Dupre, 47 Dick Maegle, 50 Jerry Tubbs, Eqp. Mgr.-Jack Eskridge

Head Coach-Tom Landry, Asst. Coach-Tom Dalms, 51 Tom Braatz, 53 Mike Connelly, 54 Chuck Howley, 56 Jack Patera, 61 Allen Green, 62 Andy Cvercko, 63 Mike Falls, 64 Bob Grottkau, 67 John Houser, Asst. Coaches-Brad Ecklund and Babe Dimancheff

70 Bob McCreary, 71 Charlie Granger, 72 Bill Herchman, 74 Bob Lilly, 75 Bob Fry, 77 Byron Bradfute, 78 Don Healy, 79 Ken Frost, 80 Ola Lee Murchison

81 Bill Howton, 82 Frank Clarke, 83 Jim Doran, 87 Nate Borden, 88 Sonny Davis

## ★ 1962 ★
### DALLAS COWBOYS

11 Buddy Humphrey, 14 Eddie LeBaron, 17 Don Meredith, 20 Bob Bercich, 21 Glynn Gregory, 22 Amos Bullocks, 23 Jerry Norton, 27 Mike Gaechter

30 Mike Dowdle, 31 Amos Marsh, 34 Cornell Green, 35 J. W. Lockett, 38 Sam Baker, 41 Warren Livingston, 43 Don Perkins, 44 Don Bishop

49 Jack Collins, 50 Jerry Tubbs, 51 Lynn Hoyem, 52 Dave Edwards, 53 Mike Connelly, 54 Chuck Howley,

56 Bob Long, 60 Joe Bob Isbell

62 Andy Cvercko, 64 Bob Grottkau, 66 George Andrie, 67 John Houser, 68 Guy Reese, 70 Dale Memmelaar, 71 Don Talbert, 73 Monte Clark, 74 Bob Lilly

75 Bob Fry, 76 Ed Nutting, 77 Clyde Brock, 78 John Meyers, 79 Ken Frost, 81 Billy Howton, 82 Frank Clarke, 83 Lee Folkins, 84 Pettis Norman, 88 Donnie Davis

## ★ 1963 ★
### DALLAS COWBOYS

Asst. Coach-Ermal Allen, 11 Sonny Gibbs, 14 Eddie LeBaron, 17 Don Meredith, 20 Jerry Overton, 21 Glynn Gregory, 22 Amos Bullocks, 27 Mike Gaechter, 31 Amos Marsh, Asst. Coach-Jim Myers

33 Wendell Hayes, 34 Cornell Green, 38 Sam Baker, 40 Jim Stiger, 41 Warren Livingston, 42 Jim Ridlon, 43 Don Perkins, 44 Don Bishop, 50 Jerry Tubbs

Asst. Coaches-Brad Ecklund, Dick Nolan, Eqp. Mgr.-Jack Eskridge, 51 Lynn Hoyem, 52 Dave Edwards, 53 Mike

Connelly, 54 Chuck Howley, 55 Lee Roy Jordan, 56 Harold Hays, 60 Joe Bob Isbell, 62 Lance Poimboeuf, 64 Jim Ray Smith, Head Coach-Tom Landry, Trainer-Clint Houy

65 Ray Schoenke, 66 George Andrie, 68 Guy Reese, 70 Dale Memmelaar, 72 Tony Liscio, 74 Bob Lilly, 75 Bob Fry, 76 Ed Nutting, 78 John Meyers

79 Larry Stephens, 80 Gary Barnes, 81 Billy Howton, 82 Frank Clarke, 83 Lee Folkins, 84 Pettis Norman

## ★ 1964 ★
### DALLAS COWBOYS

Asst. Coach-Ermal Allen, 12 John Roach, 17 Don Meredith, 18 Billy Lothridge, 20 Mel Renfro, 25 Tommy McDonald, 26 Buddy Dial, 27 Mike Gaechter, 30 Dick Van Raaphorst, 31 Amos Marsh, 34 Cornell Green, Asst. Coach-Dick Nolan

Eqp. Mgr.-Jack Eskridge, Asst. Coaches-Jim Myers and Red Hickey, 35 Pete Gent, 37 Perry Lee Dunn, 40 Jim Stiger, 41 Warren Livingston, 42 Jim Ridlon, 43 Don Perkins, 44 Don Bishop, 50 Jerry Tubbs, 51 Dave

Manders, 52 Dave Edwards, 53 Mike Connelly, Head Coach-Tom Landry, Trainer-Clint Houy

54 Chuck Howley, 55 Lee Roy Jordan, 56 Harold Hays, 60 Joe Bob Isbell, 64 Jim Ray Smith, 65 Ray Schoenke, 66 George Andrie, 67 Jake Kupp, 68 Jim Boeke

72 Tony Liscio, 74 Bob Lilly, 75 Bob Fry, 77 Jim Colvin, 78 Maury Youmans, 79 Larry Stephens, 82 Frank Clarke, 83 Lee Folkins, 84 Pettis Norman

## ★ 1965 ★
### DALLAS COWBOYS

11 Danny Villanueva, 13 Jerry Rhome, 14 Craig Morton, 17 Don Meredith, 20 Mel Renfro, 22 Bob Hayes, 24 J. D. Smith, 25 Obert Logan, 26 Buddy Dial

Trainer-Don Cochren, Asst. Coach-Ermal Allen, 27 Mike Gaechter, 30 Dan Reeves, 33 Russell Wayt, 34 Cornell Green, 35 Pete Gent, 37 Perry Lee Dunn, 40 Jim Stiger, 41 Warren Livingston, 43 Don Perkins, Trainer-Larry Gardner

Asst. Coach-Dick Nolan, Eqp. Mgr.-Jack Eskridge, 44 Don Bishop, 50 Jerry Tubbs,

51 Dave Manders, 52 Dave Edwards, 53 Mike Connelly, 54 Chuck Howley, 55 Lee Roy Jordan, 56 Harold Hays, Head Coach-Tom Landry, Asst. Coaches-Red Hickey and Jim Myers

62 Leon Donohue, 64 Mitch Johnson, 66 George Andrie, 67 Jake Kupp, 68 Jim Boeke, 71 Don Talbert, 73 Ralph Neely, 74 Bob Lilly, 75 Jethro Pugh

77 Jim Colvin, 78 Maury Youmans, 79 Larry Stephens, 82 Frank Clarke, 84 Pettis Norman

**1966**

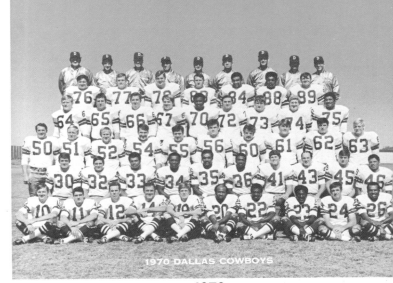

**1969**

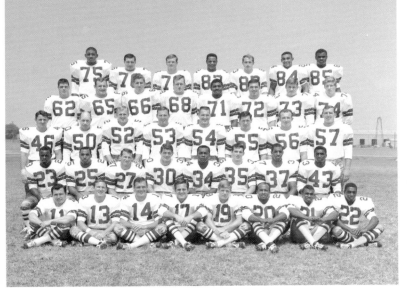

**1967**

**1970**

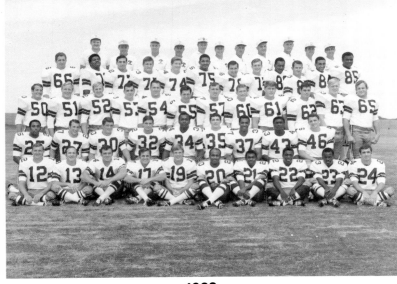

**1968**

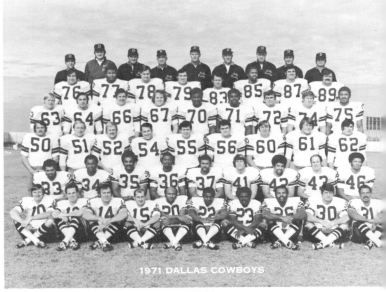

**1971**

**1960**

**1963**

**1961**

**1964**

**1962**

**1965**

## ★ 1966 ★
## DALLAS COWBOYS

11 Danny Villanueva, 13 Jerry Rhome, 14 Craig Morton, 17 Don Meredith, 20 Mel Renfro, 22 Bob Hayes, 23 Mike Johnson, 24 J. D. Smith, 25 Obert Logan, 26 Buddy Dial, 27 Mike Gaechter

30 Dan Reeves, 32 Walt Garrison, 34 Cornell Green, 35 Pete Gent, 41 Warren Livingston, 43 Don Perkins, 45 Dick Daniels, 46 Les Shy, 50 Jerry Tubbs, 51 Dave Manders

52 Dave Edwards, 53 Mike Connelly, 54 Chuck Howley, 55 Lee Roy Jordan, 56 Harold Hays, 57 Malcolm Walker, 62 Leon Donohue, 66 George Andrie, 68 Jim Boeke, 71 Willie Townes

72 Tony Liscio, 73 Ralph Neely, 74 Bob Lilly, 75 Jethro Pugh, 76 John Niland, 77 Jim Colvin, 79 Larry Stephens, 82 Frank Clarke, 84 Pettis Norman

## ★ 1967 ★
## DALLAS COWBOYS

11 Danny Villanueva, 13 Jerry Rhome, 14 Craig Morton, 17 Don Meredith, 19 Lance Rentzel, 20 Mel Renfro, 21 Dick Daniels, 22 Bob Hayes

23 Mike Johnson, 25 Les Shy, 27 Mike Gaechter, 30 Dan Reeves, 34 Cornell Green, 35 Pete Gent, 37 Phil Clark, 43 Don Perkins

46 Craig Baynham, 50 Jerry Tubbs, 52 Dave Edwards,

53 Mike Connelly, 54 Chuck Howley, 55 Lee Roy Jordan, 56 Harold Hays, 57 Malcolm Walker

62 Leon Donohue, 65 John Wilbur, 66 George Andrie, 68 Jim Boeke, 71 Willie Townes, 72 Tony Liscio, 73 Ralph Neely, 74 Bob Lilly

75 Jethro Pugh, 76 John Niland, 77 Ron East, 82 Frank Clarke, 83 Harold Deters, 84 Pettis Norman, 85 Rayfield Wright

## ★ 1968 ★
## DALLAS COWBOYS

12 Ron Widby, 13 Jerry Rhome, 14 Craig Morton, 17 Don Meredith, 19 Lance Rentzel, 20 Mel Renfro, 21 Dick Daniels, 22 Bob Hayes, 23 Mike Johnson, 24 Dennis Homan

25 Les Shy, 27 Mike Gaechter, 30 Dan Reeves, 32 Walt Garrison, 34 Cornell Green, 35 Pete Gent, 37 Phil Clark, 43 Don Perkins, 46 Craig Baynham

50 D. D. Lewis, 51 Dave Manders, 52 Dave Edwards, 53 Dave Simmons, 54 Chuck Howley, 55 Lee Roy Jordan, 57 Malcolm Walker, 60 Jackie

Burkett, 61 Blaine Nye, 62 Leon Donohue, 63 Larry Cole, 65 John Wilbur

66 George Andrie, 71 Willie Townes, 72 Tony Liscio, 73 Ralph Neely, 74 Bob Lilly, 75 Jethro Pugh, 76 John Niland, 77 Ron East, 80 David McDaniel, 83 Mike Clark, 84 Pettis Norman, 85 Rayfield Wright

Eqp. Mgr.-Jack Eskridge, Asst. Coaches-Ray Renfro, Jerry Tubbs, Ermal Allen, Raymond Berry, Bobby Franklin, Jim Myers, Ernie Stautner, Head Coach-Tom Landry, Trainers-Larry Gardner, Don Cochren

## ★ 1969 ★
## DALLAS COWBOYS

10 Ron Widby, 11 Bob Belden, 12 Roger Staubach, 14 Craig Morton, 19 Lance Rentzel, 20 Mel Renfro, 22 Bob Hayes, 23 Mike Johnson, 24 Dennis Homan, 25 Les Shy

27 Mike Gaechter, 30 Dan Reeves, 31 Otto Brown, 32 Walt Garrison, 34 Cornell Green, 35 Calvin Hill, 37 Phil Clark, 40 Bobby Joe Conrad, 42 Claxton Welch, 45 Richmond Flowers

46 Craig Baynham, 51 Dave Manders, 52 Dave Edwards,

53 Fred Whittingham, 54 Chuck Howley, 55 Lee Roy Jordan, 56 Tom Stincic, 57 Malcolm Walker, 60 Jackie Burkett

61 Blaine Nye, 63 Larry Cole, 64 Halvor Hagen, 65 John Wilbur, 66 George Andrie, 70 Rayfield Wright, 71 Willie Townes, 72 Tony Liscio, 73 Ralph Neely

74 Bob Lilly, 75 Jethro Pugh, 76 John Niland, 77 Ron East, 79 Clarence Williams, 83 Mike Clark, 84 Pettis Norman, 88 Reggie Rucker, 89 Mike Ditka

## ★ 1970 ★
## DALLAS COWBOYS

10 Ron Widby, 11 Bob Belden, 12 Roger Staubach, 14 Craig Morton, 19 Lance Rentzel, 20 Mel Renfro, 22 Bob Hayes, 23 Margene Adkins, 24 Dennis Homan, 26 Herb Adderley

30 Dan Reeves, 32 Walt Garrison, 33 Duane Thomas, 34 Cornell Green, 35 Calvin Hill, 36 Joe Williams, 41 Charlie Waters, 43 Cliff Harris, 45 Richmond Flowers, 46 Mark Washington

50 D. D. Lewis, 51 Dave Manders, 52 Dave Edwards, 54 Chuck Howley, 55 Lee Roy Jordan, 56 Tom Stincic, 60 Steve Kiner, 61 Blaine

Nye, 62 John Fitzgerald, 63 Larry Cole

64 Halvor Hagen, 65 Doug Mooers, 66 George Andrie, 67 Pat Toomay, 70 Rayfield Wright, 72 Tony Liscio, 73 Ralph Neely, 74 Bob Lilly, 75 Jethro Pugh

76 John Niland, 77 Ron East, 78 Bob Asher, 83 Mike Clark, 84 Pettis Norman, 88 Reggie Rucker, 89 Mike Ditka

Eqp. Mgr.-Jack Eskridge, Asst. Coaches-Ray Renfro, Jerry Tubbs, Ernie Stautner, Bobby Franklin, Jim Myers, Head Coach-Tom Landry, Trainers-Larry Gardner, Don Cochren

## ★ 1971 ★
## DALLAS COWBOYS

10 Ron Widby, 12 Roger Staubach, 14 Craig Morton, 15 Toni Fritsch, 20 Mel Renfro, 22 Bob Hayes, 23 Margene Adkins, 26 Herb Adderley, 30 Dan Reeves, 31 Gloster Richardson

33 Duane Thomas, 34 Cornell Green, 35 Calvin Hill, 36 Joe Williams, 37 Isaac Thomas, 41 Charlie Waters, 42 Claxton Welch, 43 Cliff Harris, 46 Mark Washington

50 D. D. Lewis, 51 Dave Manders, 52 Dave Edwards, 54 Chuck Howley, 55 Lee Roy Jordan, 56 Tom Stincic, 60 Lee Roy Caffey, 61 Blaine Nye, 62 John Fitzgerald

63 Larry Cole, 64 Tony Liscio, 66 George Andrie, 67 Pat Toomay, 70 Rayfield Wright, 71 Rodney Wallace, 72 Don Talbert, 74 Bob Lilly, 75 Jethro Pugh

76 John Niland, 77 Bill Gregory, 78 Bob Asher, 79 Forrest Gregg, 83 Mike Clark, 85 Tody Smith, 87 Billy Truax, 89 Mike Ditka

Trainer-Don Cochren, Eqpt. Mgr.-Jack Eskridge, Asst. Coaches-Ray Renfro, Jim Myers, Head Coach-Tom Landry, Asst. Coaches-Ernie Stautner, Jerry Tubbs, Bobby Franklin, Trainer-Larry Gardner

# ★ 1972 ★
## DALLAS COWBOYS

12 Roger Staubach, 14 Craig Morton, 15 Toni Fritsch, 18 Jack Concannon, 19 Lance Alworth, 20 Mel Renfro, 21 Billy Parks, 22 Bob Hayes, 23 Mike Montgomery

26 Herb Adderley, 27 Bill Thomas, 30 Dan Reeves, 31 Benny Barnes, 32 Walt Garrison, 34 Cornell Green, 35 Calvin Hill, 41 Charlie Waters, 43 Cliff Harris, 44 Robert Newhouse

46 Mark Washington, 50 D. D. Lewis, 51 Dave Manders, 52 Dave Edwards, 53 John Babinecz, 54 Chuck Howley, 55 Lee Roy Jordan, 57 Mike Keller, 61 Blaine Nye, 62 John Fitzgerald

63 Larry Cole, 66 George Andrie, 67 Pat Toomay, 70 Rayfield Wright, 71 Rodney Wallace, 72 Don Talbert, 73 Ralph Neely, 74 Bob Lilly, 75 Jethro Pugh, 76 John Niland

Eqpt. Mgr.-Jack Eskridge, 77 Bill Gregory, 81 Marv Bateman, 84 Jean Fugett, 85 Tody Smith, 86 Ralph Coleman, 87 Billy Truax, 88 Ron Sellers, 89 Mike Ditka

Asst. Coaches-Jerry Tubbs, Gene Stallings, Ermal Allen, Sid Gillman. Ray Renfro, Jim Myers, Bobby Franklin, Ernie Stautner. Head Coach-Tom Landry, Trainers-Don Cochren, Larry Gardner

# ★ 1973 ★
## DALLAS COWBOYS

12 Roger Staubach, 14 Craig Morton, 15 Toni Fritsch, 18 Jack Concannon, 20 Mel Renfro, 22 Bob Hayes, 23 Mike Montgomery, 27 Bill Thomas, 31 Benny Barnes, 32 Walt Garrison, 34 Cornell Green, 35 Calvin Hill

40 Les Strayhorn, 41 Charlie Waters, 43 Cliff Harris, 44 Robert Newhouse, 45 Larry Robinson, 46 Mark Washington, 50 D. D. Lewis, 51 Dave Manders, 52 Dave Edwards, 53 John Babinecz, 54 Chuck Howley, 55 Lee Roy Jordan

56 Rodrigo Barnes, 61 Blaine Nye, 62 John Fitzgerald, 63 Larry Cole, 64 Jim Arneson, 67 Pat Toomay,

70 Rayfield Wright, 71 Rodney Wallace, 73 Ralph Neely, 74 Bob Lilly, 75 Jethro Pugh, 76 John Niland

77 Bill Gregory, 78 Bruce Walton, 79 Harvey Martin, 81 Marv Bateman, 82 Otto Stowe, 83 Golden Richards, 84 Jean Fugett, 86 John Smith, 87 Billy Truax, 88 Drew Pearson, 89 Billy Joe DuPree

Head Coach-Tom Landry, Asst. Coaches-Gene Stallings, Jim Myers, Alvin Roy, Ernie Stautner, Ermal Allen, Jerry Tubbs, Mike Ditka, Ed Hughes, Trainer-Don Cochren, Asst. Trainer-Ken Locker, Eqp. Mgr.-Buck Buchanan

# ★ 1974 ★
## DALLAS COWBOYS

1 Efren Herrera, 12 Roger Staubach, 14 Craig Morton, 19 Clint Longley, 20 Mel Renfro, 21 Doug Dennison, 22 Bob Hayes, 30 Charles Young, 31 Benny Barnes, 32 Walt Garrison

34 Cornell Green, 35 Calvin Hill, 37 Dennis Morgan, 40 Les Strayhorn, 41 Charlie Waters, 43 Cliff Harris, 44 Robert Newhouse, 46 Mark Washington, 50 D. D. Lewis, 51 Dave Manders

52 Dave Edwards, 55 Lee Roy Jordan, 57 Louie Walker, 58 Cal Peterson, 59 Ken Hutcherson, 60 Gene Killian, 61 Blaine Nye, 62 John Fitzgerald, 63 Larry Cole, 64 Jim Arneson

67 Pat Toomay, 70 Rayfield Wright, 72 Ed Jones, 73 Ralph Neely, 74 Bob Lilly, 75 Jethro Pugh, 76 John Niland, 77 Bill Gregory, 78 Bruce Walton, 79 Harvey Martin

81 Marv Bateman, 83 Golden Richards, 84 Jean Fugett, 86 Bill Houston, 87 Ron Howard, 88 Drew Pearson, 89 Billy Joe DuPree, Eqp. Mgr.-Buck Buchanan, Asst. Trainer-Ken Locker, Trainer-Don Cochren

Asst. Coaches-John DeLuna, Jim Myers, Dan Reeves, Gene Stallings, Jerry Tubbs, Mike Ditka, Head Coach-Tom Landry, Asst. Coaches-Ed Hughes, Ernie Stautner, Ermal Allen, Alvin Roy

# ★ 1975 ★
## DALLAS COWBOYS

9 Mitch Hoopes, 12 Roger Staubach, 15 Toni Fritsch, 19 Clint Longley, 20 Mel Renfro, 21 Doug Dennison, 26 Preston Pearson, 30 Charles Young, 31 Benny Barnes

35 Scott Laidlaw, 41 Charlie Waters, 42 Randy Hughes, 43 Cliff Harris, 44 Robert Newhouse, 45 Roland Woolsey, 46 Mark Washington, 50 D. D. Lewis, 52 Dave Edwards

53 Bob Breunig, 54 Randy White, 55 Lee Roy Jordan, 56 Thomas Henderson, 57 Kyle Davis. 58 Calvin Peterson, 61 Blaine Nye, 62 John Fitzgerald, 63 Larry Cole

66 Burton Lawless, 67 Pat Donovan, 68 Herbert Scott, 70 Rayfield Wright, 72 Ed Jones, 73 Ralph Neely, 75 Jethro Pugh, 77 Bill Gregory, 78 Bruce Walton

79 Harvey Martin, 81 Percy Howard, 83 Golden Richards, 84 Jean Fugett, 87 Ron Howard, 88 Drew Pearson, 89 Billy Joe DuPree, Asst. Trainer-Ken Locker, Eqp. Mgr.-Buck Buchanan, Trainer-Don Cochren

Head Coach-Tom Landry, Asst. Coaches-Jim Myers, Ernie Stautner, Ermal Allen, Dan Reeves, Jerry Tubbs, Mike Ditka, Alvin Roy, Gene Stallings, Jim Hughes

# ★ 1976 ★
## DALLAS COWBOYS

1 Efren Herrera, 11 Danny White, 12 Roger Staubach, 20 Mel Renfro, 21 Doug Dennison, 25 Aaron Kyle, 26 Preston Pearson, 30 Charles Young, 31 Benny Barnes

35 Scott Laidlaw, 37 Jim Jensen, 41 Charlie Waters, 42 Randy Hughes, 43 Cliff Harris, 44 Robert Newhouse, 46 Mark Washington, 50 D. D. Lewis, 52 Jim Eidson

53 Bob Breunig, 54 Randy White, 55 Lee Roy Jordan, 56 Thomas Henderson, 58 Mike Hegman, 61 Blaine Nye, 62 John Fitzgerald, 63 Larry Cole, 64 Tom Rafferty

66 Burton Lawless, 67 Pat Donovan, 68 Herbert Scott, 70 Rayfield Wright, 72 Ed Jones, 73 Ralph Neely, 75 Jethro Pugh, 77 Bill Gregory, 78 Greg Schaum

79 Harvey Martin, 82 Beasley Reece, 83 Golden Richards, 86 Butch Johnson, 87 Jay Saldi, 88 Drew Pearson, 89 Billy Joe DuPree

Head Coach-Tom Landry, Asst. Coaches-Jim Myers, Ernie Stautner, Ermal Allen, Jerry Tubbs, Dan Reeves, Mike Ditka, Gene Stallings, Ed Hughes, Trainer-Don Cochren

Asst. Trainer-Ken Locker, Eqp. Mgr.-Buck Buchanan

# ★ 1977 ★
## DALLAS COWBOYS

1 Efren Herrera, 11 Danny White, 12 Roger Staubach, 18 Glenn Carano, 20 Mel Renfro, 21 Doug Dennison, 25 Aaron Kyle, 26 Preston Pearson, 31 Benny Barnes

33 Tony Dorsett, 35 Scott Laidlaw, 36 Larry Brinson, 41 Charlie Waters, 42 Randy Hughes, 43 Cliff Harris, 44 Robert Newhouse, 46 Mark Washington, 50 D. D. Lewis

53 Bob Breunig, 54 Randy White, 56 Thomas Henderson, 57 Bruce Huther, 58 Mike Hegman, 59 Guy Brown, 62 John Fitzgerald, 63 Larry Cole, 64 Tom Rafferty

65 David Stalls, 66 Burton Lawless, 67 Pat Donovan, 68 Herbert Scott, 70 Rayfield Wright, 71 Andy Frederick, 72 Ed Jones, 73 Ralph Neely, 75 Jethro Pugh

76 Jim Eidson, 77 Bill Gregory, 79 Harvey Martin, 80 Tony Hill, 83 Golden Richards, 86 Butch Johnson, 87 Jay Saldi, 88 Drew Pearson, 89 Billy Joe DuPree, Asst. Trainer-Ken Locker

Head Coach-Tom Landry, Asst. Head Coach-Jim Myers, Asst. Coaches-Bob Ward, Jerry Tubbs, Mike Ditka, Ermal Allen, Dan Reeves, Gene Stallings, Ernie Stautner, Eqp. Mgr.-Buck Buchanan, Trainer-Don Cochren

**1978**

**1981**

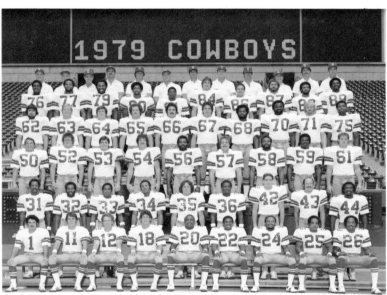

**1979**

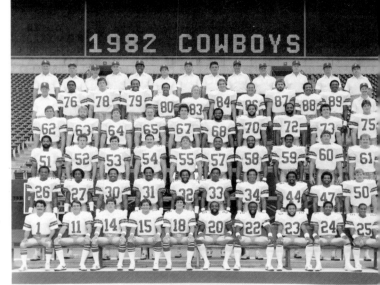

**1982**

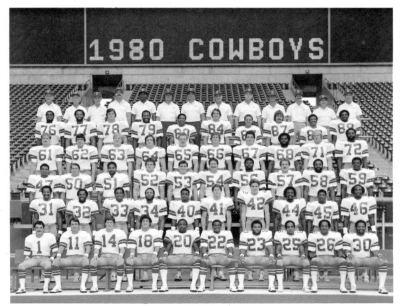

**1980**

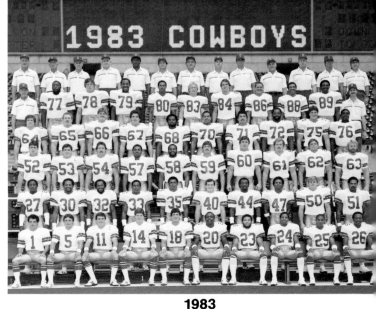

**1983**

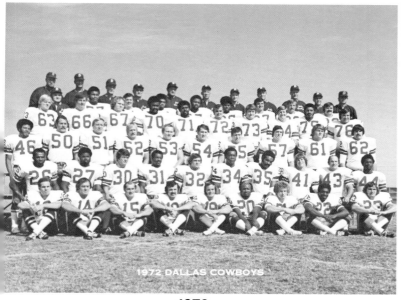

**1972**

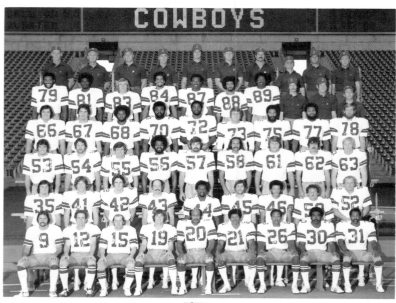

**1975**

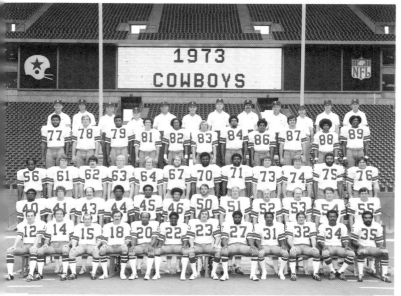

**1973**

**1976**

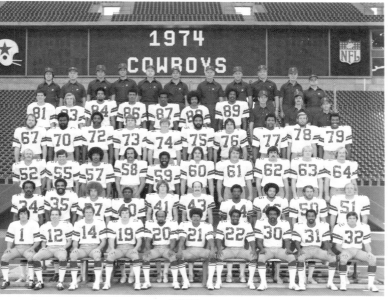

**1974**

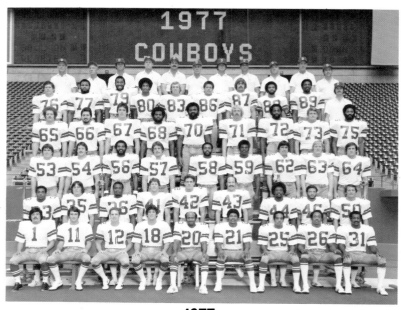

**1977**

## ★ 1978 ★
## DALLAS COWBOYS

1 Rafael Septien, 11 Danny White, 12 Roger Staubach, 18 Glenn Carano, 21 Doug Dennison, 24 Alois Blackwell, 25 Aaron Kyle, 26 Preston Pearson, 31 Benny Barnes

32 Dennis Thurman, 33 Tony Dorsett, 35 Scott Laidlaw, 41 Charlie Waters, 42 Randy Hughes, 43 Cliff Harris, 44 Robert Newhouse, 46 Mark Washington, 50 D. D. Lewis

53 Bob Breunig, 54 Randy White, 56 Thomas Henderson, 57 Bruce Huther, 58 Mike Hegman, 59 Guy Brown, 60 Tom Randall, 61 Jim Cooper, 62 John Fitzgerald

63 Larry Cole, 64 Tom Rafferty, 65 Dave Stalls, 66 Burton Lawless, 67 Pat Donovan, 68 Herbert Scott, 70 Rayfield Wright, 71 Andy Frederick, 72 Ed Jones

75 Jethro Pugh, 76 Larry Bethea, 79 Harvey Martin, 80 Tony Hill, 83 Golden Richards, 86 Butch Johnson, 87 Jay Saldi, 88 Drew Pearson, 89 Billy Joe DuPree

Head Coach-Tom Landry, Asst. Head Coach-Jim Myers, Asst. Coaches-Mike Ditka, Dan Reeves, Gene Stallings, Ernie Stautner, Jerry Tubbs, Bob Ward, Trainer-Don Cochren-Eqp. Mgr.-Buck Buchanan, Asst. Trainer-Ken Locker

## ★ 1979 ★
## DALLAS COWBOYS

1 Rafael Septien, 11 Danny White, 12 Roger Staubach, 18 Glenn Carano, 20 Ron Springs, 22 Wade Manning, 24 Alois Blackwell, 25 Aaron Kyle, 26 Preston Pearson

31 Benny Barnes, 32 Dennis Thurman, 33 Tony Dorsett, 34 Aaron Mitchell, 35 Scott Laidlaw, 36 Larry Brinson, 42 Randy Hughes, 43 Cliff Harris, 44 Robert Newhouse

50 D. D. Lewis, 52 Robert Shaw, 53 Bob Breunig, 54 Randy White, 56 Thomas Henderson, 57 Bruce Huther, 58 Mike Hegman, 59 Guy Brown, 61 Jim Cooper

62 John Fitzgerald, 63 Larry Cole, 64 Tom Rafferty,

65 David Stalls, 66 Burton Lawless, 67 Pat Donovan, 68 Herbert Scott, 70 Rayfield Wright, 71 Andy Frederick, 75 Richard Grimmett

76 Larry Bethea, 77 Bruce Thornton, 79 Harvey Martin, 80 Tony Hill, 81 Steve Wilson, 84 Doug Cosbie, 86 Butch Johnson, 87 Jay Saldi, 88 Drew Pearson, 89 Billy Joe DuPree

Head Coach-Tom Landry, Asst. Head Coach-Jim Myers, Asst. Coaches-Ermal Allen, Mike Ditka, Dan Reeves, Ernie Stautner, Gene Stallings, Jerry Tubbs, Bob Ward, Trainer-Don Cochren, Asst. Trainer-Ken Locker, Eqp. Mgr.-Buck Buchanan

## ★ 1980 ★
## DALLAS COWBOYS

1 Rafael Septien, 11 Danny White, 14 Gary Hogeboom, 18 Glenn Carano, 20 Ron Springs, 22 Wade Manning, 23 James Jones, 25 Aaron Kyle, 26 Preston Pearson, 30 Timmy Newsome

31 Benny Barnes, 32 Dennis Thurman, 33 Tony Dorsett, 34 Aaron Mitchell, 40 Eric Hurt, 41 Charlie Waters, 42 Randy Hughes, 44 Robert Newhouse, 45 Steve Wilson, 46 Roland Solomon

47 Dextor Clinkscale, 50 D. D. Lewis, 51 Anthony Dickerson, 52 Robert Shaw, 53 Bob Breunig, 54 Randy White, 56 Bill Roe, 57 Bruce Huther, 58 Mike Hegman, 59 Guy Brown

61 Jim Cooper, 62 John Fitzgerald, 63 Larry Cole, 64 Tom Rafferty, 65 Kurt Petersen, 66 Norm Wells, 67 Pat Donovan, 68 Herb Scott, 71 Andy Frederick, 72 Ed Jones

76 Larry Bethea, 77 Bruce Thornton, 78 John Dutton, 79 Harvey Martin, 80 Tony Hill, 84 Doug Cosbie, 86 Butch Johnson, 87 Jay Saldi, 88 Drew Pearson, 89 Billy Joe DuPree

Head Coach-Tom Landry, Asst. Head Coach-Jim Myers, Asst. Coaches-Ermal Allen, Mike Ditka, Al Lavan, Dan Reeves, Gene Stallings, Ernit Stautner, Jerry Tubbs, Bob Ward, Asst. Trainer-Ken Locker, Trainer-Don Cochren, Eqp. Mgr.-Buck Buchanan

## ★ 1981 ★
## DALLAS COWBOYS

1 Rafael Septien, 11 Danny White, 14 Gary Hogeboom, 18 Glenn Carano, 20 Ron Springs, 23 James Jones, 24 Everson Walls, 26 Michael Downs, 30 Timmy Newsome

31 Benny Barnes, 32 Dennis Thurman, 33 Tony Dorsett, 41 Charlie Waters, 42 Randy Hughes, 44 Robert Newhouse, 45 Steve Wilson, 47 Dextor Clinkscale, 50 D. D. Lewis, 51 Anthony Dickerson

52 Robert Shaw, 53 Bob Breunig, 54 Randy White, 55 Danny Spradlin, 56 Bill Roe, 57 Angelo King, 58 Mike Hegman, 59 Guy Brown, 60 Donald Smerek, 61 Jim Cooper

62 John Fitzgerald, 63 Glen Titensor, 64 Tom Rafferty, 65 Kurt Petersen, 67 Pat Donovan, 68 Herbert Scott, 70 Howard Richards, 71 Andy Frederick, 72 Ed Jones, 73 Steve Wright

76 Larry Bethea, 78 John Dutton, 79 Harvey Martin, 80 Tony Hill, 83 Doug Donley, 84 Doug Cosbie, 86 Butch Johnson, 87 Jay Saldi, 88 Drew Pearson, 89 Billy Joe DuPree

Head Coach-Tom Landry, Asst. Head Coach-Jim Myers, Asst. Coaches-Ermal Allen, Mike Ditka, Al Lavan, John Mackovic, Gene Stallings, Ernie Stautner, Jerry Tubbs, Bob Ward, Trainer-Don Cochren, Asst. Trainer-Ken Locker, Eqp. Mgr.-Buck Buchanan

## ★ 1982 ★
## DALLAS COWBOYS

1 Rafael Septien, 11 Danny White, 14 Gary Hogeboom, 15 Brad Wright, 18 Glenn Carano, 20 Ron Springs, 22 George Peoples, 23 James Jones, 24 Everson Walls, 25 Rod Hill

26 Michael Downs, 27 Ron Fellows, 30 Timmy Newsome, 31 Benny Barnes, 32 Dennis Thurman, 33 Tony Dorsett, 34 Monty Hunter, 44 Robert Newhouse, 47 Dextor Clinkscale, 50 Jeff Rohrer

51 Anthony Dickerson, 52 Robert Shaw, 53 Bob Breunig, 54 Randy White, 55 Danny Spradlin, 57 Angelo King, 58 Mike Hegman, 59 Guy Brown, 60 Don Smerek, 61 Jim Cooper

62 Brian Baldinger, 63 Glen Titensor, 64 Tom Rafferty, 65 Kurt Petersen, 67 Pat Donovan, 68 Herbert Scott, 70 Howard Richards, 72 Ed Jones, 73 Steve Wright, 75 Phil Pozderac

Eqp. Mgr.-Buck Buchanan, 76 Larry Bethea, 78 John Dutton, 79 Harvey Martin, 80 Tony Hill, 83 Doug Donley, 84 Doug Cosbie, 86 Butch Johnson, 87 Jay Saldi, 88 Drew Pearson, 89 Billy Joe DuPree, Asst. Trainer-Ken Locker

Head Coach-Tom Landry, Asst. Head Coach-Jim Myers, Asst. Coaches-Ermal Allen, Neill Armstrong, Al Lavan, Alan Lowry, John Mackovic, Dick Nolan, Gene Stallings, Ernie Stautner, Jerry Tubbs, Bob Ward, Trainer-Don Cochren

## ★ 1983 ★
## DALLAS COWBOYS

1 Rafael Septien, 5 John Warren, 11 Danny White, 14 Gary Hogeboom, 81 Glenn Carano, 20 Ron Springs, 23 James Jones, 24 Everson Walls, 25 Rod Hill, 26 Michael Downs

27 Ron Fellows, 30 Timmy Newsome, 32 Dennis Thurman, 33 Tony Dorsett, 35 Chuck McSwain, 40 Bill Bates, 44 Robert Newhouse, 47 Dextor Clinkscale, 51 Anthony Dickerson

52 Scott McLean, 53 Bob Breunig, 54 Randy White, 57 Angelo King, 58 Mike Hegman, 59 Mike Walter, 60 Don Smerek, 61 Jim Cooper, 62 Brian Baldinger, 63 Glen Titensor

64 Tom Rafferty, 65 Kurt Petersen, 66 Chris Schultz, 67 Pat Donovan, 68 Herbert Scott, 70 Howard Richards, 71 Mark Tuinei, 72 Ed Jones, 75 Phil Pozderac, 76 Larry Bethea

Eqp. Mgr.-Buck Buchanan, 77 Jim Jeffcoat, 78 John Dutton, 79 Harvey Martin, 80 Tony Hill, 83 Doug Donley, 84 Doug Cosbie, 86 Butch Johnson, 88 Drew Pearson, 89 Billy Joe DuPree, Ken Locker-Asst. Trainer

Head Coach-Tom Landry, Asst. Head Coach-Jim Myers, Asst. Coaches-Ermal Allen, Neill Armstrong, Al Lavan, Alan Lowry, Dick Nolan, Jim Shofner, Gene Stallings, Ernie Stautner, Jerry Tubbs, Bob Ward, Trainer-Don Cochren

# 1984 Dallas Cowboys

| | | | |
|---|---|---|---|
| 1 | Septien, Rafael | 55 | DeOssie, Steve |
| 3 | Miller, Jim | 56 | Lockhart, Eugene |
| 11 | White, Danny | 58 | Hegman, Mike |
| 14 | Hogeboom, Gary | 60 | Smerek, Don |
| 16 | Pelluer, Steve | 61 | Cooper, Jim |
| 20 | Springs, Ron | 62 | Baldinger, Brian |
| 21 | Howard, Carl | 63 | Titensor, Glen |
| 22 | Scott, Victor | 64 | Rafferty, Tom |
| 23 | Jones, James | 65 | Petersen, Kurt |
| 24 | Walls, Everson | 68 | Scott, Herbert |
| 26 | Downs, Michael | 70 | Richards, Howard |
| 27 | Fellows, Ron | 71 | Tuinei, Mark |
| 28 | Granger, Norm | 72 | Jones, Ed |
| 30 | Newsome, Timmy | 75 | Pozderac, Phil |
| 31 | Allen, Gary | 76 | Aughtman, Dowe |
| 32 | Thurman, Dennis | 77 | Jeffcoat, Jim |
| 33 | Dorsett, Tony | 78 | Dutton, John |
| 35 | McSwain, Chuck | 79 | Hunt, John |
| 36 | Albritton, Vince | 80 | Hill, Tony |
| 40 | Bates, Bill | 81 | Phillips, Kirk |
| 47 | Clinkscale, Dextor | 82 | Renfro, Mike |
| 50 | Rohrer, Jeff | 83 | Donley, Doug |
| 51 | Dickerson, Anthony | 84 | Cosbie, Doug |
| 52 | Cannon, Billy | 85 | Cornwell, Fred |
| 53 | Breunig, Bob | 89 | Salonen, Brian |
| 54 | White, Randy | | |

# Looking for the Intangible

## DALLAS SUCCESS STORY

The Dallas Cowboys have stayed near the top of the NFL through the draft and the signing of free-agents. The following breakdown of the current Cowboys team shows the year and draft choice number of each player. F.A. indicates free agent. John Dutton is the only player acquired through a trade.

### 1974
Ed Jones — 1st
Danny White — 3rd

### 1975
Randy White — 1st
Bob Breunig — 3rd
Mike Hegman — 7th
Herbert Scott — 13th

### 1976
Danny White — Had been 3rd-round choice in 1974
Tom Rafferty — 4th

### 1977
Tony Dorsett — 1st
Tony Hill — 3rd
Jim Cooper — 6th

### 1978
Dennis Thurman — 11th
Rafael Septien — F.A.

### 1979
Doug Cosbie — 3rd
Ron Springs — 5th
John Dutton —
Trade with Baltimore

### 1980
James Jones — 3rd
Kurt Petersen — 4th
Gary Hogeboom — 5th
Timmy Newsome — 6th
Anthony Dickerson — F.A.
Dextor Clinkscale — F.A.
Don Smerek — F.A.

### 1981
Howard Richards — 1st
Doug Donley — 2nd
Glen Titensor — 3rd
Ron Fellows — 7th
Everson Walls — F.A.
Michael Downs — F.A.

### 1982
Jeff Rohrer — 2nd
Phil Pozderac — 5th
Brian Baldinger — F.A.

### 1983
Jim Jeffcoat — 1st
Chuck McSwain — 5th
Chris Schultz — 7th
Gary Allen — F.A.
Bill Bates — F.A.
Jim Miller — F.A.
Mark Tuinei — F.A.
Kirk Phillips — F.A.

### 1984
Billy Cannon, Jr. — 1st
Victor Scott — 2nd
Fred Cornwell — 3rd
Steve DeOssie — 4th
Steve Pelluer — 5th
Norm Granger — 5th
Eugene Lockhart — 6th
John Hunt — 9th
Brian Salonen — 10th
Dowe Aughtman — 11th
Vince Albritton — F.A.
Carl Howard — F.A.
Mike Renfro — Trade with Oilers

Both innovative and greatly applauded, the Dallas Cowboys' draft procedure, because of its ability to select relatively unknown players from colleges no one ever heard of, has become the model for other NFL teams. In fact, the Dallas scouting department has been so successful and so highly touted that a miss on a player is as big a story as those low round picks and free-agent signees who make it.

"You've heard some criticism of some of our drafts recently," says one member of the Cowboys' front office. "But even that says something. If people weren't watching what we do pretty closely, they wouldn't be that aware of the fact a player doesn't pan out. If you're getting that much attention, you have to figure you're doing some things right, too."

It is a statement difficult to argue with. Take, for instance, the 1981 rookie crop; one which has now had a chance to bloom into veteran membership. Solid proof that the Cowboys' scouting system is alive and well is the fact that five drafted players earned spots on a team which, in that season, regained the NFC East title — and a pair of free-agents no one else showed an interest in earned starting roles in the defensive secondary.

Cornerback Everson Walls of Grambling led the league in interceptions in that first season and was named to the Pro Bowl. Michael Downs, a Rice free-agent, picked off seven passes himself as the starting free safety. Both stand as prime examples of the Cowboys' unique ability to spot talent, then mold it to their particular needs.

And the tradition seems never to end. It was in '83, remember, when a young Tennessee grad named Bill Bates fought his way onto the team and ended the season recognized as the NFL's Special Teams Player of the Year.

Over the years they have surprised their peers by signing players from other sports, gambling on their basic athletic ability, and turning them into standout NFL performers. These included basketball players like All-Pro cornerback Cornell Green and receiver Pete Gent, track men like receiver Bob Hayes and running back Mike Gaechter, and even baseball players like former defensive back Wade Manning.

And from the free-agent marketplace have come the likes of All-Pro free safety Cliff Harris and all-time receiving leader Drew Pearson and standout cornerback Benny Barnes.

The most visible person in the Dallas success story is, of course, player personnel director Gil Brandt, the man hired to coordinate the Cowboys' scouting department when the team was born back in 1960. He was there when Dallas made the pacesetting move to use computers in their draft process.

"The computer is an incredible piece of equipment," he says. "If, for instance, you ask me how many 6-3 college quarterbacks there are in the country who can run a 5.0 40 or better, it would normally take me a day and a half to go through a list of something like 600 players. With the computer, I can get the information in about 20 seconds."

Even before colleges begin spring training, Dallas scouts draw up a list of 1,500 or so prospects, assigning each player and the school he plays for a code number. "At first," Brandt explains, "it is just names and schools. But as we gather more and more information and put it into the computer we whittle things down — to a point where we have about 600 names. When we get down to that number we begin assigning data like height, weight, speed, I.Q., etc.

"Finally, we have a master list with the player's name and computer code number. Once we begin discussing whom to draft, we simply put the player's number into the computer and out comes all the data we've gathered over the two or three years we've been looking at him."

It is the ongoing draft success which has, perhaps more than anything else, enabled the Cowboys to maintain a high level of performance over the past decade and a half, going through transitional years with little visible evidence of rebuilding.

It is also worth noting that the Cowboys, historically dedicated to building through the draft, have made the most of draft picks they've traded for over the years.

*Michael Downs (above) became a regular in the Cowboys secondary after no team in the NFL bothered to select him in the draft. A product of tiny Ouitacha Baptist, safety Cliff Harris (right) went from free agent to All-Pro.*

196

Once a quarterback, Drew Pearson was judged too small and too slow to make it in the NFL. He went on to become one of the greatest wide receivers in the game's history.

*Benny Barnes came to the Cowboys as a free agent and stayed 10 years.*

"Every championship team," says head coach Tom Landry, "is built around a certain nucleus of players. Generally, to get this nucleus you have to draft in the early rounds. I mean, the first five players or so in the first round. Those are generally what I call your game-makers. Once you lose those, they are awfully hard to replace. The only reason we've stayed up as long as we have is the trades we've made for draft choices, to get the people like Ed Jones, Randy White, and Tony Dorsett."

It is no accident the three aforementioned have been selected to various All-Pro teams during their careers.

In truth, it is a process which has been ongoing for a long time. There are a number of players who have come to the squad because of a timely trade made by the Cowboys. To wit:

It was in 1970 that Dallas drafted a Clemson quarterback named Charlie Waters in the third round, using a draft pick which had come from Houston in a trade for backup quarterback Jerry Rhome. Waters went on to develop into an All-Pro safety, enjoying a 10-year career with the Cowboys. In effect, Dallas got an All-Pro starter in exchange for a backup performer who never started in a regular season game.

The next significant move came in 1972 when Dallas dealt center-guard Halvor Hagen and Honor Jackson to the New England Patriots for a second round selection. The Cowboys used that choice to pick up an All-America fullback from the University of Houston named Robert Newhouse. Score: Two long-time starters in exchange for three non-starters.

The following season Dallas had a third round pick from Houston (through New Orleans) in exchange for backup linebacker Tom Stincic. They used it to pick up a promising young defensive lineman from East Texas State. Harvey Martin would make All-Pro, be cited as the league's most outstanding defensive lineman one season, and share MVP honors in the Super Bowl. Tally: Dallas had yet to give up a starter and numbered two All-Pros and one of the league's most reliable running backs on its roster.

Then came a bonanza in 1974. The Cowboys earned the first and third round draft picks from the Houston Oilers in exchange for a pair of short-term starters, defensive end Tody Smith and wide receiver Billy Parks. They used them to pick up Ed (Too Tall)

Jones from Tennessee State and a celebrated Arizona State quarterback named Danny White. That's five starters, three of them All-Pros, in exchange for six players, none of whom were ever considered major forces on the Cowboys' teams they played with.

The Cowboys continued their hot streak in 1975 when, with Roger Staubach firmly established as the Dallas quarterback, Craig Morton was traded to the New York Giants for a No. 1 draft pick. That enabled the Cowboys to select Outland and Lombardi Trophy-winning defensive lineman Randy White of Maryland. He, too, would soon become an All-Pro and share MVP honors with teammate Martin in Super Bowl XII.

That same year the Cowboys also had a fourth round pick they had received from Houston in exchange for backup running back and wide receiver, Mike Montgomery. With it, they chose a standout Stanford grad named Pat Donovan who would go on to earn Pro Bowl honors as an offensive tackle. Score: Seven starters and a couple of backup quarterbacks gained; a pair of part-time starters and four reserves lost.

The biggest news would come in 1977 when the wheeling-dealing Cowboys pulled off an exchange with the Seattle Seahawks, giving up a first and second round pick in exchange for the right to draft Heisman Trophy-winning running back Tony Dorsett. Another part of the complex deal was the trade of a seldom-used wide receiver named Duke Ferguson for a swap of second round picks. With that second round choice the Cowboys drafted Nevada-Las Vegas quarterback Glenn Carano who would become the team's backup field general for several seasons.

The 1977 bonanza offered even more. Former All-Pro offensive guard John Niland, on the down side of his brilliant career, had been traded to the Philadelphia Eagles for a third round pick. With it, Dallas secured the services of Pro Bowl wide receiver Tony Hill, one of the most talented deep threats in the NFL.

There were no significant trades in 1978; but the following season backup defensive lineman Bill Gregory went to Seattle in return for a third round pick, resulting in Dallas' acquiring the promising tight end Doug Cosbie who advanced into a starting role in the 1983 season, earning a spot in the Pro Bowl. And linebacker Bill Roe came via a third round pick Dallas had received from Chicago in exchange for backup wide receiver Golden Richards.

Such are the moves which have kept the Cowboys ahead of the pack.

"There are very few secrets anymore," says Brandt, "because just about everyone has the same information on the players who are eligible for the draft. So you have to look to other things to maintain an edge."

Sometimes it is a free-agent signed. Or a well-thought-out trade, which results in an extra draft choice that affords them an opportunity to select a player they normally wouldn't have had a shot at.

"Our scouts," says president and general manager Tex Schramm, "are constantly in search of that intangible that so often makes the difference."

Obviously, they've managed to find it more often than not.

# The Rivals: Taking on All Comers

In a time when rivalries between certain teams have become a major fabric in the makeup of professional sport, the Dallas Cowboys, in a sense, stand alone. To be sure, there have been rivalries which developed with other teams over the last quarter century but, without exception, each has been surprisingly short-lived. Teams would rise up to challenge the Cowboys' lofty place in the structure of the NFL, battle mightily for a time, then fall back into the pack. Dallas, meanwhile, would remain at or near the top, one pretender dealt with, awaiting the next.

In a manner of speaking, then, it can be said that the rivalries the Cowboys have been involved in over the years have been relatively one-sided. The Cowboys stood apart, recognized year in and year out as one of the NFL's dominant forces. Other teams have looked to them as a formidable road block, a team and organization which has stood in the way of recognition and successes they sought.

"There's no team in the league that doesn't look forward to the opportunity to defeat the Dallas Cowboys," says one NFL executive. "Every time you do manage to beat them, you have accomplished something special. The general public has them on such a pedestal that even if you have a better team, it's always a little surprising that you defeated them. But when you do, you can rest assured you'll get people's attention. For that reason alone, everyone in the league points toward the Cowboys."

In the minds of many, then, its Dallas vs. the rest of the NFL world.

Head coach Tom Landry, however, has always made it clear that one-on-one rivalries are something he wishes to avoid. "It has always been my feeling that if you enter a season concentrating too intently on one specific team or maybe even a couple of specific teams, you're very likely to lose track of the importance of other games. Our philosophy has always been to work toward winning our division. If you do that, everything else will fall into place for you," he says.

It is, then, the membership of the NFC East which is the annual concern of the Dallas Cowboys. That in itself is rivalry enough.

No team in the NFL has served as a greater headache to the Dallas Cowboys than did the Cleveland Browns in the late sixties. Aspiring to win the Eastern Championship, the Cowboys knew they had to defeat coach Paul Brown's powerhouse to do so. In 1968 they met for the title with Cleveland scoring a relatively easy 31-20 victory. A year later, it would be the Browns triumphing over Dallas again, 42-10. Things got no better in the '69 championship game as Cleveland handled the Cowboys, 38-14.

"The first year Cleveland beat us for the championship," says president and general manager Tex Schramm, "everyone thought it was a fluke. The next year even (Browns owner) Art Modell was concerned that his team would be embarrassed. But they won that second game and it shook our entire organization. It got to a point where our players were standing around, thinking, 'Oh no, here it comes again'."

"Those championship losses to Cleveland," says coach Tom Landry, "were particularly disappointing to me because I felt we didn't accomplish a single thing in the games."

It would be in 1970, however, that the albatross would come from around the Cowboys' neck. In their drive to their first Super Bowl they managed a hard-fought 6-2 win over the Browns during a needed five-game winning streak which put them into the playoffs.

Still, the Browns own a 15-8 edge in their series with the Cowboys.

201

They were what the Dallas Cowboys wanted to be; the team recognized throughout the National Football League as the best of the best. In the mid-sixties it was the Green Bay Packers which all others were measured against. The legendary Vince Lombardi taught pride, fundamentals and togetherness — and in doing so had created a dynasty in Wisconsin.

Dallas' first chance to muscle in on that status came in the 1966 NFL Championship game. It marked the meeting of the Packer experience and mystique vs. the Dallas razzle-dazzle and enthusiasm. The Packers would win, 34-27, but not before the Cowboys had proven to the world they were worthy adversaries.

A year later the same two teams squared off for the league title in a game that would become part of the lore and legend of NFL history. It would be called the Ice Bowl, played in minus 18 degree weather. And until the fading seconds there in Green Bay, it looked as if Dallas might dethrone the champion. But with 13 seconds remaining, Packers quarterback Bart Starr scored from the two-yard line to lift his team to a 21-17 victory.

It was, Tex Schramm would later judge, those two games that convinced the nation that the Cowboys were the up-and-coming team of the NFL. Thus began a coast-to-coast love affair with the franchise in Dallas.

In time the Packers dynasty would fade to memories as Dallas continued to improve and gain in stature, winning championships of its own.

202

There was little indication in that 1961 season opener that the two teams playing before a sparse Cotton Bowl crowd would grow into the dominant forces they were eventually to become. By defeating the Pittsburgh Steelers that day, 27-24, the Dallas Cowboys would score the first ever victory in their still young history.

By the seventies they would reign as the two powerhouse teams in the NFL and would face each other twice for the world championship. In fact, throughout the decade an ongoing battle to determine who would be remembered as the greatest team of that 10-year period took place. And while the Cowboys would fashion the most impressive won-lost record over the years, it would be losses to the Steelers in Super Bowl X and Super Bowl XIII that would deny them the place in history they aspired to.

Pittsburgh would win the first meeting, 21-17, then held off a Roger Staubach-inspired rally to win in '78, 35-31.

During the seventies, Dallas would win two Super Bowls; Pittsburgh, four.

The Steelers, in fact, are one of the few teams in the NFL who can claim an edge over Dallas, having won 12 of the 22 meetings.

It is a feud which simmered through much of the seventies, then boiled into a blood rivalry briefly in 1980 when Philadelphia Eagles quarterback Ron Jaworski entertained the media with stories of how he and his Eagles had set Dallas up prior to defeating them, 20-7, in the NFC Championship game.

The Eagles went on to Super Bowl XIV while the Cowboys fumed. Jaworski's intimation was that the Cowboys, thanks to the psychological war games orchestrated by Philadelphia coach Dick Vermeil in the week leading up to the game, had fallen victim to the praise showered on them by their opposition.

In truth, there has been little love lost between Dallas and Philadelphia for some time. It was in 1971 that defensive end Mel Tom threw a chin-high forearm at Dallas quarterback Roger Staubach, knocking the Cowboys field general cold. Safety Bill Bradley used to delight in tossing verbal hand grenades toward Dallas receivers. And there was the highly publicized matter of Cowboys defender Dennis Thurman delivering a late blow to Jaworski, earning himself a 15-yard penalty and Jaworski several cracked ribs.

The Eagles threat to the Cowboys' dominance of the Eastern Division, however, was a short-lived affair. Indeed, Dallas owns a 31-16 edge in its 25-year-old series with Philadelphia.

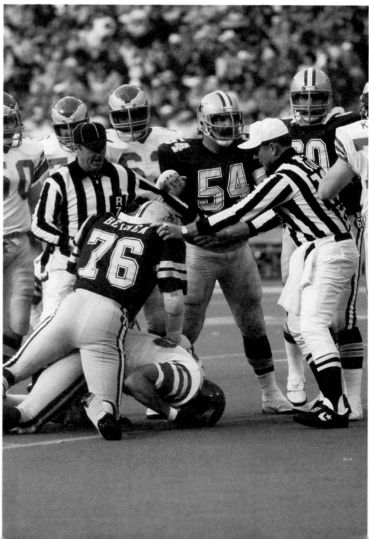

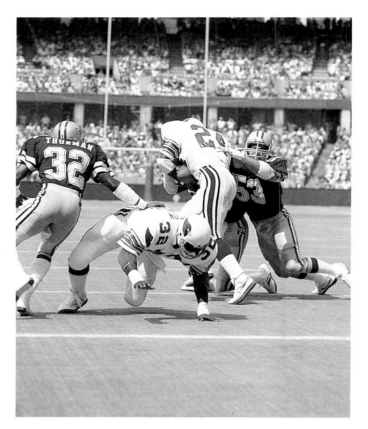

It was a Monday night in 1970 when the St. Louis Cardinals and Dallas Cowboys squared off in the Cotton Bowl for the benefit of the ABC-TV cameras. And for the first — and only — time in their history, the Cowboys were shut out. The Cardinals won the game, 38-0, administering one of the worst public humiliations Dallas has ever experienced. But from those ashes the Cowboys rose to win seven straight and gain their first trip to the Super Bowl.

Enroute to building a 27-15-1 advantage in the series, Dallas has generally dominated the Cardinals in recent years. But not without some good-natured bantering between St. Louis board chairman Billy Bidwill and Dallas president and general manager Tex Schramm. It was, for instance, in the late seventies that Bidwill decided the Cardinals would break tradition and wear white jerseys at home, forcing Dallas to wear its seldom-used blue jerseys — adding to the Blue Jersey Jinx concern that the Cowboys labored with in those days.

As with all teams in the NFL, Bidwill was looking for some kind of edge.

Today there is a bit of the Cowboys flavor in the Cardinals front office as former Dallas public relations man Curt Mosher serves as vice-president in charge of administration.

The in-fighting between the Dallas Cowboys and Washington Redskins has been going on for a long time. When the outspoken George Allen was coaching the Washington squad, he made it clear that he entertained no greater ambition than beating the Cowboys. So enthusiastic was his dislike for the team that when a young Redskins rookie arrived in the Washington camp one summer, bearing the first name Dallas, Allen immediately informed him he would never be called by that name.

Diron Talbert, a member of the Redskins defense, made it an annual habit to deride Cowboys quarterback Roger Staubach and members of the Dallas and Washington media have had a hard time keeping up with the barbs tossed around the week before the two teams play.

What has fueled the rivalry in recent years, however, is not rhetoric but the quality of both

teams. Dallas and Washington have, of late, emerged as two of the predominant forces in the NFL. Since 1970 the Cowboys have been to five Super Bowls, the Redskins three.

Though Dallas owns a healthy 28-18 edge in the series, games played during the last decade have ranked among league classics: Roger Staubach bringing Dallas back in the waning seconds to register a 35-34 victory which eliminated the Redskins from the playoffs in 1979; reserve quarterback Clint Longley coming off the bench to lift the Cowboys to a come-from-behind win on Thanksgiving Day in 1974; Lance Alworth decking defender Jack Pardee with what George Allen labeled an illegal crack-back block in the '72 showdown; and Cowboys defensive lineman Larry Cole scoring four touchdowns in his 12-year career, all against the Redskins.

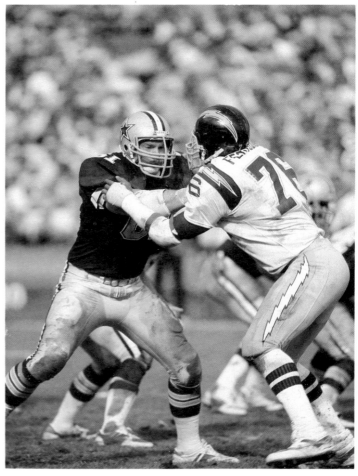

While they are generally acknowledged as two of the offensive giants of professional football, each leaning heavily on the wide open, high octane brand of offense, the Cowboys and the San Diego Chargers have squared off just three times.

Dallas won the first two, scoring a 34-28 victory in 1972, then a 42-31 win in '80. San Diego managed a 24-23 triumph in 1983.

But on that day their victory took a backseat to even bigger news. It was in the pressbox that day in San Diego that Cowboys president and general manager Tex Schramm first confirmed that Clint Murchison, Jr., was planning to sell the team he had owned since 1960.

The battles between Lamar Hunt's Kansas City Chiefs and Clint Murchison's Dallas Cowboys actually began long before there was an Arrowhead Stadium or even a team named the Chiefs. Before making the move to Kansas City they were the American Football League Dallas Texans, locked in a three-year battle with the NFL Cowboys for Dallas fans. Finally, after the 1962 season Hunt chose to move his team to Kansas City, leaving Dallas to the NFL and the Cowboys.

Since then the teams have met only three times, with Dallas owning a 2-1 edge in the series. They defeated the Chiefs, 27-16, in 1970, lost to them, 34-31, in '75, and won in 1983, 41-21. John Mackovic, formerly the Cowboys' quarterback coach, is the Chiefs' head coach.

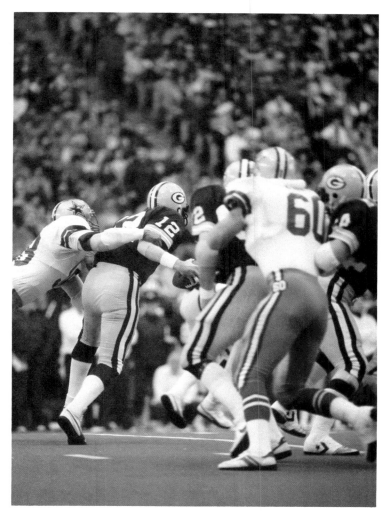

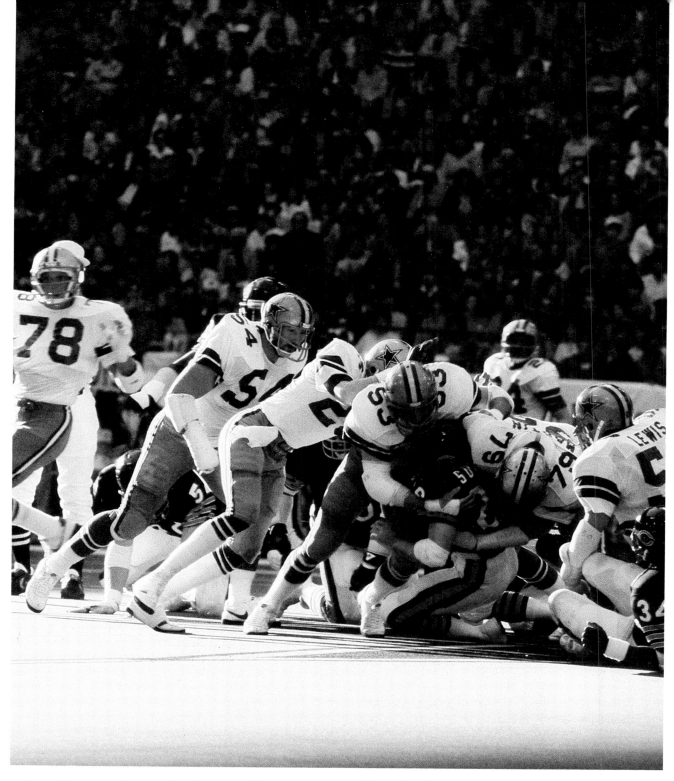

Though they have faced each other only eight times since that first game in 1960, the Dallas-Detroit Lions series has been marked by some memorable moments.

It was in the 1970 divisional playoffs that a determined Dallas defense rose to the occasion, keeping Super Bowl hopes alive with a 5-0 victory over the Lions on a mud-splattered Cotton Bowl afternoon. Then, in the 1981 meeting, in Detroit, the Lions managed a 27-24 victory with a last minute field goal. Films, however, would later show that Detroit, then coached by former Cowboys player Monte Clark, had 12 players on the field at the time of the winning kick.

Ironically, the Lions won the first, then the most recent game played between the two teams. Dallas enjoyed a six-game winning streak in between.

The Dallas-Chicago relationship goes back to the days when original Cowboys owner Clint Murchison, Jr., was trying to gain support for his expansion plans that would give life to the Cowboys. One of his strongest supporters was Bears owner George Halas.

And, since that initial meeting of the two teams in 1960, there have been some memorable games in the series which the Cowboys now lead, 7-3. It was in the troubled 1971 season that the Bears scored a 23-19 win over Dallas, dropping the staggering Cowboys to a 4-3 record. Following that game, head coach Tom Landry advised his team to relax and simply enjoy the remainder of the season. They did, launching into a 10-game winning streak that would not end until they had defeated Miami in Super Bowl VI.

Today a former Cowboys player and assistant coach, Mike Ditka, serves as head coach of the Bears.

217

Though Dallas and the Houston Oilers have faced each other only four times during the regular season, a pre-season rivalry developed back in 1965 thanks to the fact lineman Ralph Neely swore allegiance to both teams following his career at the University of Oklahoma.

Two weeks before the Sooners were to play in the Gator Bowl, Neely signed an undated contract with the Oilers, a move that would cost him the right to play in the bowl game. Later, however, he would become the property of the NFL Cowboys. But only after it was ruled that Dallas must provide compensation to the AFL Oilers in the form of a series of pre-season games that would be played in the Houston Astrodome. In time the game would come to be known as the Neely Bowl.

The pre-season series has continued since, however, with a trophy — the Governor's Cup — going to the winner each summer. Several years ago, however, someone began looking for the trophy — and neither team was able to locate it.

The Cowboys own a 3-1 lead in the brief regular season series with the Oilers.

Since 1977 the Dallas Cowboys have faced the Tampa Bay Buccaneers on six occasions, two of those meetings coming in playoff games. And, though it took a 27-24 overtime victory in 1983 to keep the streak intact, Dallas has never lost to the John McKay-coached Bucs.

They first met in what will be remembered as the most historically important games in Dallas Cowboys history. It was against the Miami Dolphins, in Super Bowl VI, that Dallas finally put to rest the "can't win the big one" talk with a near-perfect game, winning 24-3 to claim their first world championship.

Since that January day in 1972 the two teams have met three times in regular season play, Dallas winning once and the Dolphins twice.

But, even as they rarely play, there is something of an ongoing rivalry involving Dallas coach Tom Landry and Dolphins coach Don Shula, the two winningest active coaches in the game today. Going into the '84 campaign, Landry boasted 234 career wins with Shula claiming 226.

While playing cornerback for the New York Giants, Cowboys head coach Tom Landry was a Pro Bowl selection. Later he would serve the team as an innovative assistant. And, over the years, he has left little doubt that he still feels a warm spot for the city he once called home. To Landry, the annual visit to New York to play the Giants is something special.

In the early days of the Dallas franchise's existence, in fact, he would tell his players of the importance of playing well in the Big Apple. "The media gets a good look at you there," he would say. "That's where you make All-Pro, playing well in front of the New York media." The records will show that Dallas has done so on numerous occasions, leading the series 30-11-2.

Four times the Dallas Cowboys and San Francisco 49ers have met in the playoffs, and on each occasion the games were memorable.

It was in the 1972 divisional playoff in Candlestick Park that the Cowboys made a miracle comeback to win 30-28, scoring twice in the final minutes of play. An onside kick by Toni Fritsch had enabled Dallas to get possession of the ball with just 1:30 remaining and Roger Staubach directed the winning touchdown.

Coaching the 49ers at the time was former Cowboys defensive back Dick Nolan. Previously Dallas had defeated San Francisco for the divisional title in 1970 and the NFC Championship in '71.

The 49ers would gain some measure of revenge in the historic 1981 NFC title game. Coach Bill Walsh's team drove the length of the field in the waning minutes to score and manage a 28-27 triumph that blocked a sixth Super Bowl appearance by the Cowboys. Overall, Dallas owns a 8-7-1 edge in its series with the 49ers.

There was a touch of irony when the Dallas Cowboys and Denver Broncos met in New Orleans for Super Bowl XII. Quarterbacking the AFC champions was Craig Morton, the man whose previous Super Bowl experience had come as a member of the Cowboys' organization.

It would be a dismal day for the Broncos as Dallas scored a 27-10 victory, claiming its second world title. Morton would suffer four interceptions and leave the game at the half. The man who replaced him at the Dallas helm, Roger Staubach, would, on the other hand, enjoy one of his finest hours.

Only once in the four games the two teams have played has Denver managed to defeat Dallas, accomplishing the trick in 1980. Today the Broncos are coached by former Cowboys running back and assistant coach Dan Reeves.

They've only met three times yet their long distance battle is carried on every season. The Dallas Cowboys, with 18 straight winning seasons, are generally recognized by most as the owner of the best won-lost record in modern times.

Neither has had much opportunity to settle the issue on the field. The Raiders defeated Dallas, 27-23, in the first meeting of the two teams in 1974; then the Cowboys evened the score in 1980, winning 19-13. Most recently L.A. managed a 40-38 victory in 1983. The issue, fanned by Dallas general manager Tex Schramm and Raiders acting general partner Al Davis, longtime adversaries, is far from over.

On seven occasions the Dallas Cowboys and Los Angeles Rams have battled in the playoffs, twice playing for the NFC Championship. And while Dallas owns a 5-2 edge in those playoff encounters, the overall series is currently deadlocked at 9-9.

Through the years Dallas-Los Angeles games have been laced with drama and no small amount of nostalgia. It was Los Angeles that gave Tex Schramm his start in professional football and there that he learned many of the philosophies he would bring to the operation of the Cowboys in later years.

There were the years, too, when arch-rival George Allen coached the Rams, once drawing charges of spying on team practices at the Cowboys' training facility in Dallas prior to a crucial meeting.

What has emerged over the years, then, is a series matching two of the NFL's most colorful and tradition-laden teams. And each time fireworks have exploded when they met.

The Cowboys' series with the Minnesota Vikings dates back to 1961 and is filled with memorable moments. Four times they've met in the playoffs, twice for the NFC title. The Vikings defeated Dallas, 27-10, in 1973 and went on to the Super Bowl and Dallas triumphed over Minnesota in the 1977 championship game, advancing to Super Bowl XII.

Over the years the Cowboys have managed a 9-5 edge in the series.

More important, however, are the historical footnotes which have been a part of the match-ups. There was the famed Roger Staubach-to-Drew Pearson "Hail Mary" touchdown pass that won the 1975 Divisional Playoff game; then the 99-yard touchdown run by Tony Dorsett in the 1982 regular season finale.

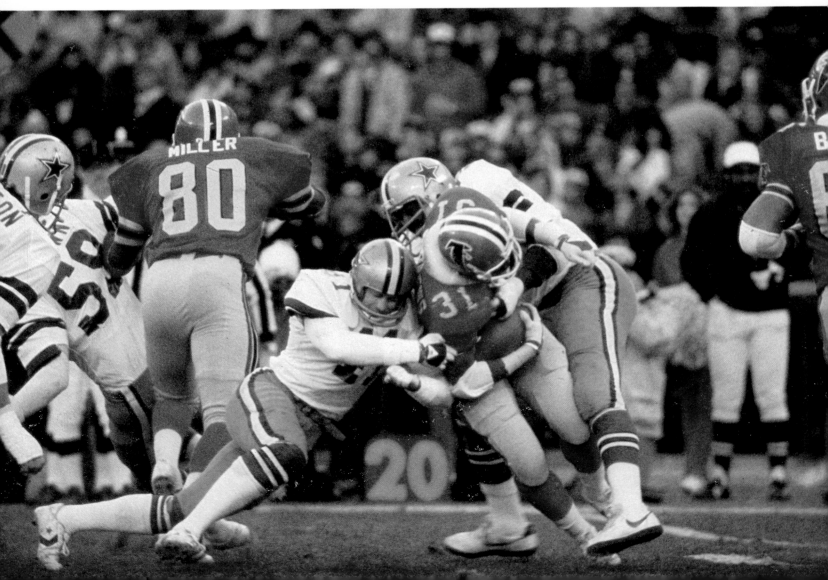

The first game ever played in Texas Stadium matched the host Dallas Cowboys against the AFC New England Patriots. Dallas would win that game, 44-21, and since has defeated the Patriots on three other occasions to manage a 4-0 record against them.

Currently serving as vice-president of the New England franchise is Francis (Bucko) Kilroy, once a scout for the Dallas Cowboys. And Ron Meyer, another former Dallas scout, is now the Patriots' head coach.

Though there have been only eight games in the Dallas-Atlanta Falcons series (the Cowboys own a 7-1 edge, including two division playoff victories), each encounter has drawn considerable interest. With former Cowboys quarterback Eddie LeBaron serving as executive vice-president and chief operating officer and one-time Dallas linebacker Tom Braatz operating as general manager, the Falcons' organization and philosophy are closely patterned after that of the Cowboys.

It was in the 1978 divisional playoff game in Atlanta when quarterback Danny White fashioned his first major come-from-behind victory, quarterbacking the Cowboys to an upset 27-20 victory with a pair of touchdown passes late in the fourth quarter.

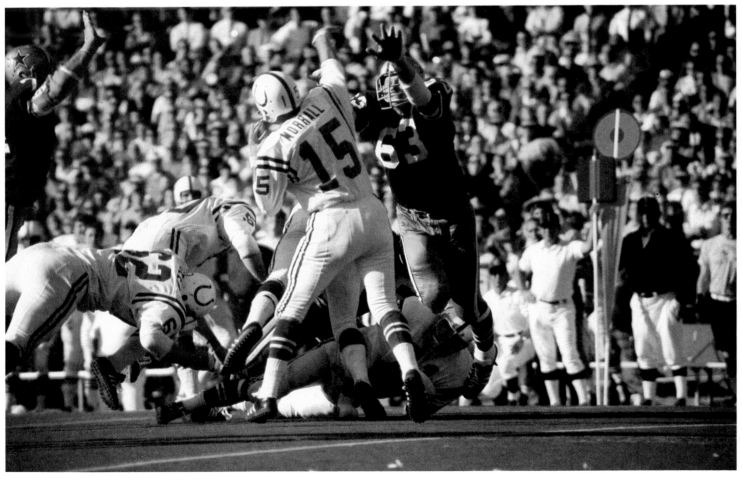

The Dallas Cowboys and the Baltimore-to-Indianapolis Colts go back a long way. In 1952 they were known as the NFL Dallas Texans and Clint Murchison, Jr., a man eager to see pro football succeed in Texas, was the owner of 20 season tickets.

It would be 18 years later when Murchison would watch his own Dallas Cowboys meet the Baltimore Colts in Super Bowl V. Some called it the Blooper Bowl because of all its mishaps and freak plays. Baltimore would win that day, 16-13, on a field goal by Jim O'Brien in the final minute. But Dallas' presence in the championship game would serve as a signal of good

things to come. Five times during the just-beginning decade they would play in the NFL championship game.

None of which might have happened had things worked out the way Murchison would have liked in the fifties. When the Texans ran into financial trouble he had offered to buy the team. But the owners, in a hurry to sell, refused to allow him two days to go over the books. Thus they went to Baltimore and Murchison had to wait another eight years for a team of his own.

Now the Cowboys can claim a 6-3 edge in their series with the Colts.

The rivalry between the Cowboys and the Seattle Seahawks began not on the playing field but in the drafting room when the Dallas front office arranged a wheeling-dealing trade prior to the 1977 draft. In exchange for Seattle's first round selection, Dallas swapped the Seahawks a No. 1 and three second round picks — and got the right to pick Heisman Trophy winning running back Tony Dorsett of the University of Pittsburgh. Today none of the players the Seahawks got in the historic deal are still on their roster while Dorsett has emerged as one of the finest running backs in NFL history. On the field, the Seahawks have fared no better against Dallas, losing in each of their three regular season meetings.

There was a time when many were certain a strong geographic rivalry involving Dallas and the New Orleans Saints would develop. In fact, when they first met in 1967 the Cowboys managed a slim 14-10 win in Dallas, then later traveled to New Orleans to learn quickly that the city was going to be anything but hospitable. It was in that second meeting, in fact, that it took an amazing 17 minutes for Cowboys quarterback Don Meredith to get an offensive play in motion because of the thunder of boos he faced each time he advanced to the line of scrimmage. Nonetheless, Dallas won the game.

Only in 1971, in fact, did the Saints manage to defeat the Cowboys (24-14) and now trail 10-1 in the series.

If linebacker Lee Roy Jordan had anything to say about it the Dallas Cowboys would have played the Cincinnati Bengals more often. It was in the first meeting of the two clubs in 1973 that he accomplished a still-standing club record with three interceptions in a single quarter of play, gathering 49 yards in returns along the way. Dallas would win that one, 38-10, then score a 38-13 victory in the only other meeting of the two teams in 1979.

Another of the NFL teams never to have beaten the Cowboys is Buffalo. Dallas scored a wild 49-37 victory in the first meeting of the two clubs back in 1971 and added wins in 1976 and 1981 to up its record to 3-0 against the Bills.

Dallas and the New York Jets have met on just three occasions and the Cowboys have been decisive winners on each occasion. They triumphed in the 1971 series opener, 52-10, then followed that up with a 31-21 victory in '75 and a 30-7 win in '78.

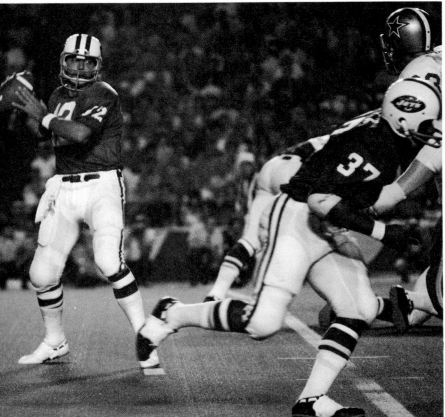

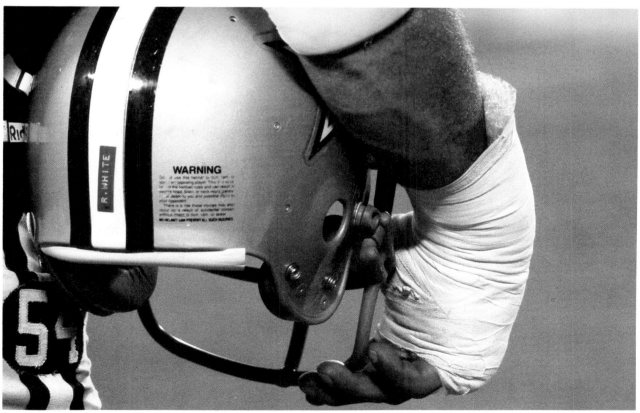

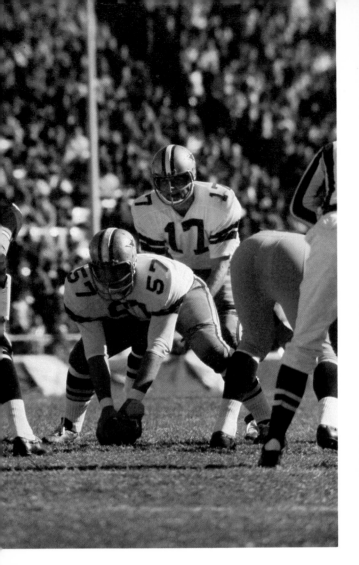
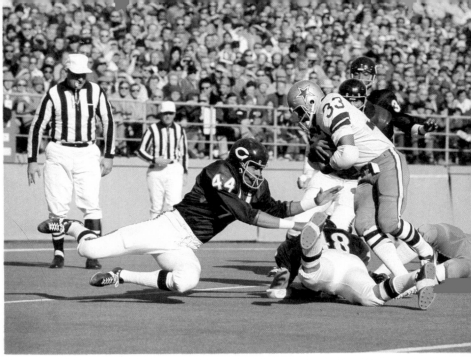

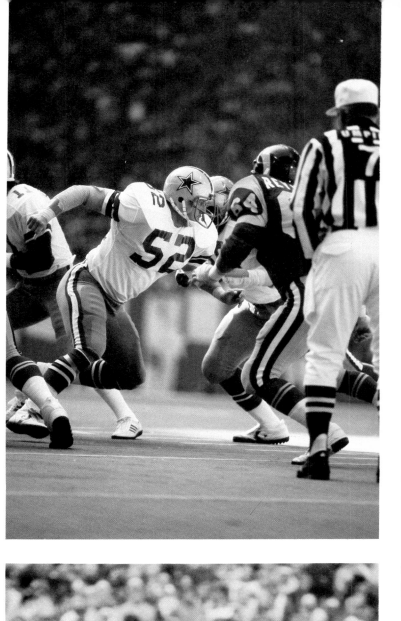

# The Future

He is a man who admits to superstitions and commands great order in his business life. H.R. (Bum) Bright always puts his right shoe on first, knocks on wood when the necessity arises, and organizes the cash in his pockets by the Federal Reserve Bank district numbers on the bills.

It is, friends say, that combination of orderliness and the search for good fortune which has enabled him to amass a fortune, which *Texas Business Magazine* recently estimated at $500 million, give or take a few bucks.

Equal parts quiet and tenacious, the 63-year-old Dallas resident, who was cited in 1983 as one of Texas' most powerful citizens, flew to Hawaii in Spring 1984 to be officially welcomed as the new majority owner of the Dallas Cowboys. Insisting he would model his involvement after that of former owner, Clint Murchison, Jr., Bright told members of the media that there would be no noticeable change in the operation of what has now gained recognition as the most expensive franchise in professional sports.

"If you thought Clint Murchison was an invisible owner, you will be shocked at me," Bright said. "The group of investors that I represent will be even more invisible than he was. It is not our intent to get involved with the running of the club." His, then, is a 'if it ain't broke, don't fix it' kind of philosophy.

Announcing that Tex Schramm, who served Murchison as president and general manager, would assume the role of managing partner in the new organizational structure, Bright made it clear he will leave the operation of the team to the man who has been at the helm since before Dallas was even officially granted an NFL franchise.

The purchase price of the Cowboys, the new team headquarters being built on thirty acres in The Valley Ranch, and various other Murchison holdings has been reported at $60 million, the highest figure ever recorded in the sale of a pro sports team.

Additionally, Bright personally bought the Texas Stadium Corporation from Murchison for $20 million and appointed Schramm to oversee that operation as well.

"So far as the operation of the club goes and what the Dallas Cowboys stand for," Bright said, "you will not notice a blip in the way things are done. Tex will have absolute authority to run the club. It will be his responsibility to do everything that is necessary for the Cowboys to continue to be a strong, winning organization."

The New Era, then, sounds as if it will be something of a carbon copy of the Old.

The announcement that Bright and his group would assume ownership of the Cowboys ended months of speculation, which had finally been confirmed in November of 1983 when Murchison, wishing to settle the estate of his late brother, John, began looking for a buyer.

The task of actually finding a new owner fell to Schramm. In essence, he was dispatched to go in search of his own boss. With the only guideline

*A new owner, a new home, a new promise for vitality in the decades ahead.*

being that a low profile ownership be sought, Schramm approached Bright about the possibility of entering the race for the franchise. The suggestion appealed to him and he set about to collect a group of Texas businessmen. Soon thereafter negotiations were underway. And, while there were several other prospective buyers in the derby, Bright insists there was little doubt in his mind that he would become the new Cowboys owner.

"When I'm in a race," he said, "everyone else is a long shot. We are organizers, we are planners, we are tenacious, we are reticent when we need to be, and we are deal-makers."

Bright looked over the Cowboys' books in mid-January and began to formulate the plan to collect a limited partnership. He later explained that he did not want to tie up the amount of money necessary to become the majority owner because of the low-yield nature of pro sports ownership. Despite league policy which requires that a franchise have a majority owner — a policy but not a hard-and-fast rule — Bright decided to put together a solid group and see what the league's attitude would be.

Seeking fellow owners who, as he put it, "would not be on a big ego trip," Bright quickly formed his group and made Murchison an offer. The deal was underway.

The league owners, who would vote for or against the plan, were quickly made aware of the fact Schramm would serve as acting general partner. It was a big plus. The voting procedure at the league meeting took only ten minutes.

Long regarded as one of the most astute executives in the league, Schramm's role is basically the same now as it was before the change of ownership. During his relationship with Murchison, Schramm was dealt the responsibility of the day-to-day running of the team.

*H. R. (Bum) Bright*

236

"It was great to finally get the sale done and over," Schramm admits. "For me personally it was a sad project because of my relationship with and feelings for Clint. He's the man who built this team to what it has become. On the other hand, I feel we have excellent ownership now."

While Bright and Schramm have repeatedly insisted there will be few, if any noticeable changes in the way the Cowboys are run, they have, at the same time, pointed to new and exciting developments which promise a bright new future for the organization.

Already under construction is the state-of-the-art Cowboys headquarters and training facility at The Valley Ranch. Once completed, it will serve as the new home of every phase of the Cowboys operation, from practice facilities to front office, ticket sales to Cheerleader rehearsals.

The new facility will include three football fields, locker and training room facilities, meeting rooms, weight training areas, running trails, basketball and racquetball courts, and a film lab. All administration offices as well as those for the coaches and members of the scouting department will be located in the 80,000-square foot building.

Then, there will be a unique 200-acre project adjacent to the headquarters called Cowboys Center.

The focal point of the Cowboys Center will be the Dallas Cowboys Show Place offering something of a historical museum for fans. The focal point of the Center will be a theater area programmed to exhibit a Cowboys multi-media presentation and films highlighting the history of the team and organization.

The Cowboys Center will also serve as the site of a hotel, conference center, office sites, a sports club, a retail and restaurant pavilion, a sports arena, and a residential area. It will, in fact, become something of a city within a city.

The overall focal point, however, will be the Dallas Cowboys, a team that enters its second quarter century with much the same enthusiasm and determination it displayed back in 1960 when it arrived as the new kid on the NFL block, uncertain of what the future held, but eager to make its presence felt.

"What Clint Murchison and his people did with the organization in the first 25 years," says Bright, "was incredible. They built the Dallas Cowboys into the finest sports operation in the country. What we hope to do is see that things run the same for the next 25 years."

It is an ambitious pledge, one typical of the Dallas Cowboys' philosophy.